# Trisha Yearwood's Family Recipes

includes the *New York Times* bestselling titles *Georgia Cooking in an Oklahoma Kitchen* and *Home Cooking with Trisha Yearwood*

with Gwen Yearwood and Beth Yearwood Bernard
foreword by Garth Brooks

in loving memory of
Gwendolyn Paulk Yearwood
November 8, 1937–October 1, 2011

Clarkson Potter/Publishers
New York

# trisha yearwood

## Georgia Cooking in an Oklahoma Kitchen

### Recipes from My Family to Yours

with Gwen Yearwood
and Beth Yearwood Bernard
foreword by Garth Brooks

clarkson potter/publishers
new york

# dedication

In memory of
Jack Howard Yearwood,
a wonderful husband, father, friend,
and one hell of a good cook.
We miss you every second of every minute
of every day.

Love,
your girls,
Gwen, Beth, and Patricia

# contents

OPPOSITE: Skillet Almond Shortbread (page 209)

# foreword

Why is it that two people can make the same dish, following the same recipe from beginning to end, and one will taste ten times better than the other? We all judge food on how it smells and how it tastes, but when you find a dish that is amazing, there is always that "something" you can't describe. I believe that "something" is love. Loving to cook is the difference between making food that is good and food that is *great*.

Watching Miss Yearwood (as I often call my wife) in the kitchen, it is easy to see how much she loves to cook. In fact, she defines what loving to cook means to me. Peeling potatoes and snapping green beans are chores that I rush through to get them over with; Trisha looks upon these tasks not as chores but as the careful, loving steps she takes on the way to making a meal that will bring joy to whoever is seated at our table.

When I think of Thanksgiving or Christmas, it is always with the pleasure of knowing this year's meal will be amazing. The anticipation of the German chocolate cake she bakes each year for my birthday makes me not mind getting a year older. And I know how happy it makes her that all of our friends feel the same way, because she always makes their favorite cake, pie, or pudding for their special days, too.

Be it for family or guests, Trisha always wants the meal to be something worth remembering. Which brings me to this: To make truly delicious meals, not only must you love to cook, you must also love those for whom you are cooking. *That is what makes Miss Yearwood's cooking . . . simply the best.*

—Garth Brooks

# introduction

Other than for the "singing thing" I do, I'm best known among my friends for my cooking. It's something I take great pride in. I don't think people expect me to be a good cook, so it's always fun to watch their expressions as they taste whatever I've made. Their liking my food gives me the same feeling I get when an audience applauds one of my performances—it feels good!

Food seems to always be a topic of conversation when my friends and I get together. Somebody's got some new recipe we all need to try, or we're talking about a new restaurant that's just opened and finding out if anyone's been there yet. Sharing recipes and memories about food has always been a great way to connect with friends and family.

When I first moved to Oklahoma, what I missed most of all was my family. We make every effort to see one another often, but there are those times when we can't get together, and I found myself on those lonely days making my mom's chicken noodle soup or baking a batch of my niece Ashley's banana bread. For my birthday a few years ago, my mom and my sister put together a notebook full of our favorite family recipes and called it *Georgia Recipes for an Oklahoma Kitchen*. Ashley even did artwork on her computer, using pictures of both states for the cover. We've come a long way from that binder full of typed recipes, and we found many "lost" or never-written-down recipes along the way.

That compilation planted the seed for this very special family cookbook. Some of these recipes go back to my grandmothers, Elizabeth Yearwood and Elizabeth "Lizzie" Paulk. I love the idea of making a meal I can imagine

OPPOSITE: Lizzie's Chicken and Dumplings (page 40)

my grandmother Lizzie making for Grandaddy to enjoy when he came in from working the tobacco fields back in the 1930s. It's yet another way we stay connected from generation to generation. My mom, my sister, and I had a wonderful time organizing, compiling the recipes, and sometimes recreating an old recipe entirely to make it workable for modern kitchens and lives. You'll also find that the ones that do take a bit more time and effort, like the frosted birthday cakes and the super-huge Just Married Pound Cake, create wonderful memories you will share with your family for generations to come.

My sister and I have really high standards when it comes to cooking, because we learned from the best. Mama taught us the basics of cooking and to use what you have available. I think one of the biggest lessons she taught me is that it's okay to change a recipe to make it work for me. I used to follow every recipe to the letter, afraid that if I left out something or added something else, it wouldn't turn out right. She also taught us simple rules of thumb—the ratio of flour to fat to liquid in a white sauce or a biscuit dough, for example—that are at the heart of every successful recipe. I learned that as long as I observed those basic guidelines, I could change the rest around. My husband recently asked if we could try to create a heartier, meatier lasagna recipe, and I said, "Sure! Let's experiment." If it turns out well, maybe it'll make the next cookbook!

From my daddy I learned about laughing, having fun in the kitchen, and the satisfaction that comes from seeing the pleasure others take in a meal you have prepared. He was always happy when folks appreciated his cooking, and he passed that down to me. I think comfort food gets its name from the wonderful memories associated with specific meals. My daddy's barbecued chicken recipe still makes my mouth water when I think about all of those chicken-cues we had on the town square in Monticello when I was growing up. Other recipes, like the Chicken

CLOCKWISE (from top left): Kyle Bernard; Bret Bernard and Beth; Joanne Jordan; Gwen, brother Wilson Paulk; John Bernard, Beth, Trisha, Gwen, and Joanne; Betty Maxwell; Ashley Bernard and Gwen; Trisha
CENTER: Beth, Trisha, Gwen, and Joanne

Broccoli Casserole, always bring a smile to my face because I know how much my family loves it when they find out that's what's for supper.

You'll also love how easy everything in this book is to make. I never want to try something new if I think it's going to take all day to cook. Who has time for that? These are easy-to-make recipes that use everyday seasonings you already have in your kitchen. Don't worry that I'll send you to a gourmet store to buy one specialty spice you'll never use again. As far as I'm concerned, there's really not much you can't do with a little salt and pepper—and maybe a jalapeño thrown in occasionally!

Garth says my cooking is good because it's made with love. I used to think that was just a sweet thing to say to your wife, but now I think it's true. If you truly love what you do, it shows—in life, love, good music, and good food. I hope you will love using these recipes as much as my family and I have enjoyed sharing them with the people who are important to us.

# Useful Equipment

In many of my recipes I've included suggestions about pan sizes, ingredient substitutions, information sources, and so on. This is a list of my favorite small appliances and kitchen gadgets and why they're my choices.

1. **Measuring spoons.** Three sets of metal spoons that include a $\frac{1}{2}$ tablespoon measurement. Choose sets that can be separated and stored each one with its equal. No need to wash an entire set when you've used only one.

2. **Measuring cups.** Two sets of dry measuring cups and 2 sets for liquid measuring. To dry-measure, overfill the cup and then scrape off the excess evenly with a flat-edged knife or spatula. Liquid measure has space above the top line and is easily read at eye level. OXO has designed liquid measuring cups that allow you to view the liquid from the top. No bending over!

3. **Cookie sheets.** Two cookie sheets of your choosing that fit in your oven with 2 inches of space on all sides. Sheets with a dark, nonstick finish bake a browner, crispier cookie, especially on the bottom, more quickly than a light, shiny sheet. An insulated sheet bakes a softer cookie. Don't wash insulated sheets in the dishwasher or soak in dishwater.

4. **Jelly roll pan.** Two pans with low sides, $\frac{1}{2}$ to 1 inch deep. Even if you never bake a jelly roll, these pans are a must for recipes that have juicy drippings, such as Roasted Carrots (page 123). They can also be used for baking cookies or biscuits.

5. **Fat separator or basting bulb.** The ideal way to remove fat from broth is to allow the broth to cool and then chill it so the fat solidifies and can be lifted off. If you don't have the time, fat can be removed from hot broth by lowering a ladle just below the fat line and allowing the fat to flow into the ladle. A fat separator is a clear, heat-resistant cup with a spout coming out from the side near the bottom. When the cup is tilted, the broth pours off, leaving the fat behind. You can get the same effect with a basting bulb. Squeeze the bulb to expel the air before plunging the tube to the bottom of the broth. Release the bulb, and the broth is drawn up into the tube, leaving the fat.

6. **Electric stand mixer.** KitchenAid with attachments that include a flat beater, wire whip, food grinder, and roto slicer with shredder. Two mixer bowls are handy when things such as egg whites are to be beaten separately.

7. **Kitchen blender.** Choose a brand such as Oster that has a glass, square-topped pitcher for even blending and ease of cleaning.

8. **Electric skillet.** Rival 12 x 15 x 3-inch pan with a cover. Temperature control is useful for frying chicken or cooking pancakes.

9. **Slow cookers.** One large, 4-quart, for cooking and keeping bigger batches of food warm, and a smaller, such as Rival 1-pint dip pot for hot dips. A removable liner makes cleanup easy.

10. **Pressure cooker.** Four to 6-quart. Mine is 6-quart because I make lots of creamed potatoes.

11. **Roasting pan with rack and cover.** Should be large enough to hold a 20-pound turkey or ham. Cameron manufactures a heavy-duty stainless-steel pan with a flat top that can be used as a separate pan. The handles of the pan and top are offset, making this very large cooker easier to store.

12. **Digital kitchen scale.** Salter weighs amounts up to 11 pounds.

13. **Cookie press.** Manual Mirro press with attachments.

14. **Cast-iron Dutch oven.**

15. **Cast-iron skillet.** Nine or 10 inches in diameter. Directions for seasoning are usually included with the pan. They are also given in this cookbook following the Buttermilk Cornbread recipe (p. 154).

16. **Electric ice-cream churn.** Wooden bucket with a tall metal canister that holds 1 gallon.

# Substitutions and Helpful Hints

- 1 tablespoon = 3 teaspoons
- 1 tablespoon flour = $1\frac{1}{2}$ teaspoons cornstarch
- 1 cup self-rising flour = 1 cup sifted all-purpose flour + $1\frac{1}{2}$ teaspoons baking powder + $\frac{1}{8}$ teaspoon salt
- 1 cup buttermilk = 1 tablespoon lemon juice or white vinegar + enough milk to make 1 cup
- Half-and-half = $1\frac{1}{2}$ tablespoons melted butter + enough whole milk to make 1 cup
- 1 teaspoon vinegar = 2 teaspoons lemon juice
- Make 1 cup confectioners' sugar by streaming $\frac{3}{4}$ cup granulated sugar into the small opening of a blender set at high speed.
- To correct an oversalted soup or stew, add a couple of peeled and quartered white potatoes and cook.
- When selecting cuts of meat, such as hams and roasts, allow 8 ounces, uncooked, per person.

# snacks and appetizers

**Everybody in my family LOVES good food.** We're not much into finger foods because they're just too dainty for us—those tiny servings are usually just enough to whet our appetites! These dips and snacks are so hearty they should probably be called fist foods. I remember how, back when Mama made wedding cakes for extra income, she would also sometimes make cocktail foods for the wedding reception. My sister and I would usually go along to help carry the cake. Beth, being the oldest, was in charge of sitting in the backseat of the station wagon and holding the top layer of the wedding cake, the one with the bride and groom on top. She never dropped one! My job was usually holding one of the bottom layers that could be repaired easily at the church if it got dented along the way. At the reception, I would watch in amazement as people took one or two cheese straws and maybe one sausage hors d'oeuvre, and think that if I could make my own plate, I would pile it high with those yummy treats. Maybe that's where it all began for me, knowing that if I could learn to make this wonderful food myself, I could eat as much of it as I wanted. I have been known, for instance, to make an entire batch of sausage hors d'oeuvres when nobody at all was coming over!

Any of the recipes in this chapter are great whether you have a big party planned, a small gathering of family trickling in for the holidays, or if you're just craving something good!

# Cheese Straws

From Gwen:
If you find a Mirro cookie press, either vintage or new, that includes the star tube, grab it!

I *love* cheese! I would eat a piece of Cheddar cheese over a piece of chocolate cake any day. That probably makes me a little weird, but if you love cheese like I do, you'll love these cheese straws. My mom used to make them for baby showers and wedding receptions. In 1991, the year my career started to really take off, she made them for me to give as Christmas gifts to everyone who had been so supportive. We laughed about how these cheesy treats were baked in a small kitchen in Monticello, Georgia, and ended up on the desks of some of the biggest movers and shakers in Nashville.

3  10-ounce bricks sharp Cheddar cheese, room temperature

1  cup (2 sticks) butter, softened

4  cups sifted all-purpose flour

2  teaspoons salt

⅛  teaspoon black pepper

⅛  teaspoon cayenne pepper

   Dash of garlic powder

Preheat the oven to 325°F.

Put the softened cheese and butter in the bowl of a heavy-duty electric mixer. Using the heaviest mixer attachment, beat the cheese and butter until the mixture has the consistency of whipped cream, about 30 minutes.

On a sheet of waxed paper, sift 3 cups of the flour with the salt, black pepper, cayenne, and garlic powder. Gradually add the seasoned flour to the cheese mixture by large spoonfuls, beating well after each addition. Add the unseasoned flour until the dough is somewhat stiff but still soft enough to be pushed through a cookie press; you may not need to add all of the flour.

Lightly spray a cookie sheet with cooking spray. Put a portion of the dough into a cookie press fitted with the star tube and press the dough onto the cookie sheet in long strips that run the length of the pan (see Note). Bake for 20 minutes. The cheese straws should be golden brown and crisp. With a sharp knife, cut the long strips into 3-inch lengths. Use a flat, thin spatula or egg turner to remove the cheese straws from the pan. Allow them to cool on a wire rack. When they are completely cool, store in a tightly covered container.

Note: If you don't have a cookie press, form the dough into 1-inch balls and flatten them with a fork.

# Sausage Hors d'Oeuvres

Makes 50

I've laughed a lot while writing this cookbook—and gotten very hungry! I laugh because most people consider these tasty meatballs the perfect small bite for a party or wedding reception, but I sometimes make them just to satisfy a craving! They are usually served cold, but when I make them at home, I serve them warm, right out of the oven, and they are awesome! So to answer the burning question, can you make an entire meal out of sausage ball appetizers? *Yes!*

*From Beth:*
Double this recipe, bake, and freeze half for use at a later time.

 1  pound spicy pork sausage

10  ounces Cheddar cheese, grated

 3  cups baking mix, such as Bisquick, or self-rising flour

    Salt and pepper

Preheat the oven to 375°F.

*From Trisha:*
I like Jimmy Dean's sage sausage for this recipe.

Using a stand mixer fitted with the paddle attachment, combine the sausage, cheese, and baking mix and beat on low speed until blended. Add salt and pepper to taste. Shape the mixture into 1-inch balls and place them 1 inch apart on an ungreased cookie sheet. Bake for 20 minutes, or until browned. Drain on paper towels, and serve hot, warm, or at room temperature.

# Kim's Black-Eyed Pea Dip

Note: The electric mixer makes this a smooth dip, and I use the Crock-Pot because I usually serve the dip at parties and like to keep it warm. You can also put the dip in an 8 x 10-inch casserole dish and warm it in the oven at 375°F for 7 to 8 minutes before serving.

I'm sort of a snob when it comes to trying new recipes. I just seem to like my old tried and true ones best, and it takes a lot for something new to grab my attention. I had to have the recipe for this dip after I tried it on Super Bowl Sunday 2006. Garth is a die-hard Steelers fan, so it was an exciting day. Everybody always brings something for the party, and this was my friend Kim's contribution. Being a good southern girl, I love anything with black-eyed peas in it, but for you folks who are right now turning up your noses at the idea of eating black-eyed peas, all I can say is just try it. In fact, maybe I should name it something else for those skeptics. How about Pea Dippy?

- 3   15-ounce cans black-eyed peas, rinsed and drained
- ½   cup finely chopped canned pickled jalapeños, juices reserved
- 10  ounces Cheddar cheese, grated
- 1   medium sweet onion, finely chopped
- ¼   cup (½ stick) butter, softened
- ¼   teaspoon garlic powder

In an electric mixer or large mixing bowl, mix together the peas, jalapeños, 3 tablespoons of the reserved jalapeño juice, Cheddar, onion, butter, and garlic powder until blended. Heat the dip in a medium Crock-Pot and serve it warm with corn chips.

# Warm Feta Dip with Artichokes

Spinach artichoke dips seem to be on every restaurant's appetizer list these days, and I like them okay but have never been a big spinach fan. Feta cheese, on the other hand, is something I'm very fond of, so I was excited to find this recipe. It's also one of those really easy recipes that tastes like it must have been really hard to make. You gotta love those!

Serves 8

1   14-ounce can artichoke hearts, drained and finely chopped

5   ounces feta cheese, crumbled

¾   cup mayonnaise

½   cup grated Parmesan cheese

1   2-ounce jar pimientos, drained and diced

2   teaspoons minced garlic

    Pita chips or Melba toast, for dipping

Preheat the oven to 350°F.

In a medium bowl, stir together the artichoke hearts, feta cheese, mayonnaise, Parmesan cheese, pimientos, and garlic until thoroughly combined. Transfer the mixture to a small casserole or glass pie plate and bake, uncovered, for 25 minutes, or until lightly browned. To serve, place the dish on a larger platter and surround with pita chips or Melba toast.

# Ranch Dressing Cheese Ball

Makes 2 cheese balls; serves 24

*From Beth:*
Let this sit at room temperature for about 30 minutes before serving for easier spreading.

This is my sister's go-to appetizer for church socials, Super Bowl Sundays, and Christmas munchies. Several years ago, she put too much of the ranch dressing mix into the recipe, and it was hard to serve. My dad renamed it the "cheese wad." We think Ranch Dressing Cheese Ball sounds more appetizing, but at our house, it will forever be known as Cheese Wad!

1 4-ounce package Hidden Valley Ranch dressing mix

½ cup mayonnaise

½ cup buttermilk, well shaken

16 ounces Cheddar cheese, grated, room temperature

12 ounces cream cheese, room temperature

1 cup pecans, finely chopped

In a medium bowl, combine the dressing mix, mayonnaise, buttermilk, Cheddar, and cream cheese until thoroughly blended. Divide the mixture into two equal portions in two separate bowls. Cover the bowls and place them in the freezer for 30 minutes. When each portion is firm, use your hands to shape it into a ball. Place the nuts in a shallow bowl or on a piece of waxed paper. Roll each ball in the nuts to coat it on all sides. Serve with crackers or bagel chips.

# Pimiento Cheese Spread

A pimiento cheese sandwich made on very fresh white bread is a true southern staple. Nothing goes better with Gwen's Fried Chicken (page 93). Mama slices the crusts off the sandwiches and cuts them in half for family reunions—very southern belle!

Makes 4 cups

*From Gwen:* Make a lot of these. One triangle disappears in only three bites!

2   7-ounce jars canned, sliced pimientos, drained

3   10-ounce bricks sharp Cheddar cheese, finely grated

1   cup mayonnaise

Place the drained pimientos in a blender or food processor and purée until smooth. Using an electric mixer, combine the cheese and pimiento, beating until smooth. Beat in the mayonnaise. Spread on slices of white sandwich bread while the mixture is room temperature. Trim the bread crusts and cut the sandwiches into triangles.

The spread may be stored, covered, in the refrigerator for up to 1 week. Remove the spread from the refrigerator and allow it to reach room temperature before serving.

# His 'n' Hers Deviled Eggs

Makes 24

You won't go to a southern picnic or covered-dish supper and *not* see deviled eggs. Garth and I grew up eating different versions of this dish, so both varieties are included here. Honestly, I never met a deviled egg I didn't like, so these are both yummy to me!

12  large eggs

## His Filling

¼  cup mayonnaise

2  teaspoons yellow mustard

1  tablespoon butter, softened

Salt and pepper to taste

## Her Filling

¼  cup mayonnaise

1½  tablespoons sweet pickle relish

1  teaspoon yellow mustard

Salt and pepper to taste

Paprika for garnish

*From Trisha:* Cool, crack, and peel the eggs like the recipe says, or your yolks will turn green on the outside! I guess that's where green eggs and ham came from.

Place the eggs in a medium saucepan with water to cover and bring to a boil. Remove from the heat, cover the pan, and let stand for 20 minutes. Pour off the hot water and refill the saucepan with cold water. Crack the eggsshells all over and let them sit in the cold water for 5 minutes. Peel the eggs, cover, and chill for at least 1 hour.

Halve the eggs lengthwise. Carefully remove the yolks and transfer them to a small bowl. Mash the yolks with a fork, then stir in the filling ingredients of your choice. Season with salt and pepper. Scoop a spoonful of the mixture into each egg white half. Sprinkle the tops with paprika.

This is one time when freshest isn't bestest. Very fresh eggs are hard to peel, so use eggs near the sell-by date on the carton. Also, invert each egg in the carton the night before cooking so the yolk will become more centered in the white. It makes a prettier deviled egg. Who knew?

# Boiled Peanuts

If you've ever driven through a small town in Georgia, you no doubt have seen signs for boiled peanuts along the roadside. I've found that they're a love-hate thing; people are rarely undecided about boiled peanuts! I include the recipe here because I absolutely love them. When I make them at home in Oklahoma, it takes me back to our family vacation trips to Florida, when we'd stop on the roadside and eat the warm peanuts in the car. Yum!

5   pounds fresh green peanuts
    Salt

Wash the peanuts and put them in a 3-quart stockpot. Add enough water to barely float the peanuts, measuring the amount of water required. Add ⅔ cup salt for each gallon of water used. Stir to distribute the salt. Bring the water to a boil and reduce the heat to medium. Cover the pan and cook the peanuts for 1½ hours, or until the shelled peanuts are tender. Add water during cooking if the peanuts are no longer floating in the liquid. Remove from the heat and cool in the cooking liquid.

The peanuts will become saltier as they sit in the liquid, so taste them at intervals as they are cooling. When they are as salty as you like them, drain the peanuts (do not rinse) and store them in the refrigerator or freezer. (If the boiled peanuts are too salty, soak them in plain water to dilute the saltiness.)

Makes 10 cups

*From Gwen:* Use green peanuts for this. Dried nuts in the shell are just not as tender.

# Green Punch

Makes 20 cups

Serve this punch with Cheese Straws (page 20). It's a Yearwood family tradition—perfect to serve at Christmas parties, because it's a beautiful bright green and makes a pretty punch bowl.

2   .13-ounce packets unsweetened lemon-lime soft drink mix, such as Kool-Aid

2   cups sugar

1   46-ounce can pineapple juice

12   ounces frozen lemonade concentrate, thawed

32   ounces (1 quart) ginger ale

Put 2 quarts of water in a 1-gallon container. Add the drink mix and sugar and stir until the sugar is dissolved. Add the pineapple juice and lemonade concentrate and stir well. Just before serving, add the ginger ale.

*From Gwen:* Monticello ladies often act as hostesses for everything from bridal showers to baby showers. This easy punch is a favorite for those occasions.

# Jerry's Sugared Pecans

Makes 4 cups

I think making someone else's recipes is a wonderful way to remember them when they're no longer with us. Garth's brother Jerry loved my cooking, and he was a good cook himself. He always made me feel he truly appreciated the meals I made for him, and I loved him for it. He had a wonderful smile and a great spirit. Jerry brought these pecans out to the house one day, and I only stopped eating them when they were gone! The butter and sugar make them crunchy, sweet, and rich.

½  cup (1 stick) butter, melted

3  large egg whites

1  cup sugar

1  teaspoon ground cinnamon

4  cups pecan halves

*From Gwen:* These pecans will still be a bit wet and gooey when you take them out of the oven. As they cool on the baking sheet, they will get crunchy.

Preheat the oven to 350°F.

Line a large baking sheet with sides with aluminum foil. Pour the butter onto the lined sheet. In a large bowl, mix the egg whites, sugar, and cinnamon. Add the pecan halves and toss until they are fully coated. Spread the pecans onto the baking sheet. Bake for 30 minutes, stirring the pecans every 10 minutes. Cool on the baking sheet for 10 to 15 minutes before serving.

# Grandma Yearwood's Sweet Iceberg Pickles

Makes 6 quarts

These are sweet and crunchy, like no other pickle I've ever tasted. They're great on salads, but I eat them right out of the jar with a fork!

3  cups pickling lime (see Note on page 36)

7  pounds small cucumbers (no bigger than 1 inch in diameter), unpeeled, sliced crosswise ⅛ inch thick

5  pounds sugar

6  cups apple cider vinegar

1  tablespoon whole cloves

1  ounce fresh ginger

1  tablespoon whole allspice berries

1  tablespoon celery seed

2  cinnamon sticks, broken into pieces

*From Gwen:* Chill before serving. Store leftover pickles in the refrigerator.

Note: Five tablespoons mixed pickling spices may be used instead of the individual spices.

Mix 2 gallons water with the lime in a 3-gallon stockpot. Add the cucumbers, stir, and soak for 24 hours, stirring occasionally to redistribute the lime.

Stir the pickles and drain the lime water. Replace the lime water with 2 gallons fresh water. Some lime will remain in the pickles at this point. Soak for 1 hour, then drain and replace with fresh water again. Continue soaking the pickles in fresh water and draining every hour until the pickles have soaked in fresh water for 4 hours. Drain again.

In a separate large saucepan, mix the sugar and vinegar. Place the cloves, ginger, allspice, celery seed, and cinnamon on a square of cheesecloth and bring the sides in to make a small bag; tie it closed with cotton string or thread (see Note at left). Bring the vinegar mixture to a boil and pour it (including the cheesecloth bundle) over the

continued . . .

Note: You can find pickling lime in the canning section of a grocery store, or ask at your local farmer's market. You can also order pickling lime at www.kitchen krafts.com and www.canning pantry.com.

pickles. Bring the pickles and vinegar to a boil. Remove from the heat and let stand overnight.

The next day, bring the pickles back to a boil and simmer for 1 hour. Wash and rinse 12 1-pint canning jars. Fill the jars with pickles and liquid, leaving ½ inch head space at the top of each jar. Wipe the edges of the jars and close with canning lids and rings, hand-tightening each. Seal the jars in a hot-water bath (instructions follow) or in a large pressure canner, following the manufacturer's instructions.

## Hot-Water Bath Method for Sealing Canning Jars

Place a wire rack with handles in the bottom of a large, deep pot with a lid. The rack will keep the jars off the bottom of the pot, and the handles make it easier to add and remove the jars. Fill the pot half full of water and bring to a boil. Lower the jars slowly and carefully into the water. The water should cover the jars by 1 inch. Add more boiling water if necessary to reach this level. Cover the pot and boil the jars for 30 minutes after the water has returned to a boil. Carefully remove the jars from the water and set aside to cool. The jar lids will pop and invert as they seal.

When the jars are cool, remove the rings if the pickles are to be stored before use. The rings may rust during lengthy storage, making them difficult to remove. When the rings are removed, the jars should be wiped clean and handled in such a way as not to disturb the sealed lid. Lift by the sides or the glass rim only.

# Vi's Garlic Dill Pickles

If you're not a sweet pickle fan, you should try these wonderful dill pickles that my friend Lisa's grandmother makes. Sweet pickles are generally sliced, but these are served whole. They are deliciously dilled and better than any store-bought pickle, I guarantee it!

| | |
|---|---|
| 12 | large sprigs fresh dill |
| 6 | garlic cloves, peeled |
| 6 | pounds small cucumbers, no more than 1 inch in diameter |
| 2 | cups cider vinegar |
| ½ | cup sugar |
| ½ | cup rock salt |

Wash and rinse 6 1-quart canning jars. Place a sprig of dill and a clove of garlic in the bottom of each jar. Pack the cucumbers into the jars and place a large sprig of dill on top of each. In a saucepan, combine 1½ quarts water and the vinegar, sugar, and salt. Bring to a boil, then remove from the heat. Pour the vinegar mixture over the cucumbers. Wipe the tops of the jars and close with canning lids and rings. Seal the jars by processing in a hot-water bath (page 36) for 3 minutes.

Makes 5 to 6 quarts

*From Gwen:* I first ate these wonderful pickles when Lisa brought them to supper in Oklahoma. Those large sprigs of dill were beautiful in the jar.

# soups and salads

There's nothing like walking into the kitchen on a cold, rainy day and smelling a warm, inviting soup simmering on the stove. I love soup, all kinds of soup. I love soups with thin broth and rich, hearty soups that are meals all by themselves. Because a soup is only as good as the broth it is based on, we give our recipe for homemade boiled hen and broth, which we use to make chicken and dumplings, among many other soothing, homey soups.

Any of these salads would make a nice meal with a warm bowl of soup. Because I like a lot of texture and interest in my salads, you'll find many of these have something extra thrown in at the end, like a sprinkle of bacon or chopped nuts or sunflower seeds. The southern nut of choice is most often the pecan (here and throughout the book), but I would encourage you to try almonds, walnuts, or whatever nut strikes your fancy. Served on their own or paired up, these soups and salads will leave you satisfied!

# Lizzie's Chicken and Dumplings

Serves 6

My grandmother, Lizzie Paulk, was an amazing woman. She worked the fields in South Georgia with my grandfather Winnes, raised three children, and somehow still found time to put three home-cooked meals on the table every single day. She passed away when I was in junior high, but I have wonderful memories of her laughter and her love for her family. Mama had always complained she could never get her dumplings to come out as thin as her mom's, but the first time she made them after Grandma died, she said it was as if Lizzie were guiding her. Maybe she finally decided it was okay for Mama to be able to make her dumplings! They've come out perfectly every time since. (See photo, page 10.)

- 1  5-pound hen (makes about 4 pounds cooked, after bones and skin are removed)
- 1  tablespoon salt
- 1  teaspoon pepper

## Dumplings
- 2  cups unsifted all-purpose flour
- 1  teaspoon salt
- ¾  cup water

    Salt and pepper

*From Gwen:*
My mom would drape the dough strips over her fingers as she transferred the pieces to the broth. It was fun for me, many years later, to allow my grandchildren to handle the dough the same way.

Put the hen, breast side down, in a very large (8-quart) stockpot and add water to within 2 inches of the top of the pot; this will vary according to the size of your pot, but the hen should float clear of the bottom of the pot and be covered completely. Add the salt and pepper. Bring the water to a boil and reduce the heat to simmer. Cover the pot and cook for 2 hours, or until the chicken is tender and the drumstick joint twists easily. Allow the chicken and broth to cool slightly, and then remove the chicken to a colander.

Strain the broth into a very large bowl. Cover the broth and place it in the refrigerator. When the fat solidifies on the top of the broth, remove and discard it. Remove the chicken from the bones and cut or shred the meat by hand into small pieces. Set aside 2 cups and refrigerate or freeze the rest for another use. (Leftover broth may also be frozen in individual containers to be used another time.)

To make the dumplings, heat 2 quarts of the defatted chicken broth in a 3-quart saucepan. While it heats, put the flour in a medium bowl. Dissolve the salt in the water and stir the mixture into the flour to make a stiff dough. Turn the dough out onto a heavily floured surface and knead until smooth, 1 to 2 minutes. Divide it into 4 parts. Heavily flour a rolling pin. Roll one portion of the dough very thin. With a very sharp knife or pizza cutter, cut the dough into 2 x 4-inch strips.

When the broth reaches a rolling boil, add the strips of dough. Reduce the heat to a simmer, cover the pot, and roll out another portion of dough, cut it into strips, and drop them into the broth. Continue preparing each portion of the dough and adding the strips in this manner. Always raise the heat to bring the broth back to a rolling boil before dropping in more dough strips, and then reduce the heat to simmer before covering the pot again. Sprinkle in the salt and pepper to taste. Add the 2 cups of cooked chicken and cover the pan. Simmer for 15 minutes.

Many cookbooks assume we all know the basics of cooking, and instructions for boiling a hen, like you'll find in this recipe, are seldom included. When I first moved away from home and started asking my mom for recipes, I needed her help with everything from boiling corn on the cob to making chicken broth from scratch. If I don't use all the broth from a hen in the recipe I'm making, or if I'm just cooking the chicken to use in a salad, I save the broth and freeze it for the future. Canned chicken broth is good, but homemade is always better! A hen is a mature chicken that produces eggs. A fryer is a younger, more tender chicken. Using a hen for chicken stock gives you a richer broth, because hens have more fat than fryers. Mama taught me that!

# Mama's Awesome Chicken Noodle Soup

Serves 10

I love living in Oklahoma. I do miss my family in Georgia, but luckily I get to travel back and forth a lot for visits. My Georgia family has also made the trek to Oklahoma several times, so now both places feel like home. Only once have I gotten so homesick I thought I wouldn't make it, and that was because I was really sick with the flu and Mama wasn't there to take care of me. Sometimes nobody will do except Mama! She made this soup for me, froze it in quart containers, packed it in dry ice (who knew you could get dry ice in Monticello?), and shipped it overnight to me in a Styrofoam cooler. When I got it the next morning, I cried, ate some soup, cried, ate some more soup, and thanked God for the most awesome mom on the planet!

*From Gwen:* I would never have guessed that sending this simple soup would bring such pleasure to my child *and* to me!

- 1   4-pound hen
- 3   celery stalks with leafy tops, chopped
- 3   carrots, peeled and chopped
- 3   garlic cloves, sliced
- 1   large sweet onion, such as Vidalia, chopped
- 2   tablespoons salt
- ½   teaspoon black pepper
- ½   teaspoon chopped fresh parsley
- 2   bay leaves
- 1   16-ounce package frozen green peas
- 8   ounces noodles, such as egg noodles or very thin spaghetti, broken into small pieces

Put the hen in a large stockpot and pour in water to cover (about 8 cups). Add the celery, carrots, garlic, onion, salt, pepper, parsley, and bay leaves. Bring to a boil over high heat, then immediately reduce the heat to a simmer. Skim off any foam that rises to the surface. Simmer the hen for 2 hours, or until the meat comes off the bone easily. Remove the hen to a large bowl and cool. Strain the broth into a large bowl and discard the vegetables. Chill the broth and skim off and discard any fat that has risen to the top.

When the chicken is cool enough to handle, remove the meat from the bones, discarding the bones and skin, and shred the meat into bite-sized pieces.

Return the broth to a large pot. Add the shredded chicken, the frozen peas, and the noodles. Bring the soup to a boil, then simmer over medium heat for 10 minutes, or until the pasta is tender. Add extra salt to taste if desired.

# Trisha's Chicken Tortilla Soup

Chicken tortilla soup became really popular in restaurants a few years ago, but it was never something I made at home. Garth loves this soup and orders it almost every time he sees it on a menu, so I started studying the different versions at each restaurant and questioning Garth about what he liked and didn't like about each one. This recipe I finally came up with doesn't actually taste like any of those we tasted in restaurants, but we love it—and now we can enjoy it whenever we want!

- 3 tablespoons butter
- 1 teaspoon minced garlic
- 1 medium onion, finely chopped
- 2 tablespoons all-purpose flour
- 3 14-ounce cans chicken broth
- 4 cups half-and-half
- 1 10.75-ounce can cream of chicken soup
- 1 cup prepared salsa, mild or spicy, according to your taste
- 4 boneless, skinless chicken breasts, boiled, drained, and shredded
- 1 15-ounce can kidney beans, drained
- 1 15-ounce can black beans, drained
- 1 15-ounce can whole kernel corn, drained
- 2 teaspoons ground cumin
- 1 1.27-ounce packet fajita seasoning
- 1 16-ounce bag tortilla chips
- 8 ounces Monterey Jack cheese, grated
- 8 ounces sharp Cheddar cheese, grated
- ½ cup sour cream

Melt the butter in a large pot over medium heat; add the garlic and onion and sauté for 5 minutes, or until softened. Add the flour and stir well, cooking for 1 minute more. Add the broth and the half-and-half. Bring to a boil over medium heat, about 10 minutes, then reduce the heat to low. Stir in the cream of chicken soup, salsa, chicken, beans, corn, cumin, and fajita seasoning. Continue to simmer over low heat for 15 minutes. Crumble the tortilla chips into individual bowls and top with a ladle of soup. Sprinkle each serving with cheese and add a dollop of sour cream.

# Jack's Brunswick Stew

Makes 16 1-cup servings

*From Gwen:* The "stew-cooking day" started before sunrise, and the early helpers were rewarded with coffee and sausage biscuits prepared by Jack.

My daddy was a great cook, and many of the recipes in this cookbook are his. If there was a fund-raiser in Monticello, people would always ask, "Is Jack making the Brunswick Stew?" or "Is Jack cooking the chickens?" before they bought their tickets. The food was usually prepared outside in very large quantities with the help of members of the sponsoring organization. Brunswick Stew is one of those classic southern dishes that varies from region to region, but I've never had Brunswick Stew that tasted like my dad's. In his version, everything is ground through a food grinder, so it's more like a wonderfully rich soup than a stew. His version also fed 160 people, so we've reduced our recipe to serve a cozy 16!

| | |
|---|---|
| 1 | pound Boston butt pork roast |
| 1 | pound fresh chicken or hen, bone in |
| 1 | pound boneless beef chuck roast |
| 1 | pound red or white potatoes |
| 1 | small (3 ounces) sweet onion, such as Vidalia |
| 6 | cups canned tomatoes |
| 2½ | teaspoons salt |
| 2½ | teaspoons ground black pepper |
| ⅛ | teaspoon ground cayenne (red) pepper |
| ¾ | cup ketchup |
| 2 | tablespoons Worcestershire sauce |
| 32 | ounces (4 cups) cream-style white corn |

Place the pork and chicken in a 1½-gallon stockpot with water to cover. Bring to a boil, then immediately reduce the heat to a simmer. Skim off any foam that rises to the top and cook for 2 hours, or until the meat is very tender, skimming occasionally. Remove the meat to a bowl and reserve the stock.

At the same time, place the beef in a separate large stockpot with water to cover and cook for 2 hours, or until tender. Remove the beef and discard the broth.

Peel, quarter, and cook the potatoes in water until tender (see Note).

Remove and discard the bones and skin from all the cooked meat, and grind the meat with a heavy-duty meat grinder. Put 2 pints of the pork and chicken stock into a 1½-gallon stockpot. (Reserve the rest for another use.) Add the ground meats to the stock.

Peel and grind the onion and add it to the meat mixture. Grind the tomatoes, add them to the stockpot, and bring the mixture to a boil. When the stew is hot, grind and blend in the cooked potatoes, stirring until any lumps are removed. At this point, the stew should be soupy but not watery. If the stew is too thick to stir easily with a flat spatula or pancake turner, thin it slightly with the reserved pork and chicken stock.

Stir in the salt. Dissolve the black pepper and cayenne pepper in 1 tablespoon water, then add to the stew along with the ketchup and Worcestershire sauce. Cook for 30 minutes, stirring constantly.

Grind and add the corn, then continue to cook the stew over very low heat for 1 hour, stirring often and scraping the bottom of the stockpot with a flat spatula or pancake turner to avoid scorching.

Note: Cooking the potatoes before grinding them makes the stew cook more quickly. This method also makes the stew smoother and gives it the signature texture only Jack's stew has.

*Daddy stirring Brunswick Stew for 160 people!*

# Winter Vegetable Soup

Serves 6

Some recipes in this book have been passed down from generation to generation, and some are newer recipes discovered in the past few years that have become family classics. This is one of the old-timers. My mom used to make this soup when I was a child, and I remember how much my dad loved it served over biscuits. For me, when a recipe has a great memory attached to it, it tastes even better. I make this soup at the first sign of cold weather every year and serve it poured over Buttermilk Cornbread.

*From Gwen:*
If you're lucky enough to have a ham hock, cook it in water for seasoning instead of chicken broth.

2   14-ounce cans chicken broth

3   red potatoes, about 4 ounces each, peeled and diced into ¾-inch pieces

1   12-ounce can diced tomatoes

1   8-ounce package frozen lima beans

2   tablespoons finely chopped onion

1   12-ounce can cream-style corn

Salt and pepper to taste

In a medium saucepan, combine the broth with the potatoes, tomatoes, beans, and onion. Bring to a boil, then reduce the heat and cook the soup over medium heat for 20 to 25 minutes, or until the potatoes are tender. Remove from the heat, stir in the corn, and serve. Salt and pepper to taste. This soup goes great with Buttermilk Cornbread (page 154).

# Baked Potato Soup

*From Beth:*
For a pretty presentation, top individual bowls of soup with a sprinkling of shredded cheese, crumbled bacon, and chopped green onions.

The best description I can offer of my sister's baked potato soup is that it tastes just like the best potato bar you ever tried. I always used to love twice-baked potatoes, mainly because the work of "fixing" a baked potato with the sour cream, cheese, and so on, was all done for you. It's the same with this soup. It's like someone fixed the ultimate baked potato just for you and put it into a bowl. All you have to do is enjoy it.

4  large baking potatoes

6  bacon slices

$\frac{2}{3}$  cup ($1\frac{1}{3}$ sticks) butter

$\frac{2}{3}$  cup all-purpose flour

6  cups milk

$\frac{3}{4}$  teaspoon salt

$\frac{1}{2}$  teaspoon pepper

2  green onions (scallions), finely chopped

5  ounces Cheddar cheese, shredded

8  ounces sour cream

Preheat the oven to 400°F.

Wash the potatoes and prick them several times with a fork. Wrap them individually in foil, and bake them for 1 hour, or until they are soft when squeezed (see Note). Let the potatoes cool slightly.

While the potatoes bake, cook the bacon in a small skillet, in a microwave, or on an indoor grill until crisp. Drain the bacon on paper towels and, when cool enough to handle, crumble it into small pieces. Set aside.

In a large, heavy saucepan, melt the butter over low heat. Add the flour, stirring constantly for 1 minute until smooth. Gradually whisk in the milk and cook over medium heat, stirring constantly, for 5 to 10 minutes, until the mixture is thick and bubbling. Cut the potatoes in half lengthwise, and scoop the flesh into the thickened milk mixture. Add the salt, pepper, green onions, reserved bacon, and Cheddar. Cook over low heat just until heated through. Stir in the sour cream and serve.

Note: Wrapping the potatoes in foil before baking makes them cook faster. To shorten the preparation time even more, peel the potatoes, cut them into 1-inch cubes, and cook them in a pressure cooker for 5 minutes. Leftover baked potatoes may also be used for this recipe. Peel and mash them coarsely before adding to the milk mixture.

*Bret, Ashley, and Kyle Bernard*

# Potato Salad

When it comes to potato salad, you like what you like. This recipe is mayonnaise-based, but if you like a mustard-based potato salad, just experiment a little. Add some yellow mustard and leave out a little bit of the mayonnaise. Make these recipes your own by finding out what works for you. Our traditional potato salad uses peeled potatoes, but unpeeled work too, and the skins add some color to your dish.

Serves 12

5   pounds red potatoes, peeled and cut in ½-inch cubes

2   teaspoons salt, plus more to taste

4   hard-boiled eggs, peeled, and diced

¾   cup mayonnaise

½   cup sweet pickle relish

    Black pepper

*From Gwen:* Don't overcook the potatoes. They should hold their shape during mixing.

Place the potatoes in a medium saucepan or pressure cooker (see Note). Add 2 teaspoons salt and enough water to cover the potatoes. Boil the potatoes for 30 minutes, or until they are tender when pierced with the point of a knife but hold their shape. Drain the potatoes, transfer them to a large mixing bowl, and allow them to cool completely. Add the chopped eggs, mayonnaise, and sweet relish, and fold gently to combine. Add salt and pepper to taste. Refrigerate until ready to serve.

Note: The potatoes may be cooked in a pressure cooker. Sprinkle salt over the potatoes. Follow the manufacturer's instructions and pressure-cook for 5 minutes. Release the pressure immediately and drain and cool the potatoes.

# Fourth of July Coleslaw

There are as many varieties of coleslaw as there are shades of pink, especially in the South! A lot of coleslaw recipes have sugar as an ingredient, but this one gets that bit of sweetness from sweet salad pickles, which don't mask the fresh flavors of the cabbage and carrots. We serve this every Fourth of July with Barbecued Pork Ribs (page 84) and Easy Baked Beans (page 133).

*From Gwen:* The sweetest cabbage I've ever had was brought to us by friends from Spruce Pine, North Carolina.

1   firm head green cabbage, about 2 pounds

1   large carrot, peeled

½   small sweet onion, such as Vidalia, peeled and chopped fine

¼   cup diced salad pickles

½   cup mayonnaise

½   teaspoon salt

    Pinch of black pepper

Remove and discard any bruised or undesirable outside leaves from the head of cabbage. Quarter the cabbage and grate it into a large bowl using the coarse side of a hand grater or the shredding blade of a food processor. Grate the carrot and add it to the cabbage, tossing together to combine. Add the onion, pickles, mayonnaise, salt, and pepper. Stir together until thoroughly mixed. Chill for 1 hour before serving.

# Pink Salad

We always made this to take to Family Night suppers at church. Its official name was Congealed Fruit Salad, but it was known at our house as pink salad, because, well, it's pink! Besides, anything with the word *congealed* in the title just sounds gross to me, and this is anything but.

Serves 8

1   cup boiling water

1   3-ounce package strawberry-flavored gelatin

1   3-ounce package cream cheese, room temperature

1   15-ounce can crushed unsweetened pineapple, drained

2   ripe but firm bananas, peeled and diced

1   6–ounce jar maraschino cherries with juice, stems removed

½   cup chopped pecans

1   cup heavy cream

*From Gwen:* Substituting orange-flavored gelatin gives this salad a soft, appealing peach color.

Pour the boiling water into a large mixing bowl. Add the gelatin and stir until dissolved. Blend in the cream cheese, stirring until it is thoroughly mixed and the gelatin is completely dissolved. Cool in the refrigerator until the mixture thickens but is not fully gelled, about 45 minutes. Add the pineapple, bananas, cherries, and nuts, and mix gently.

In a separate bowl, use an electric mixer or whisk to beat the cream until stiff. Gently fold the whipped cream into the thickened gelatin mixture, and pour into a 6 x 9 x 2-inch dish. Refrigerate overnight, or until firm.

# Lettuce Wedge Salad with Trisha's Easy Thousand Island Dressing

Serves 4

*From Trisha:* This dressing also makes a great topping for burgers.

*From Gwen:* There are no pickles in the dressing, thus no "islands." I call it Rushin' Dressing because you can mix it quickly when you are rushing to get dinner on the table.

I'm the hick who always asks the uptown restaurant waiter if they have Thousand Island dressing. They usually give me that look (you know the one), then politely inform me it is not on the menu. I know there are lots of wonderful dressings out there, and I've sampled most of them, but I always come back to this one. I usually whip it up and pour it over a big iceberg lettuce wedge.

- 1 head iceberg lettuce
- ½ cup mayonnaise
- 3 tablespoons ketchup

  Dash of Tabasco sauce

  Dash of black pepper

Wash the lettuce and remove any damaged or wilted outer leaves. Remove the lettuce core and discard. Cut the head into quarters and set it aside.

In a medium bowl, whisk together the mayonnaise and the ketchup. Add the Tabasco sauce and pepper to taste. Place a lettuce wedge on each serving plate. Drizzle with the dressing.

## Quick Lettuce Core Removal Tip

Slam the head of lettuce down on a cutting board, core-side down. The core will separate from the rest of the head with a twist and come out easily.

# Minty Greek Salad

I am a big fan of Greek salads, but at restaurants I seem to find myself always picking the vegetables and cheese out of the lettuce. One day I thought, why make it with lettuce at all? This recipe is just veggies and feta. I love it!

|  |  |
|---|---|
| 2 | cucumbers, peeled and cut into chunks |
| 16 | pitted green olives |
| 16 | pitted black olives, such as kalamata |
| 24 | grape tomatoes, halved |
| 2 | cups feta cheese, crumbled |
| ¼ | cup olive oil |
| 2 | tablespoons fresh lemon juice |
|  | Pinch of salt and pepper |
| 1 | tablespoon fresh mint, chopped |

In a large bowl, combine the cucumbers, olives, tomatoes, and feta cheese. In a small bowl, mix the olive oil and lemon juice. Pour the dressing mixture over the vegetables. Season with salt and pepper to taste. Garnish with the mint.

# Broccoli Salad

This is great served with Barbecued Pork Ribs (page 84) or prepared to take to a covered dish supper, because it's sturdy enough to stand at room temperature for a while without wilting. It also adds great color to a picnic spread.

*From Beth:* Low-fat mayonnaise can be substituted for regular without significantly changing the taste or texture.

½  pound bacon

2  cups small broccoli florets

1  cup mayonnaise

1  tablespoon cider vinegar

⅓  cup chopped onion

¼  cup sugar

¾  cup raisins

½  cup sunflower kernels

In a medium skillet, cook the bacon over medium heat just until crisp; drain on paper towels. When cool enough to handle, crumble the bacon and set aside.

Bring a large saucepan of salted water to a boil. Add the broccoli and blanch until bright green and slightly softened, about 3 minutes. Drain well, run under cold water to stop the cooking, and drain again.

In a mixing bowl, combine the mayonnaise, vinegar, onion, sugar, and raisins. Add the broccoli and toss to coat with the dressing. Refrigerate for 1 hour.

Just before serving, fold in the sunflower kernels and all but 2 tablespoons of the crumbled bacon. Sprinkle the reserved bacon over the salad to garnish. Serve immediately.

# Chicken Salad with Fruit

Serves 12

This unusual take on chicken salad is a meal in itself, with the rice, fruit, and almonds as well as cooked chicken. Just add bread or crackers.

*From Beth:*
I know this sounds like an odd combination of ingredients, but don't leave anything out! That's what makes it so interesting.

5   boneless, skinless chicken breasts, cooked (see page 61)

1   cup mayonnaise

2   tablespoons olive oil

2   tablespoons orange juice

1   teaspoon salt

3   cups cooked rice, cooled

1½   cups green grapes, halved

1   13-ounce can pineapple tidbits in juice, drained

1   15-ounce can mandarin oranges, drained

1   cup slivered almonds

    Pepper

In a large bowl, stir together the mayonnaise, oil, orange juice, and salt. Dice the cooled chicken, then add to the dressing with the rice, grapes, pineapple, oranges, and almonds, folding gently to coat the ingredients with the dressing. Add pepper to taste and gently mix again.

Cover the bowl and refrigerate overnight to allow the flavors to develop. Serve chilled.

# Trisha's Homemade Chicken Salad

I keep this chicken salad in the refrigerator pretty much year round. It's easy to make, and it keeps in the fridge for a week. Of course, at my house, it only lasts a few days! I serve this on toasted bread, or with wheat crackers as an appetizer.

- 6   medium boneless, skinless chicken breasts
- ½   teaspoon salt
- 4   hard-boiled eggs, peeled and diced
- ½   cup sweet pickle relish
- 1   cup mayonnaise
- Salt and pepper to taste

Place the chicken in a large pot with water to cover. Add the salt, bring to a boil, then reduce the heat to a low simmer and cook the chicken until tender, about 45 minutes (see Note). Drain the chicken, cover, and refrigerate until cool, or up to 24 hours.

Pull the cooled chicken into shreds and place in a large bowl. Add the eggs, relish, and mayonnaise, and stir together gently until well mixed. Season with salt and pepper.

Serves 10

*From Gwen:* It may sound weird, but I love this for breakfast on a slice of toasted bread!

Note: You may also cook the chicken in a pressure cooker, in which case you should reduce the cooking time to 15 minutes.

# Margaret's Cranberry Salad

From Gwen:
A Monticello friend prepared this recipe at my request and gave it a big thumbs-up!

Note: To toast pecans, place them on a baking sheet. Place in a 350°F oven or toaster oven for 10 minutes, or until they are fragrant and golden brown.

My sister Beth's sister-in-law, Margaret, makes this salad, and it's a nice alternative to plain cranberry sauce for holiday meals. In fact, it's rich enough to serve as a dessert!

1   13.5-ounce can crushed pineapple in juice

2   3-ounce packages lemon gelatin

7   ounces ginger ale

1   16-ounce can whole cranberry sauce

2   ounces Dream Whip, prepared (or 8 ounces Cool Whip)

1   8-ounce package cream cheese, room temperature

½   cup toasted pecans, chopped (see Note)

Drain the pineapple and pour the juice into a measuring cup, reserving the pineapple separately. Add enough water to the pineapple juice to make 1 cup. Bring the liquid to a boil in a medium saucepan. Add the gelatin and stir until it dissolves. Chill the gelatin until it is cool but not set. Stir in the ginger ale and chill for 1 additional hour, or until partially set.

Combine the cranberry sauce and the reserved pineapple and add to the gelatin mixture. Pour into a 9 x 9 x 2-inch dish and refrigerate until firm, 4 hours or overnight. Prepare the Dream Whip according to package directions, and then blend in the softened cream cheese. Spread the cheese mixture over the gelatin salad like frosting, then sprinkle with the chopped pecans.

# Spinach Salad with Garlic Dressing

I'm not a cooked spinach fan, but I do like spinach served fresh in a salad. (And I love any salad that has bacon as an ingredient!) I'm also not a mushroom gal, so I leave those out when I make it, but it's good either way.

½   pound bacon

¾   cup olive oil

¼   cup red wine vinegar

½   teaspoon salt

1   teaspoon minced garlic

    Freshly ground pepper

1   pound leaf spinach, tough stems removed

½   pound mushrooms, thinly sliced

In a medium skillet, cook the bacon over medium-high heat until just crisp. Drain on paper towels and, when cool enough to handle, crumble. Set aside.

In a small bowl, whisk together the oil, vinegar, salt, garlic, and pepper. Chill and beat vigorously before using.

Wash the spinach leaves very well and spin dry. Tear the leaves into small pieces and place in a medium salad bowl. Add the mushrooms and bacon and toss to combine. Pour ⅔ cup of the dressing over the salad (reserve the rest for another use) and toss again. Serve immediately.

# Sweet and Crunchy Garden Salad

Browning the almonds in sugar gives a great sweet crunch to this salad. I have to state for the record that this is one of the best salads I've ever tasted.

- 1   cup sliced or slivered almonds
- ½   cup sugar
- 1   head iceberg lettuce, rinsed
- 1   head romaine lettuce, rinsed
- 1   cup vegetable oil
- ¼   cup red wine vinegar
- 1   tablespoon chopped fresh parsley
- 1   teaspoon salt
-     Dash of black pepper
-     Dash of cayenne
- 3   green onion (scallion) tops, thinly sliced
- 1   22-ounce can mandarin oranges, drained and chilled

Mix the almonds with ¼ cup of the sugar in a medium saucepan. Cook over medium heat, stirring as the sugar melts and the almonds brown. Carefully spread the almonds on an ungreased baking sheet to cool, using a metal spatula; the nuts will be very hot. When completely cooled, break the candied almonds into tiny pieces.

Tear the iceberg and romaine lettuce into pieces and wash well. Dry the greens thoroughly and transfer them to a salad bowl. Cover and refrigerate if not serving immediately.

Combine the oil, vinegar, remaining ¼ cup sugar, and the parsley, salt, pepper, and cayenne in a bowl, and mix well. Chill covered, in the refrigerator, until ready to serve.

Combine the lettuce, sliced green onions, candied almonds, and orange segments in a large salad bowl. Just before serving, toss the salad with enough dressing to coat the greens.

*From Gwen:* Seeing is believing! This salad is consumed rapidly even by self-professed salad haters!

# Mexican Salad

Serves 12

*From Beth:*
This is a fun dish for children to help with.

What's great about this salad is that it only involves opening a few cans and layering the veggies with shredded cheese. It's simple, healthy, and looks pretty in a glass bowl to boot!

1   15-ounce can black beans, drained and rinsed

1   15-ounce can diced tomatoes with green chiles, drained

1   15-ounce can whole kernel corn, drained

1   8-ounce jar chopped, pickled jalapeños, drained

2   cups shredded Cheddar cheese

2   tablespoons chopped fresh cilantro (optional)

1   lime, cut in wedges

1   large bag corn chips (I like the scoop-type chips for this)

In a large bowl, combine the beans, tomatoes, corn, and jalapeños, and mix well.

Spread one-third of the bean mixture in the bottom of a large serving bowl. Sprinkle with one-half of the grated cheese. Top with half of the remaining bean mixture, and all but $\frac{1}{4}$ cup of the remaining cheese. Finish with a final layer of the bean mixture and garnish with the reserved $\frac{1}{4}$ cup cheese and the chopped cilantro. Serve with lime wedges and chips for scooping up the salad.

# Trisha's Pasta Salad (The Original)

Like most families, we struggle to get enough vegetables into our diets. This pasta salad, served cool, is full of great greens and reds, and it is so tasty! The sunflower kernels give it a nice crunch.

Serves 6

- 12 ounces rotini pasta
- 5 ounces Cheddar cheese, grated
- 2 tablespoons olive oil
- 2 tomatoes, diced
- 2 broccoli florets, blanched
- 1 bell pepper, seeded and diced

  Salt and pepper to taste
- ½ cup salted, roasted sunflower kernels

Bring a large saucepan of salted water to a boil. Add the pasta and cook for 9 minutes, or until it is tender; you don't want it too al dente. Drain the pasta and transfer it to a mixing bowl. When the pasta has cooled to room temperature, add the cheese, olive oil, tomatoes, broccoli, and bell pepper, and mix well. Season with salt and pepper and mix again. Top with the sunflower kernels.

# Garth's Pasta Salad

Garth has to claim this recipe because he modified my basic pasta salad to suit his tastes and changed it completely! He likes to eat it warm because he loves the way the cheese melts into the other ingredients, so he doesn't wait for the pasta to cool down at all. He also says the secret to making the tomatoes taste so good is salting them separately. Who knew he was Gartha Stewart?

- 12 ounces rotini pasta
- 12 ounces spinach tortellini
- 2 dozen grape tomatoes, sliced in halves
- 1 teaspoon salt
- ½ teaspoon pepper
- 10 ounces Cheddar cheese, shredded
- 3 tablespoons olive oil

In a large saucepan, cook the rotini and tortellini for 10 minutes, or until they are at a desired tenderness. Drain the noodles. In a small bowl, toss the sliced tomatoes with the salt and pepper. While the pasta is still warm, toss it with the tomatoes, cheese, and olive oil. Serve warm.

# beef and pork

Most of the meat dishes cooked in my family were made using ground beef, because it was inexpensive and readily available. When I was six years old, my parents moved us from town to a 30-acre farm just outside the city limits where we had a huge garden and also raised our own beef. After that, I remember we had steak a lot more often! You won't find a recipe for grilling steak in this cookbook, because my daddy always said a great steak is one that was cut properly and had just the right amount of fat on it before you laid it on the grill; all it needed was salt and pepper. When I would break out the Heinz 57 at the table (still my steak sauce of choice), he would say that any sauce at all ruined a good steak!

In the South, pork is most often used for barbecue, but my mother also made it lots of other tasty ways. When I was a child, getting really juicy pork chops from the grocery store was easy. Hogs are raised to be leaner these days, so be sure when you're shopping to pick a thicker-cut pork chop or loin if you can. I recommend at least a 1-inch-thick cut for pork chops and 1½ inches to 2 inches for stuffed pork chops. If you start out with a great piece of pork, whether it be ham, ribs, roast, or chops, your meal will taste better, no matter what the recipe.

# Roast Beef with Gravy

Roast beef is all about Sunday afternoons after church for me. Mama would get up early and put the roast on to cook, then turn off the oven when we left for church and let it sit until we got home again. The memory of walking through the door and smelling that amazing aroma still makes my mouth water! The hardest part about this meal was waiting for the gravy to be made before you could sit down to eat it!

*From Gwen:* Choose a well-marbled roast so you'll have lots of good juice for gravy.

I've never been a fan of canned gravies or gravy starters, so I don't usually make gravy unless I have drippings from roasting beef or turkey. I like the gravy on the roast and on the white rice I usually cook to go with dinner; Garth puts the gravy on everything!

- 1 5-pound boneless chuck roast
  Salt and black pepper to taste
- 1 large red onion, sliced
- ¼ cup cider vinegar
- 4 tablespoons all-purpose flour

Preheat the oven to 450°F.

Line a 9 x 13 x 2-inch pan or your oven's broiler pan with a sheet of heavy-duty aluminum foil large enough to fully wrap the roast. The shiny side of the foil should be up. Sprinkle the roast on all sides with salt and pepper and place it in the center of the foil. Spread the onion slices over the top of the roast and pour the vinegar around it. Bring the ends of the foil together and fold several times, then fold the ends together to completely enclose the roast. Pour about 1 inch water into the pan around the foil-wrapped roast. Bake for 3 to 4 hours, or until the meat is fork-tender and brown. Check the water level in the pan regularly during cooking and replenish it if necessary. If any juice seeps from the foil seals during roasting, save it to use in making the gravy.

When the roast is done, remove the package from the baking pan and let it cool for a few minutes. Open the package carefully to preserve all the juices and transfer the meat to a platter; cover with a tent of foil to keep it warm while you make the gravy.

Pour the roasting juices into a measuring cup and let the fat rise to the surface. Skim off the fat, reserving 4 tablespoons in a saucepan and discarding the rest. (If the fat measures less than 4 tablespoons, add enough butter to make up the difference.)

Measure the remaining defatted pan juices; if you have less than 2 cups, add water to make 2 cups.

Add the flour to the fat in the saucepan and stir with a wire whisk to make a roux. Cook over medium-low heat until the flour is lightly browned, about 1 minute. Slowly whisk in the reserved pan juices and stir until thickened.

Slice the roast or cut it into chunks (it will be very tender), and serve it with the gravy.

# Gwen's Old-Fashioned Potato-Beef Casserole

Serves 6

My family likes casseroles because they get the whole meal in one pan, and this is a favorite. It was probably born as a result of my mom's trying to put food on the table on a budget, and while a lot of people cook with ground beef because it is relatively inexpensive, I would pay big bucks to get to eat this every now and then! This is similar to a shepherd's pie, but a bit heartier, I think.

*From Gwen:* Potatoes cook quickly. Test often for tenderness and don't overcook them.

| | |
|---|---|
| 3 | pounds white or red potatoes, peeled and sliced ¼-inch thick |
| 1 | pound lean ground beef |
| ½ | cup chopped onion |
| 4 | tablespoons (½ stick) butter |
| ¼ | cup flour |
| 1 | teaspoon salt |
| ¼ | teaspoon black pepper |
| 2 | cups milk |
| 2 | cups grated sharp Cheddar cheese |
| ½ | cup unseasoned dry bread crumbs |

Place the potatoes in a large saucepan with water to cover by 1 inch. Add a generous pinch of salt and cook for 15 minutes, or until tender. Alternatively, cook the potatoes in a pressure cooker for 5 minutes, releasing the pressure immediately to prevent overcooking. Drain the potatoes and arrange them in a 6 x 9 x 2-inch casserole dish.

In a large skillet, combine the beef and onion and cook together over medium heat until the beef is browned and the onion softened, 12 to 15 minutes. Pour off the excess fat.

Preheat the oven to 350°F.

Melt the butter in a medium saucepan and whisk in the flour to make a roux. Cook over medium heat, whisking constantly, until the mixture bubbles and the flour turns light brown in color. Gradually whisk in the milk and continue to stir while cooking over medium heat. When the mixture thickens, whisk in the salt and pepper, then stir in the cheese and browned beef.

Pour the ground beef mixture over the potatoes and bake the casserole for 20 minutes until heated through and bubbling. Sprinkle the bread crumbs on top of the casserole and bake until the crumbs are toasted, about 5 minutes longer.

Note: Because all the ingredients are fully cooked, if they are still hot when you assemble the casserole, the baking time can be greatly reduced or even eliminated; simply brown the crumb topping under the broiler for a couple of minutes.

*Daddy and Mama, 2005.*

# Ribbon Meatloaf

Serves 6 to 8

I love homemade biscuits, and I love meatloaf, so it's no surprise I'm pretty fond of this recipe. The sauce is so terrific, especially poured over that wonderful homemade biscuit dough with a little ground beef rolled inside. Yum!

1 pound lean ground beef

1 tablespoon minced onion

1½ teaspoons salt

½ teaspoon pepper

⅓ cup self-rising flour (see Note)

2 cups canned tomatoes, drained and juices reserved

1¾ cups frozen peas, thawed

1 recipe biscuit dough (page 151)

*From Gwen:* This is one time it's okay to knead extra flour into the biscuit dough recipe to make it easier to roll and cut.

Combine the beef, onion, salt, and pepper in a large skillet and cook over medium heat until the meat is browned, 12 to 15 minutes. Remove from the heat. Stir in the flour and ⅓ cup of the reserved tomato liquid. Remove 1 cup of this meat mixture and set aside. Add the tomatoes, crushing them with your hands as you add them, and the peas to the skillet. Set aside.

Preheat the oven to 450°F.

Note: If you do not have self-rising flour, substitute ⅓ cup regular flour, ½ teaspoon baking powder, and a pinch of salt.

On a well-floured surface, roll the biscuit dough into a large rectangle about ½ inch thick. Spread the reserved cup of meat mixture thinly over the dough, then roll the dough like a jelly roll, beginning from one long edge. Place the roll on a greased baking sheet. Using kitchen shears or a very sharp knife, cut 1-inch slices almost through to the bottom of the roll. To expose some of the filling, pull alternate slices to the left and right. Bake for 15 minutes, or until browned.

Reheat the beef and vegetable mixture. Slice the baked loaf and spoon some of the hot vegetable and meat mixture over each slice.

# Meatloaf

I probably make meatloaf once a week, and I've developed some pretty strong opinions about what works and what doesn't. I have sampled meatloaf across the country, and when it's good, it's usually because it's a simple rendition. If I don't like it, it's usually because someone tried to get fancy with it and put something in it that didn't belong there! This is the one I make most often. I prefer to use lean ground beef because it keeps the meatloaf from being too moist. Also, be sure to remove the meatloaf from the pan as soon as it's done; otherwise, the fat that has rendered into the pan will be absorbed back into the meat—not good!

Serves 8 to 10

*From Trisha:*
If you've never had a cold meatloaf sandwich the next day, you don't know what you're missing.

  2  pounds lean ground beef

 20  saltine crackers, crumbled

  1  large egg, lightly beaten

 ¼  cup ketchup

  1  tablespoon yellow mustard

  1  teaspoon salt

 ½  teaspoon pepper

  1  medium onion, finely chopped

Preheat the oven to 350°F.

Gently mix the beef, cracker crumbs, egg, ketchup, mustard, salt, pepper, and onion until blended. Shape the mixture into two loaves and place side by side crosswise in a 9 x 13 x 2-inch pan. Bake the loaves for 1 hour, or until they are browned. Transfer to a platter immediately and allow the loaves to cool slightly and firm up before slicing.

# Creamed Beef

This is one of those old-fashioned dishes that people either love or hate. I *love* creamed beef on toast. In fact, it's what I have for breakfast on my birthday every year! In our house, this dish is affectionately known by another name I can't print in this cookbook, but whatever you choose to call it, it's yummy!

| | |
|---|---|
| 1 | pound lean ground beef |
| ¼ | cup all-purpose flour |
| 2 | cups milk |
| 1½ | teaspoons salt |
| ¼ | teaspoon pepper |
| 4 | bread slices, toasted and cut in half diagonally |

Sauté the beef in a large skillet over medium heat, breaking it up with a wooden spoon and cooking until it is no longer pink, 12 to 15 minutes. Drain off the excess fat and sprinkle the meat with the flour (see Note). Stir and cook the beef and flour over medium heat until the flour has completely coated the beef and cooked slightly. Stir in the milk and continue to cook until the mixture becomes smooth and thickens, about 8 minutes. Add the salt and pepper. Serve over toast triangles.

*From Gwen:* This recipe is traditionally made with salted chipped beef from a jar, but I found my family preferred the lightly salted flavor of very lean ground beef. Put a pat of real butter on top before serving.

Note: If you use very lean beef, there will be just enough fat to mix with the flour without draining the excess fat.

# Pork Chops and Rice

Serves 6

Sometimes it's nice to make a meal that takes only a couple of steps to get into the oven, and then you can forget about it for an hour while it cooks. The beef broth gives the rice a great flavor. I serve this with Cooked-to-Death Green Beans (page 130).

| | |
|---|---|
| 4 | tablespoons butter |
| 1 | cup long-grain white rice |
| 6 | pork chops, bone in |
| | Salt to taste |
| 1 | 10-ounce can beef broth |
| ¾ | cup water |
| 6 | onion slices, separated into rings |
| ¼ | teaspoon pepper |

Preheat the oven to 350°F.

In a medium skillet, melt the butter over medium-low heat. Add the rice and sauté until it is light brown, about 5 minutes.

Spread the rice in 9 x 13 x 2-inch casserole. Season the pork chops with the salt and arrange them on top of the rice. Pour the broth and water over the chops. Spread the onion rings over the chops and sprinkle with the pepper. Cover the dish with aluminum foil and bake for 45 minutes, or until the pork chops are tender. Remove the pork chops to a plate and keep warm, then cover the dish and return the rice to the oven for an additional 15 minutes. If the rice is dry, add a bit more water before returning it to the oven. Serve the pork chops on a bed of the rice.

# Stuffed Pork Chops

This dish takes a bit of attention, but the results are well worth the effort for a special meal. The steam that rises from the water in the bottom of the pan keeps the pork chops tender and moist. Mom used canning jar rings instead of a rack to elevate the chops above the water.

- 3 tablespoons butter
- 1 medium onion, finely chopped
- 2 tablespoons chopped fresh parsley
- ½ cup bread crumbs
- 1 teaspoon salt
- ¼ teaspoon pepper
- ⅛ teaspoon garlic powder
- 1 large egg, lightly beaten
- 4 bone-in pork chops, about 1½ inches thick, with pockets
- 1 cup all-purpose flour
- ¼ cup vegetable oil

Preheat the oven to 325°F.

Melt the butter in a large skillet over medium-high heat. Add the onions and sauté until they are translucent, about 7 minutes. Remove the pan from heat and stir in the parsley, bread crumbs, salt, pepper, and garlic powder. Stir in the beaten egg.

If your pork chops don't have pockets cut into them, insert the point of a small sharp knife horizontally into the fat-covered edge. Move the knife back and forth to create a deep pocket about 1½ inches wide.

Fill the pocket of each chop with the bread crumb mixture. Secure the openings with toothpicks and cotton thread or twine.

Dredge the stuffed chops lightly in flour, shaking off the excess. Wipe out the skillet used previously in making the stuffing and place over medium-high heat. Add the oil and, when hot, add the chops. Sear over medium heat until lightly browned, about 3 minutes on each side.

Put water in the bottom of a roasting pan with a rack, being careful not to cover the rack with water. Place the chops on the rack and cover the roaster with the lid or aluminum foil. Bake the chops for 1 hour, then uncover and continue baking for 20 minutes longer, to crisp the surface a bit.

# Barbecued Pork Ribs

Serves 8

Since moving to Oklahoma, I have noticed that a lot of the barbecue there is made with beef. I started making these Georgia pork ribs a couple of years ago for the Fourth of July, and they quickly became tradition around here. Cut the racks into two-rib portions and serve them with Easy Baked Beans (page 133) and Fourth of July Coleslaw (page 54) for an awesome holiday feast!

*From Gwen:*
These take some extra time and effort, but it really pays off! Hint: The marinade can really bake onto the pan during cooking. Using a baking bag makes cleanup a lot easier.

2   cups soy sauce

1   cup water

½   cup light brown sugar, packed

1   tablespoon dark molasses

1   teaspoon salt

5   pounds meaty pork ribs

Barbecue Sauce

⅓   cup water

1   14-ounce bottle ketchup

1   12-ounce bottle chili sauce

½   cup light brown sugar, packed

1   teaspoon dry mustard

In a medium saucepan, combine the soy sauce, water, ½ cup brown sugar, molasses, and salt. Bring the marinade to a boil and set aside to cool.

Put the ribs in a large, turkey-size oven baking bag or sealable plastic bag. Support the bag in a 12 x 14-inch baking pan. Pour the marinade over the ribs and seal the bag. Marinate the ribs in the refrigerator overnight, turning the bag occasionally to thoroughly coat the meat.

The next day, preheat the oven to 375°F.

Drain and discard the marinade from the bag. Cut 4 slits in the top of the baking bag if you are using one. Otherwise, drain the marinade, transfer the ribs to the baking pan, and cover the pan with foil. Bake the ribs for 2 hours.

While the ribs are baking, prepare the barbecue sauce. In a large saucepan, blend the water, ketchup, chili sauce, brown sugar, and dry mustard. Bring this mixture to a boil, stir well to dissolve the sugar, and set aside to cool.

When the ribs are cooked and tender, open the bag and discard the drippings. Lower the oven temperature to 350°F.

Brush the ribs on both sides with the barbecue sauce and return them to the oven to bake for 30 minutes longer. Just before serving, throw the ribs onto the barbecue or blacken them under the broiler to give them a bit of a char.

# Pork Barbecue Sauce

Makes
1½ quarts

I respect people who won't share old family recipes, but when I find something good, I want everybody to be able to make it for themselves, and that's how I feel about my daddy's barbecue sauce. I truly believe Daddy could have bottled and sold this sauce, it was so popular! It's a personal preference, but I like a thin, vinegar-based barbecue sauce instead of the thick, ketchup-based sauces.

1   small onion, ground fine

1   quart cider vinegar

12  ounces tomato juice

1   tablespoon pepper

1   tablespoon sugar

*From Gwen:*
Use this on chopped, sliced, or pulled pork.

Chop the onion finely and purée it in a blender with ½ cup water. Place the puréed onion in a 2-quart saucepan with additional water to cover. Bring to a boil, and reduce the heat. Cook, stirring constantly, until the water has almost evaporated. Add the vinegar, tomato juice, and pepper, and mix well. Bring to a boil, and then stir in the sugar. Immediately remove from the heat to cool and store. Serve with your favorite barbecue dish.

*Gwen on her childhood farm in Willacoochee, Georgia, 1958.*

# Pork Roast with Sauerkraut

Even those who say "No!" to sauerkraut will love this specialty dish from family friend Betty Maxwell.

- 2    pounds sauerkraut, undrained
- 1    4-pound Boston butt pork roast
- ½    cup packed light brown sugar

Preheat the oven to 375°F.

Spread the sauerkraut and its liquid in the bottom of a 10 x 12 x 3-inch roasting pan. Push the pork roast down into the sauerkraut and sprinkle with the brown sugar.

Cover the pan and bake for 1 hour and 30 minutes, or until the roast registers 170°F on a meat thermometer. Remove the meat to a platter and spoon the drained sauerkraut around the roast.

Serves 8 to 10

*From Gwen:* Betty loves to cook but doesn't like to eat alone. (Who does?) I'm fortunate to be on her invitee list!

# Baked Ham with Brown Sugar Honey Glaze

Serves 20 to 30

*From Gwen:*
If you don't want or need a whole ham, you can bake half a ham, but choose the butt (meatier) end rather than the shank end.

This is the main attraction of our traditional Easter meal, and we think those spiral-sliced prebasted hams take a backseat to our version. Ask your butcher to order a whole smoked water-added ham such as Gwaltney, Hamilton, or Smithfield, and have him remove and quarter the hock. This not only makes the ham fit more easily into your pan but also gives you the hock pieces to use another time and contribute unbeatable seasoning to soups and veggies. Serve with Potato Salad (page 53) and Baby Lima Beans (page 132).

18–20-pound smoked ham, water added, ham hock removed

1   16-ounce box light brown sugar

1   cup (8-ounce jar) clover honey

Adjust the oven racks to accommodate a large covered roasting pan. Fit the pan with a shallow rack. Preheat the oven to 350°F.

Unwrap the ham and rinse it in cold water. Place it on the rack in the roasting pan. Cover the pan with the lid and open the vents in the lid slightly to allow steam to escape. Bake the ham for half the estimated cooking time. (Total cooking time is about 20 minutes per pound.) Halfway through the estimated cooking time, in a separate saucepan, mix the sugar and honey until smooth. Pour the mixture over the ham. Continue baking the ham, basting occasionally with the drippings in the roaster.

Check for doneness at the end of the estimated cooking time by inserting a meat thermometer at a meaty point (not into fat or touching the bone). It should register 160°F.

Allow the ham to stand for 15 minutes before slicing to allow the juices to set.

# Breakfast Sausage Casserole

You see this recipe a lot in the South. It's great because you do all the work the night before; the next morning, this wonderful meal bakes while you're having a nice, leisurely cup of coffee! Beth makes this on Christmas Eve so it can bake Christmas morning during the present-opening frenzy.

 6   slices white loaf bread

 1   pound fresh bulk pork sausage with sage

10   ounces sharp Cheddar cheese, grated

 5   large eggs, lightly beaten

 2   cups half-and-half

 1   teaspoon salt

 1   teaspoon dry mustard

Cut the bread into 1-inch cubes and spread in the bottom of a greased 9 x 12 x 2-inch casserole.

In a medium skillet, brown the sausage over medium heat until fully cooked and no longer pink. Drain off and discard the rendered fat. Spread the cooked sausage over the bread and top with the cheese. Stir together the eggs, half-and-half, salt, and dry mustard. Pour this mixture over the cheese. Cover the casserole with aluminum foil and refrigerate for 8 hours or overnight.

The next day, preheat the oven to 350°F.

Bake the covered casserole for 50 minutes, or until set and slightly golden. Remove from the oven and allow the casserole to set for 15 minutes before serving.

# poultry, fish, and pasta

I remember one diet I went on several years ago that included grilled chicken at just about every meal. To this day, I have difficulty eating plain grilled chicken, and I'm always looking for ways to make chicken interesting. These dishes give you every choice: basic southern fried chicken, a leaner, baked "fried" chicken in cornflake crumbs, and everything in between.

I've included only a few fish recipes in this cookbook, mainly because I'm just not a fan of fishy-tasting recipes. But I know it's good for you, and I'm trying to eat more of it. Growing up in middle Georgia certainly dictated the kinds of fish we ate; the only salmon we ate came out of a can, and the only fresh fish we ate was the fish we caught ourselves. You can't beat a day filled with baiting your own hook (or asking Daddy to handle the icky worms!) and catching your own dinner.

I also didn't grow up eating much pasta, though it's one of my passions now. For the most part, I believe in leaving pasta dishes to the professionals, but a few dishes have become mainstays for me. You don't have to be Italian to serve a flavorful spaghetti sauce with your plain old spaghetti noodles, and I would put my fettucine Alfredo up against any version you can find!

# Chicken Baked in Cornflake Crumbs

Serves 4 to 6

*From Gwen:*
To make crumbs, place cornflakes in a sturdy resealable plastic bag and roll over the sealed bag with a rolling pin. Remove the chicken skin for less fat.

This is a nice recipe for southern girls like me who love fried chicken but realize they can't eat it everyday. The cornflakes give you that crispy crust like fried chicken without all of the added fat of deep-frying—not that I'm saying there's a thing wrong with deep-frying! My motto is "Everything in moderation, including moderation."

2–3 shakes of Tabasco sauce (optional)
  1 cup buttermilk, well shaken
  1 cup cornflake crumbs
  8 chicken pieces (drumsticks, thighs, breasts), with skin
  1 teaspoon salt
  ¼ teaspoon pepper

Preheat the oven to 350°F.

Line a cookie sheet with aluminum foil and spray the foil with cooking spray. Shake the Tabasco sauce into the buttermilk and pour into a shallow bowl. Place the cornflake crumbs in another bowl or on a piece of waxed paper. Dip each piece of chicken in the buttermilk, and then roll it in the crumbs. Place the coated chicken pieces on the cookie sheet and sprinkle with the salt and pepper.

Bake the chicken for 1 hour, or until the crust is golden brown and the thigh meat is no longer pink at the bone. Check this with the point of a sharp knife. Remove the pieces from the pan and serve while the chicken is warm.

# Gwen's Fried Chicken with Milk Gravy

My biggest complaint about fried chicken is that all of the flavor ends up on the outside, and the meat is usually bland. Not my mama's! The secret is in the prep. When you soak the chicken overnight in salt brine, the salt infuses into the meat and makes it so tasty! When I asked my mom how long to fry the chicken, she said, "Just cook it 'til it sounds right." I have since fried enough chicken to completely understand this sentence, but at the time— you can imagine! As chicken begins to fry, it's loud because of all the water cooking out into the fat. It gets quieter as it gets done. Who knew? Now you do!

Serves 4 to 6

*From Gwen:* Milk makes the gravy rich and smooth.

- 8  serving pieces of chicken, light or dark meat
- 2  tablespoons salt
- 2  cups peanut oil
- 1  teaspoon black pepper
- 2  cups all-purpose flour

## Milk Gravy

- 4  tablespoons oil
- 4  tablespoons all-purpose flour
- 2  cups milk
   Salt and pepper to taste

Put the chicken pieces in a large bowl and cover them with water. Sprinkle the salt in the water, cover the bowl, and refrigerate for 4 hours or overnight.

Pour oil into an electric frying pan or deep, heavy skillet to a depth of 1 inch. Heat the oil to 375°F. (Check the temperature by sprinkling flour over the oil. If the flour sizzles, the oil is hot enough.)

continued . . .

Drain the water from the chicken, sprinkle each piece with pepper, and coat the pieces with flour. Carefully place the chicken in the hot oil. Place the cover on the pan and open the vent to allow a small amount of steam to escape. Cook for 15 minutes. Remove the cover and, using tongs, turn each piece of chicken. Replace the cover and cook for 15 minutes more, or until done. Use a sharp, thin-bladed knife to check for doneness by slicing a drumstick to the bone. Neither the meat nor the juices should be pink. Drain the chicken on paper towels and keep warm while you make the gravy.

Pour off all but 4 tablespoons of the oil from the pan in which the chicken was fried, leaving the bits of browned flour in the pan. Sprinkle in the 4 tablespoons flour. Stirring with a wire whisk, cook the flour and drippings until the flour is browned, about 1 minute. Slowly stir in the milk and cook until the gravy thickens, 5 to 10 minutes. Season with salt and pepper.

Pass the chicken and gravy separately.

# Barbecued Chicken

As a young man, my dad worked with the State of Georgia Extension Service, where he learned to barbecue chickens by the hundreds. Over the years, he cooked thousands of chickens that were sold on the town square, at football games, or horse shows. He and his friends would build a huge pit with cement blocks and top them with specially made racks that could hold about 50 chicken halves each. To turn the chickens, another rack was placed on top, and two men, one on each end of the racks, would flip the entire rack at once! My mom has adapted Dad's recipe to serve a family, not the whole town.

3   2½-pound frying chickens, split (see Note)

4   tablespoons salt

1   cup cider vinegar

¾   cup peanut oil

1   teaspoon Tabasco sauce

⅛   teaspoon black pepper

¼   cup water

1   teaspoon cayenne pepper

*Daddy with Bank of Monticello grill.*

Put the chicken halves in a very large bowl or deep pot and cover with water. Sprinkle 3 tablespoons of the salt in the water. Cover the bowl or pot and refrigerate the chickens in this brine for 6 hours or overnight.

Prepare a fire in a grill with the grilling rack set 16 inches above the coals (see Note).

In a saucepan, mix together the vinegar, remaining tablespoon salt, peanut oil, Tabasco sauce, black pepper,

¼ cup water, and the cayenne. Bring this mixture to a boil, stir well, and remove from the heat.

When the coals are uniformly covered with gray ash, spread them in a single layer. Drain the chicken, pat dry, and place the halves on the grill, skin side up. Baste with the sauce and cook for 30 minutes. Using tongs, turn the chickens skin side down and baste the top with sauce. Continue to grill the chickens for an additional 1½ hours, turning and basting the chicken every 15 minutes. Add charcoal as needed to maintain a hot layer of coals. Check for doneness by twisting a drumstick. It should move easily.

Note: If you cannot find small chickens, use larger ones (3–3½ pounds) and quarter them. If the grill rack cannot be adjusted, cook the chickens closer to the coals and turn the halves more often to avoid burning.

# Chicken Pie

Comfort food. That's all I've got to say!

- 3  cups cooked, shredded chicken
- 2  cups chicken broth
- 1  10-ounce can cream of chicken soup
- 1  cup self-rising flour (see Note)
- ½  teaspoon pepper
- ½  cup (1 stick) butter, melted
- 1  cup buttermilk, well shaken

Preheat the oven to 425°F.

Put the chicken in a 2-quart casserole dish. Combine the broth and soup in a medium saucepan and bring the mixture to a boil. Pour the broth mixture over the chicken.

In a separate medium bowl, mix the flour with the pepper. Stir in the melted butter and the buttermilk. Pour this mixture over the casserole and smooth the top; do not stir. Bake the casserole for 45 minutes, or until the crust is brown and the filling beneath is hot and bubbly.

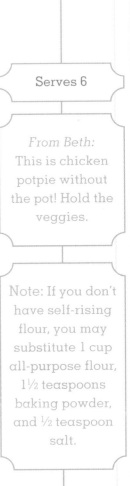

Serves 6

*From Beth:*
This is chicken potpie without the pot! Hold the veggies.

Note: If you don't have self-rising flour, you may substitute 1 cup all-purpose flour, 1½ teaspoons baking powder, and ½ teaspoon salt.

# Chicken Broccoli Casserole

This casserole is hearty and contains everything you could want on the table in one dish. It's a favorite of our whole family. It makes ten servings, but my husband likes it cold for breakfast the next day, so in my house you'd better take your serving at dinner the night before, 'cause that's all you're gonna get!

- 2 cups cooked rice
- 3 cups cooked chopped broccoli
- 1 cup sour cream
- ½ cup mayonnaise
- 1 tablespoon lemon juice
- 1 10-ounce can condensed cream of chicken soup
- 10 ounces Cheddar cheese, grated
- ½ teaspoon salt
- ¼ teaspoon pepper
- 4 chicken breasts, cooked and shredded (see page 61)

Preheat the oven to 350°F. Grease a 9 x 13 x 2-inch baking dish with butter or nonstick cooking spray.

Spread the rice in an even layer in the baking dish. Make a second layer with the broccoli.

In a large bowl, mix the sour cream, mayonnaise, lemon juice, condensed soup, half of the grated cheese, and the salt, pepper, and chicken. Pour this mixture over the broccoli and top with the remaining grated cheese. Bake for 40 minutes.

Let stand for 5 minutes before serving.

# No-Baste, No-Bother Roasted Turkey

Serves 20 to 25

*From Gwen:*
This turkey is tender and produces lots of pan juices for the gravy.

Every Thanksgiving, I hear cooks groaning about having been up all night basting the big turkey, and I just smile. I've found a foolproof, easy way to make a great turkey and get your sleep too! It also makes the most tender, moist turkey I've ever tasted. The first time I cooked Thanksgiving dinner for my family, Garth couldn't believe this method would actually work, so he politely asked me to cook a "stunt" turkey so he could taste it for himself before the big day. Most of my friends have been just as hesitant, but once they have tried it my way, they never go back to the old way. To make sure the oven temperature doesn't drop too quickly, I put a sign on it threatening bodily harm to anyone who even thinks about opening the oven door during this process!

1   12-pound turkey, completely thawed, all giblets removed

½   cup (1 stick) salted butter, softened

2   tablespoons salt

2   teaspoons pepper

2   stalks celery, cut in lengths to fit turkey cavity

1   medium sweet onion, such as Vidalia, cut in half

1   large carrot

2   cups boiling water

Adjust the oven racks so the covered roasting pan fits easily inside the oven. Preheat the oven to 500°F.

Rub the butter on the outside and in the cavity of the turkey. A self-basting turkey will not require all of the butter. Sprinkle the salt and pepper on the inside and on the outside of the turkey. Put the celery, onion, and carrot in the cavity. Place the turkey, breast side up, in a large roasting pan. Pour the boiling water into the pan. Cover with a tight-fitting lid and put the pan in the preheated oven.

Start a timer when the oven temperature returns to 500°F. Bake for exactly 1 hour and turn off the oven. Do not open the oven door. Leave the turkey in the oven until the oven cools; this may take 4 to 6 hours. Reserve the pan juices and refrigerate the turkey if it will not be served soon after roasting.

Serve with Grandma Lizzie's Cornbread Dressing (page 145) and Giblet Gravy (recipe follows).

*Daddy holding a wild turkey.*

# Giblet Gravy

*From Gwen:*
*Give it a try!*
*Giblets are*
*people, too!*

For some people, it just isn't Thanksgiving without giblet gravy for the turkey and potatoes. Mom has included directions for a giblet-free version for those of us who have seen a giblet and never want to eat one!

Giblets and neck from turkey (see Note)
1 teaspoon salt, plus more to taste
4 tablespoons fat skimmed from the turkey roasting pan
4 tablespoons all-purpose flour
2 cups turkey broth
2 large eggs, hard-boiled, peeled, and chopped fine
Pepper to taste

Place the giblets in a saucepan with 3 cups water and 1 teaspoon salt. Bring to a boil, then reduce the heat, skim off any foam that rises to the surface, and simmer until tender, about 25 minutes. Cool the giblets in the cooking liquid. When cool, strain the broth into a measuring cup; if it is less than 2 cups, add chicken stock to make a full 2 cups. Pull the meat off the bones and shred the giblets. Cover and reserve.

In a medium saucepan, mix the flour with the skimmed fat and cook until the roux is lightly browned, about 3 minutes. Slowly whisk the turkey broth into the roux and cook until the gravy thickens. Stir in the shredded giblets and chopped eggs. Season to taste.

Note: There are those, Trisha included, who pass on the giblet gravy because they don't care for giblets, which traditionally include the liver, heart, gizzard, and the dark meat from the neck. For giblet-free gravy, substitute a bit of shredded white meat from the turkey or boiled and shredded chicken breasts for the giblets.

# Baked Orange Roughy

This recipe is a nice alternative to fried fish, and the spices give the fish plenty of flavor. You can substitute any mild fish for the roughy.

Serves 6

*From Gwen:* Choose only the freshest fish. If you are in an area where fresh fish isn't readily available, use frozen.

- 2 cups dry bread crumbs
- ½ cup grated Parmesan cheese
- ½ cup chopped fresh parsley
- 1 teaspoon paprika
- ½ teaspoon dried oregano
- ¼ teaspoon dried basil
- 2 teaspoons salt
- ½ teaspoon pepper
- 6 orange roughy fillets, 3–4 ounces each
- 1 cup buttermilk, well shaken
- Lemon wedges, for serving

Preheat the oven to 375°F.

In a large, flat dish, mix the bread crumbs, cheese, parsley, paprika, oregano, basil, salt, and pepper. Spray a 9 x 13 x 2-inch baking dish with cooking spray. Dip each fillet in the buttermilk, and then coat it with crumbs, pressing to be sure they adhere. Arrange the fillets in the baking dish and bake uncovered for 25 minutes, or until the fish flakes easily with a fork. Serve with the lemon wedges.

# Herb's Fried Catfish

Growing up, I was lucky to have a catfish pond just down the hill on our farm. My daddy had created the pond from a natural spring when I was a little girl and stocked it with catfish and bream. We had many a wonderful fish fry with freshly caught catfish from our pond all through my childhood. Fresh fried fish served with Mama's Cornmeal Hushpuppies (page 140)—you couldn't ask for a better meal! My only suggestion is that you let someone else dress the catfish. Yuck!

- 6 pounds catfish fillets, cut into 2-inch strips
- 3 tablespoons plus ½ teaspoon salt
- 1 cup self-rising cornmeal
- 1 cup cracker meal
- ½ teaspoon pepper
- 4 tablespoons Cajun seasoning
- 1½ gallons peanut oil

In a large bowl, prepare a salt-water brine by combining 3 tablespoons salt with 2 quarts water. Add the fish and more water if needed to just cover the fish. Soak the fish in the brine for 30 minutes.

Mix the cornmeal, cracker meal, remaining ½ teaspoon salt, pepper, and Cajun seasoning in a 1-gallon plastic bag.

In a large (3-gallon) catfish cooker or deep Dutch oven, heat the oil to 350°F. Preheat the oven to 150°F.

Coat the fish by shaking a few pieces at a time in the plastic bag with the crumbs.

*Opposite: Mama, the great fisherman . . . um, woman! (1960)*

Drop 8 to 10 of the coated fish fillets into the hot oil. Cook until the coating is light brown; the fillets will cook quickly, in less than 5 minutes. Pieces will float to the top of the oil when they're done. Drain the cooked fish on paper towels and keep warm in the oven while you fry additional batches. Let the oil return to 350°F before adding and cooking more fish.

# Salmon Croquettes with Creamed Peas

Makes 30 croquettes

Cooking fish is not one of my specialties, but I do love this recipe because it doesn't taste fishy. I think it was probably my mom's attempt to get us girls to eat some fish by disguising it in fried bread crumbs. What can I say? It worked. The creamed peas give the croquettes a slightly sweet accent. This topping tastes good on other meats too, like baked chicken and ham.

*From Gwen:* Forget the creamed peas where Trisha's dad was concerned. Pass the creamed potatoes!

- 3 tablespoons butter
- 2 tablespoons finely chopped onion
- ⅓ cup all-purpose flour
- ½ cup milk
- 2 teaspoons fresh lemon juice
- ¼ teaspoon salt

  Dash of pepper

- 1 14-ounce can pink salmon, drained (see Note)
- 1 cup fine dry bread crumbs
- 2 large eggs, beaten

Note: If you like, substitute ¾ pound shrimp, cooked, shelled, and chopped, or 14 ounces tuna for the salmon in this recipe.

## Creamed Peas

- 2 pounds fresh green peas, shelled
- 3 tablespoons salted butter
- 2 tablespoons all-purpose flour
- 2 cups milk
- 1 teaspoon salt
- ¼ teaspoon pepper

- 3 cups peanut oil, for frying

Melt the butter in a medium skillet over medium-high heat. Add the onion and sauté until softened, about 3 minutes. Use a wire whisk to stir in the flour. Cook for 1 minute, and then stir in the milk. Cook until the mixture is very thick, stirring constantly for 1 minute. Remove from the heat and add the lemon juice, salt, and pepper.

Allow the white sauce to cool slightly, and then stir in the salmon. Shape the mixture into small balls or cones about 1½ inches in diameter. Place the bread crumbs in a shallow dish. Mix the beaten eggs with ¼ cup water. Double-coat the croquettes by rolling them first in the crumbs, then in the egg mixture, and then in the crumbs again. Place each coated croquette on a baking sheet. Cover the croquettes and set them aside.

To make the creamed peas: Bring 1 cup lightly salted water to a boil. Add the peas and cook for 6 to 7 minutes, or until tender. Drain and set aside. Melt the butter in a medium saucepan over medium heat. Stir in the flour and cook until smooth and lightly browned, about 1 minute. Slowly whisk in the milk and continue cooking on medium heat, stirring often. Add the salt and pepper. Cook until the mixture is smooth and thick, about 6 minutes. Stir in the cooked peas and keep warm while you fry the croquettes.

Heat the oil to 375°F in a deep, heavy pot. Preheat the oven to 150°F.

Add about 12 croquettes at a time to the hot oil and cook until they are golden brown. Drain the croquettes on paper towels and keep them warm in the oven as you fry the remaining croquettes. Make sure the oil returns to 375°F before adding and cooking more croquettes, or they will be heavy and greasy.

# Black Bean Lasagne

Everybody has a tried and true basic lasagne recipe, but occasionally it's nice to try something different. Somewhere along the way, I decided to replace the meat with beans, and the result was a hit. This lasagne keeps well in the refrigerator, and if you have leftovers, they freeze well. When I was single and living in Nashville, I would cool this lasagne and freeze portions in individual freezer bags. It was perfect to pull one out of the freezer in the morning before I went to work in the studio, then microwave it for a minute or two when I got home in the evening.

- 1 16-ounce can diced or stewed tomatoes
- 1 12-ounce can tomato paste
- 2 teaspoons salt
- ½ teaspoon black pepper
- ¼ teaspoon garlic powder
- 1 tablespoon dried oregano leaves
- 1 small onion, finely chopped
- 8 ounces lasagna noodles
- 2 15-ounce cans black beans, rinsed and drained
- 1 16-ounce container ricotta cheese
- 16 ounces Cheddar cheese, shredded
- 16 ounces mozzarella cheese, shredded

In a large saucepan, combine the tomatoes and their juices, the tomato paste, 2 cups water, and the salt, pepper, garlic powder, oregano, and onion. Bring to a boil over medium-high heat, then reduce the heat and simmer, uncovered, for 30 minutes.

Meanwhile, bring a large pot of salted water to a boil. Add the lasagna noodles and cook according to package directions. Drain the noodles well and spread them on a baking sheet to prevent them from sticking together.

Preheat the oven to 375°F.

Spread 1 cup of the prepared sauce in a 9 x 13 x 2-inch baking pan. Make three layers each of noodles, sauce, black beans, ricotta, Cheddar, and mozzarella, ending with mozzarella. Bake for 40 minutes, uncovered. Allow the dish to stand for 15 minutes before cutting into squares and serving.

# Fettuccine Alfredo

Serves 6

*From Trisha:* If you try this recipe, make sure you don't have to drive afterward. Maybe it should come with a warning not to operate heavy machinery after eating!

I *love* pasta—and who doesn't? Because I didn't grow up cooking Italian food, I usually save my Italian experiences for my favorite Italian restaurants, like La Mela in the heart of New York's Little Italy and Anna's in Los Angeles. But a gal's gotta make fettuccine Alfredo occasionally. This is the very first home-cooked meal I tried on Garth, and I'm surprised he ever allowed me to cook for him again! It was early on in our relationship, and I wanted to impress him with my cooking skills, so I thought this recipe would be perfect. It is so rich it makes you full fast. That particular night, however, my Alfredo sauce came out so thick it was almost impossible to serve it from the pan. Garth, being the gentleman he is, took a big serving and attempted to eat it. I don't know if he finished it all, but it was so rich and filling he almost fell asleep in his plate! He says he has no memory at all from about halfway through the meal until he woke up hours later on the couch.

12  ounces fettuccine noodles

¾  cup (1½ sticks) butter

1  cup whipping cream

¼  teaspoon white pepper

2  cups freshly grated Parmesan cheese

1  teaspoon cornstarch

2  tablespoons snipped fresh chives or parsley

Bring a large pot of salted water to a boil. Add the pasta and cook according to the package directions.

In the meantime, make the sauce. In a medium saucepan over low heat, melt the butter. Whisk in the whipping cream and pepper, stirring frequently, until the mixture thickens slightly, about 5 minutes. Gradually stir in 1¼ cups of the Parmesan cheese. Cook and stir just until the cheese is melted. Whisk in the cornstarch and stir until slightly thickened, about 3 minutes.

Drain the pasta and add the hot noodles to the cheese mixture. Toss until the pasta is well coated. Transfer individual servings of the pasta to plates. Sprinkle 2 tablespoons Parmesan cheese over each serving, and garnish with the chopped chives or parsley.

# Spaghetti with Meat Sauce

I am allergic to canned spaghetti sauce! Well, maybe not *really*, but I just can't eat spaghetti sauce out of a can or jar. This sauce is easy, and it is even better warmed over the next day, after the flavors have had a chance to settle in.

- 1  pound lean ground beef
- ¾  cup finely chopped onion
- 2  teaspoons minced garlic
- 2  16-ounce cans crushed tomatoes
- 2  6-ounce cans tomato paste
- 1½  teaspoons dried oregano
- 1  teaspoon salt
- ½  teaspoon pepper
- 2  1-pound packages spaghetti

Put the ground beef, onion, and garlic in a medium saucepan and cook together over medium-high heat until the beef is browned and the onions are softened, about 10 minutes. Add the tomatoes and their juices, the tomato paste, 1 cup water, and the oregano, salt, and pepper. Simmer uncovered, stirring occasionally, for 1 hour.

While the sauce simmers, bring a large pot of salted water to a boil. Add the spaghetti and cook until al dente, about 8 minutes, or according to package directions. Drain well and divide among plates. Spoon the sauce over the spaghetti and serve.

# Baked Macaroni and Cheese

My mom made this cheese sauce when I was a child, mostly to pour over vegetables she was trying to get us to eat. I was a grown woman before I realized that steamed broccoli didn't have to be served with cheese sauce! It does make this homemade mac and cheese taste amazingly good, though!

2   teaspoons salt

1   pound elbow macaroni

### Cheese Sauce
4   tablespoons (½ stick) butter

4   tablespoons all-purpose flour

1   teaspoon salt

2   cups milk

2   cups grated sharp Cheddar cheese

### Topping
½   cup bread crumbs

¼   cup (½ stick) butter, melted

Preheat the oven to 350°F. Butter a 2-quart casserole dish.

Bring 4 quarts of water to a boil in a large saucepan. Add 2 teaspoons of salt and the macaroni. Bring the water back to a boil and cook the macaroni for 12 minutes, or until tender. Drain well.

Make the sauce while the macaroni cooks. Melt the butter in a 1-quart saucepan. Using a wire whisk, stir in the flour and 1 teaspoon of salt, stirring and cooking over medium heat until the roux bubbles and the flour turns pale brown, about 3 minutes. Remove the pan

continued . . .

from the heat and slowly whisk in 1 cup of the milk. Return the pan to the heat and whisk in the remaining 1 cup milk. Continue to cook, stirring constantly, until the sauce thickens. Add the cheese and stir until it melts.

Add the drained macaroni to the cheese sauce and mix thoroughly. In a small bowl, stir the bread crumbs together with the melted butter until the crumbs are moistened. Transfer the macaroni and cheese to the prepared baking dish, top with the buttered bread crumbs, and bake for 15 minutes, or until the dish bubbles around the edges.

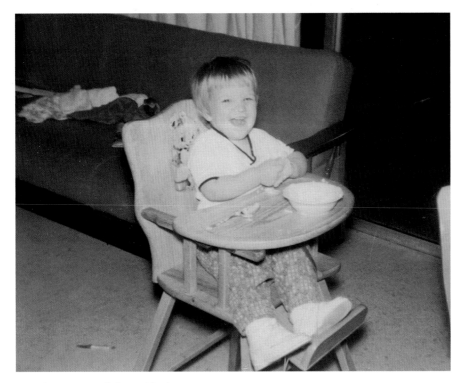

*Me, showing an early love of food at age one.*

# sides

Once you've decided what entrée you're cooking for supper, the next step is figuring out what goes along with it. In this section you'll find plenty of healthy, colorful side dishes to expand your repertoire—maybe a few will become your stand-bys, as they are mine. You'll also find a really basic how-to on cooking fresh vegetables, like green beans. It's not hard to do—unless you've never done it before and have no idea how—so we show you. Many of these recipes have been made for so many generations in my family they were never written down; coming up with exact amounts involved trying something, making changes, and trying again. In general, when it comes to vegetables, we've taken the less-is-more approach, especially with seasonings like salt. It's always easier to add salt at the table than it is to take salt out of the finished dish! And while we've mentioned which entrées we typically serve with these side dishes, you should feel free to serve what you like with the entrées you like.

# Betty's Cabbage Medley

Growing up in a classic meat-and-potatoes family, I can't remember a meal that didn't include meat. As an adult, I've learned you don't always have to have meat at dinner. This dish is a perfect choice for a meal that is all veggies and will leave you full and satisfied.

1 cup sliced carrots, ¼-inch rounds

1 cup thinly sliced onion

1 cup diced celery

1 small head cabbage, cut in chunks (about 6 cups)

1 tablespoon sugar

2 cups warm water

¼ cup corn oil

*From Gwen:* Get your veggie vitamins in one quick and pretty dish.

In a large heavy saucepan with a tight-fitting lid, arrange the vegetables in layers in the following order: Spread the carrots on the bottom of the pan, then top with the onions, celery, and cabbage. Sprinkle the sugar on top, and then pour in the warm water and oil. Cover the pan tightly and cook over high heat for 10 minutes, or until the vegetables are done but still crunchy. Remove the lid, stir the vegetables, then replace the lid and let the vegetables stand for 20 minutes, or until you are ready to serve.

# Sautéed Cabbage

Serves 4

It's hard for families on the go to eat enough vegetables, so we decided to have one night every week that is only veggies. When we do, I always make this recipe. As the cabbage cooks, it sweetens a bit. I like to let it brown a little in the pan because I like the crispness and the flavor. Try it!

1  large head cabbage

3  tablespoons olive oil

3  tablespoons water (optional; see Note)

Salt and pepper to taste

Note: The cabbage will steam in its own juice. If the low setting on your stove is not low enough, add water to prevent scorching.

Peel off and discard any bruised or wilted leaves from the cabbage, and use a sharp knife to remove the core. Cut the head in half lengthwise, then cut the halves crosswise into thin shreds.

In a large skillet or saucepan, heat the oil and sauté the shredded cabbage over medium-high heat for 5 minutes, tossing and stirring often until wilted. Reduce the heat to very low, cover the pan with a tight-fitting lid, and cook for 30 minutes, or until the cabbage is tender. Stir frequently, as the cabbage can scorch easily. Season the cabbage with salt and pepper to taste.

# Roasted Carrots

Here's another dish that's a hit on veggie night!

- ½  cup (1 stick) butter, melted
- 1  teaspoon salt
- ½  teaspoon pepper
- 2  pounds carrots, peeled and cut diagonally into 3 x ½-inch sticks
- 2  tablespoons chopped fresh dill or parsley (optional)

Serves 6

*From Beth:*
Try this same treatment on fresh asparagus. It's good!

Preheat the oven to 400°F. Line a large jelly roll pan with aluminum foil.

In a medium bowl, mix the melted butter, salt, and pepper. Spread the carrots on the jelly roll pan and pour the butter mixture over them, stirring to coat. Roast for 25 to 30 minutes or until tender, stirring once. Toss with the chopped herbs, if using, and serve.

# Zucchini Sauté

When Beth first made this very simple zucchini dish (which she created for our parents), Daddy asked, "Honey, how'd you learn to cook?" I thought that was funny because I think what he was really wondering was how she'd learned to cook something that Mama didn't make at home!

Serves 8

1  tablespoon olive oil

½  teaspoon minced garlic

4  zucchini squash, thinly sliced

½  teaspoon salt

¼  teaspoon pepper

¼  cup grated Parmesan cheese

Heat the olive oil in a medium skillet over medium heat. When hot, add the garlic and sauté for 2 minutes, or until fragrant; don't let it brown. Add the squash, salt, and pepper and cook until the squash is tender but still slightly crisp, about 5 minutes. Transfer the squash to a serving dish and sprinkle with the Parmesan cheese.

# Collards

*From Gwen:*
I cook and freeze these for Trisha every summer.

I could live on collard greens and corn bread! I like collard greens better than turnip greens because I think collards are sweeter. When I make my corn bread and greens bowl (crumbled-up buttermilk corn bread covered with collard greens and a little juice), I add a little hot pepper just for fun. In the South, collard juice, or the cooking liquid that accumulates, is often called *pot likker*. My daddy always planted a big collard patch every spring, not only for the family but also to share with friends. Through the years, friends knew the patch was just out back of the barn and they were free to drive in and help themselves.

*Daddy with a collard plant.*

2   large bunches collards, homegrown or from the produce section

½   pound cured ham hock or salt pork

½   cup salt, for brine (optional; see below)

Prepare the collards for cooking by cutting the large stems from the center of the leaves. Wash the leaves thoroughly. If the collards are homegrown, soak the leaves briefly in a salt-water brine made by adding ½ cup salt to enough water to cover the leaves. Rinse well to rid the leaves of any insects. Stack and roll the leaves and cut them crosswise into 1-inch strips.

Put 2 inches of water in a saucepan large enough to hold the raw collards (the leaves can be pushed down tightly and will wilt to about one-quarter volume as they cook). Add the ham hock or pork and bring the water to a boil. Add the collards and toss with tongs until the water returns to a boil and the leaves wilt down into the pan. Reduce the heat, cover, and simmer over low heat for 1 hour, or until tender. Stir occasionally, checking to be sure there is enough liquid to prevent scorching. Taste the liquid and add salt if needed. Serve with Buttermilk Cornbread (page 154).

# Fresh Green Beans (a.k.a. Tom Cruise Green Beans)

Serves 4

Garth and the girls and I went to Colorado one spring break and spent the week in the guesthouse of some friends. We skied all day and came home exhausted in the evenings. Our friends provided a chef for us, and it was great to come back to the cabin after a long day to a beautifully prepared meal. I had always made Cooked-to-Death Green Beans, but the chef made these green beans one night and we fell in love with them. (The girls also fell in love with the chef, who looked a little bit like Tom Cruise.) When we have veggie night, the girls always ask, "Are we having Tom Cruise?" You can imagine the looks we get from guests who've never been to our house on veggie night!

2  pounds fresh green beans, tips removed

4  tablespoons butter, melted

   Salt to taste

Wash and drain the beans. Put 1 cup water in a medium saucepan. Add the beans and cook until tender but still very crisp, about 6 minutes.

Drain the beans and add the butter, tossing to coat as it melts. Season with salt to taste.

# Cooked-to-Death Green Beans

Serves 4

Note: Salt pork or Goya Ham-Flavored Seasoning may be substituted for the ham hock.

I make this with our home-canned green beans, but canned green beans from your grocery store cook down nicely with a little help from a ham hock. The recipe says to cook these for 30 minutes. I would really say just to cook them to death, but 30 minutes sounds sweeter.

2   quarts home-canned green beans or canned Blue Lake variety, with their liquid

½   pound cured ham hock (see Note)

Put the beans, their liquid, and the ham in a large, heavy saucepan. Cook, uncovered, on medium heat for 30 minutes. The beans are ready when the liquid has cooked down.

# Cream-Style Corn

Serves 6

In the country, we planted a large garden every spring. It never seemed like a chore to shell peas or shuck corn because I always knew how good they were going to taste when they were cooked! If you've never had homemade cream-style corn, you don't know what you're missing. We always had a huge corn crop, so we made a lot of creamed corn and froze it in quart containers to enjoy year round. The kind of fresh corn you use can determine the thickness of the cooked dish. If it's too thick, add a little water. If it's too thin, add a little cornstarch.

12   ears fresh sweet corn, such as Truckers' Favorite or Merritt

4   tablespoons (½ stick) butter

Salt to taste

Shuck the corn and remove all the silks. Wash and drain the corn. Shave just the tips of the kernels using a very sharp knife or vegetable peeler. Cut away from you, allowing the tips to fall into a large bowl. Using the back of the knife, scrape the creamy juice from the kernels into the same bowl.

Melt the butter in a skillet over medium heat and add the corn. Cook the creamed corn for 20 minutes, stirring often, until thickened. Add water if the mixture becomes too thick. Season with salt to taste.

*From Gwen:* Be sure you use juicy corn for this; otherwise, you won't get the right creamy texture.

If fresh creamed corn is a favorite, you might want to think about purchasing a corn cutter, which removes the tips and juice with one motion. You can order one online at www.homesteadharvest.com.

# Baby Lima Beans

We call these *butterbeans* in Georgia. I serve them with Baked Ham with Brown Sugar Honey Glaze (page 88) and Potato Salad (page 53). In college I had a friend named Tina, who is from Mississippi. When I would go home with her for the weekend, she would put mayonnaise in her butterbeans. Don't try this at home, because you will love it and it's more added fat that none of us need! (Okay, try it once!)

- 2 pounds baby lima beans, fresh in the shell, or 1 10-ounce package, frozen
- 2 tablespoons butter
- ½ teaspoon salt
- ¼ teaspoon coarse ground pepper

Shell the beans and wash thoroughly. Put 2 cups water and the salt in a medium saucepan and add the beans. Cook the beans for 30 minutes, or until tender. Drain the liquid and add the butter. Sprinkle lightly with black pepper before serving.

# Easy Baked Beans

I serve baked beans with everything from hot dogs to Barbecued Chicken (page 96). They are a great side dish, and the bacon, molasses, and brown sugar in this version make them irresistible (see photo page 118).

Serves 10

- 1 pound bacon
- 1 large onion, such as Vidalia, finely chopped
- 4 15-ounce cans pork and beans
- ½ cup dark molasses
- ¼ cup light brown sugar, packed
- 2 tablespoons prepared yellow mustard

Preheat the oven to 350°F.

Fry the bacon in a large skillet over medium-high heat until crisp. Remove the bacon from the pan, leaving the drippings, and drain it on paper towels. Crumble and set aside.

Pour out and discard all but 4 tablespoons of the bacon drippings. Add the onion to the pan and sauté until softened, about 7 minutes. Stir in the beans, molasses, sugar, mustard, and bacon, and mix well.

Pour the beans into a 3-quart casserole and bake, uncovered, for 45 minutes.

# Uncle Wilson's Baked Onions

Serves 12

*From Gwen:* My brother, Wilson, loves to cook. His baked onions can be served with anything but are especially good with Barbecued Pork Ribs (page 84) and Baked Ham with Brown Sugar Honey Glaze (page 88).

Note: Cook onions on the grill by sealing the packets more securely. Cover the grill and check for tenderness after 1 hour of cooking.

If you have access to real Vidalia onions, by all means use them here. Onions from Vidalia, Georgia, are the sweetest onions on the face of the earth! (But how do I really feel about them?) My uncle Wilson made these onions one Fourth of July, and they were a huge hit.

- 6 large sweet white onions, such as Vidalia
- 12 strips bacon
- 2 tablespoons butter

Preheat the oven to 350°F.

Peel and wash the onions. With the point of a small, sharp knife, cut a 1-inch core from the top of each onion. Wrap 2 slices of bacon around each onion, securing it with toothpicks, and put 1 teaspoon butter in each core. Place each onion on a square of aluminum foil and bring the edges loosely together at the top. Put the foil-wrapped onions in a large pan and bake for 1 hour and 20 minutes, or until the onions are tender when pierced with the tip of a knife. Cool the onions for a few minutes, then unwrap and cut in quarters to serve.

# Steamed Yellow Squash

Cook out as much liquid as you can by uncovering and stirring often. A little browning doesn't hurt. You know, I don't even *like* squash, but this sounds yummy to me!

Serves 6

- 4   tablespoons (½ stick) butter
- 1   small sweet onion, such as Vidalia, peeled and finely chopped
- 12   medium yellow crookneck squash, trimmed and sliced ¼-inch thick
- ½   teaspoon salt
- ¼   teaspoon pepper

Melt the butter in a large skillet over medium-high heat. Cook the onion in the butter until it browns slightly, about 5 minutes. Layer the squash slices into the skillet and sprinkle with the salt and pepper. Cover the pan, reduce the heat to low, and cook the squash for 20 minutes, or until tender. Remove the cover. Stir the squash and continue cooking until the liquid has cooked out, another 3 or 4 minutes.

# Fried Okra

My daddy loved boiled okra, but it's too slimy for me. Fried okra, on the other hand, is great with *everything*!

12 tender okra pods, 4 inches or smaller

½ cup all-purpose flour

1 large egg, beaten

½ cup cornmeal

½ teaspoon salt

2 cups peanut oil

Wash the okra and trim the stem ends. Slice each pod crosswise into ½-inch rounds. Place the flour, egg, and cornmeal in separate shallow bowls. Coat the rounds with flour, then drop them into the beaten egg. Use a slotted spoon to transfer the okra rounds to the bowl with the cornmeal and toss to coat.

In a deep-fryer or large cast-iron Dutch oven, heat the oil to 350°F. Lift the okra out of the cornmeal, again using a slotted spoon, and shake off the excess cornmeal. Carefully drop the okra into the oil piece by piece so it doesn't stick together while cooking. Don't overcrowd the pan; you will need to cook 2 or 3 batches. Cook until light brown, about 15 minutes. Remove the cooked okra with a slotted spoon and drain on paper towels. Sprinkle with salt.

# Garlic Grits Casserole

I think people who say they hate grits just haven't had them prepared correctly. Basic grits are pretty simple, and you can add what you like to make them tastier. My sister experimented with this flavorful herb and garlic cheese version for a yummy twist on an old southern favorite.

Serves 12

*From Beth:* Even non-grits-lovers should try this recipe from my mother-in-law, Blanche Bernard.

1 cup grits

4½ cups boiling water

1 teaspoon salt

10 ounces herb and garlic cheese, such as Boursin

¼ cup (½ stick) salted butter

2 medium eggs

½ cup milk

1 tablespoon salted butter, melted

1 cup crushed cornflakes

Preheat the oven to 350°F. Grease a 9 x 12 x 2-inch casserole dish.

Cook the grits in the boiling water with the salt until thickened, about 5 minutes. Add the garlic cheese and butter to the hot grits and stir until melted and incorporated. Beat the eggs and add the milk to the beaten eggs. Slowly stir the egg mixture into the grits. Pour the mixture into the prepared dish. Pour the melted butter over the cornflakes and stir to distribute the butter. Sprinkle the crumb mixture on top of the grits. Bake for 45 minutes.

# Asparagus Casserole

This casserole belongs on a plate with roast beef, rice, and gravy for Sunday lunch. We probably didn't have it every Sunday, but it was often part of the standard after-church meal. I'm a little surprised that as children we ate asparagus, but Daddy always said we'd eat anything with Mama's cheese sauce on it!

*From Gwen:* Using the liquid from the canned asparagus intensifies the flavor of the sauce.

4  tablespoons butter

4  tablespoons all-purpose flour

   Asparagus liquid plus enough milk to equal 2 cups

½  teaspoon salt

5  ounces Cheddar cheese, grated

2  15-ounce cans asparagus spears, drained, liquid reserved

4  hard-boiled eggs, cracked and peeled

½  cup saltine cracker crumbs (about 10 crackers)

Preheat the oven to 350°F.

*From Beth:* You can substitute fresh asparagus for canned, but be sure to trim the tough ends and steam before using. Because you won't have any extra asparagus liquid from the can, use 2 cups milk.

Melt the butter in a medium saucepan. Whisk in the flour to make a roux. Cook for 1 minute, and then whisk in the milk and the asparagus liquid. Add the salt and continue cooking until the sauce thickens, about 5 minutes. Add the grated cheese and stir until it's melted, about 1 minute.

Arrange the asparagus in the bottom of a 9 x 12 x 2-inch baking dish, alternating the stem ends so each serving includes both heads and stems. Thinly slice the eggs and arrange them over the asparagus. Pour the cheese sauce over the eggs and asparagus and sprinkle with the cracker crumbs. Bake the casserole for 20 minutes, or until it is lightly browned and bubbles appear around the edges.

# Spanish Rice

I guess because most of my recipes are southern, we'll just have to say this one is way south of the border! This is a hearty side dish that can be used any time you serve rice. We serve this rice on the Fourth of July with Barbecued Pork Ribs (page 84).

Serves 8

*From Gwen:*
Great with chicken, beef, or pork.

2   tablespoons butter

1   cup long-grain white rice

½   cup chopped onion

½   cup chopped green pepper

2½  cups canned tomatoes, diced or stewed

½   cup chopped pimiento

1   teaspoon salt

    Dash of cayenne pepper

    Tabasco sauce to taste

Preheat the oven to 375°F. Grease a 9 x 12 x 2-inch casserole dish

Melt the butter in a medium saucepan over medium-low heat. Add the rice, onion, and green pepper and sauté for 8 to 10 minutes, or until the rice is slightly browned and the vegetables are softened. Stir in the tomatoes, pimiento, salt, cayenne, and Tabasco. Transfer the rice to the prepared baking dish, cover tightly with aluminum foil, and bake for 30 minutes. Remove the dish from the oven, stir the rice, and check for tenderness. If the rice is tender but too soupy, cook another 5 minutes. If the rice is dry but not tender, add ½ cup water and return to the oven, covered, for another 5 minutes, or until the rice is done.

# Mama's Cornmeal Hushpuppies

Makes 48

*From Gwen:* The idea for adding jalapeños comes from Herb's sister, Patty.

Note: If you can't find self-rising cornmeal, substitute 2 cups cornmeal plus 3 teaspoons baking powder and ¼ teaspoon salt.

You can't have fried catfish without hushpuppies! Sometimes I add a few more jalapeños to the mixture for a little extra jolt.

There are several stories about how hushpuppies got their name. My favorite is the one where an old southern cook was frying them one day and heard her dog howling nearby, so she gave him a plateful and said, "Hush, puppy!" It might just be folklore, but I like it.

2 cups self-rising cornmeal (see Note)

1 large jalapeño, seeded and chopped fine

¾ cup finely chopped onion

2 cups buttermilk

8 cups peanut oil, for frying

In a large bowl, mix the cornmeal, jalapeño, and onion. Add enough of the buttermilk to make a stiff batter. You may not need the whole 2 cups.

Heat the peanut oil to 250°F. (If you are making these to serve with fried catfish, just let the oil cool until it reaches 250°F.)

Drop the batter into the hot oil by teaspoonfuls. The hushpuppies will turn over in the oil as they cook. They are done when they are brown all over, 4 to 5 minutes. Remove them from the oil with a slotted spoon and drain on paper towels. Keep the hushpuppies warm while you fry the remaining batter. Serve hot.

# Home-Style French Fries

I'm not sure if I ever had a store-bought French fry before high school! Mama made these home fries and served them with fresh-off-the-grill burgers. They're the perfect side for Herb's Fried Catfish (page 106) and Mama's Cornmeal Hushpuppies (page 140).

6    medium white or red boiling potatoes

1    tablespoon salt

4    cups peanut oil

Peel the potatoes and slice them into ¼ x ¼-inch sticks. Put the sticks in a large bowl and cover with cold water. Sprinkle the salt into the water. Refrigerate the potato sticks in the salt water for 1 hour.

In a deep-fryer or cast-iron Dutch oven, heat the peanut oil to 375°F. Transfer half of the potatoes to a colander and drain thoroughly, leaving the rest in the cold water. Carefully drop the drained potatoes into the hot oil and fry until light brown, about 15 minutes. Using a slotted spoon, remove the potatoes to a paper towel–lined plate and sprinkle with additional salt while still hot, if desired. Bring the oil back to 375°F. Drain the remaining potato sticks and add to the oil. Keep the first batch of fries hot in a 150°F oven while you fry and drain the second batch. Serve piping hot.

# Real Mashed Potatoes

If I had to name the dish that is requested most often at home it would be this one. My family will eat almost anything if they can have these whipped potatoes on the side! I have been asked many times what secret ingredient makes this recipe so good. The answer is—potatoes! You'll be amazed at how simple it is to make really great mashed potatoes. Everyone has his or her own preference, but I like to use red potatoes, as I think they are lighter and don't get gummy like other kinds can. I also peel the potatoes completely, leaving no trace of skin, but if you like the skins, simply leave them on. For this recipe alone, I would encourage everyone who doesn't have a pressure cooker to get one. They are safe and save a ton of time in the kitchen. A pressure cooker cuts the prep time for this recipe from 1 hour to 15 minutes.

- 5 pounds medium red-skinned potatoes
- 1 tablespoon salt, plus more to taste
- ½ cup (1 stick) butter, at room temperature
- 2 tablespoons milk
  Pepper to taste

Peel the potatoes and cut them in 1-inch cubes. Place the potatoes and 1 tablespoon salt in a large saucepan with water to cover and bring to a boil. Reduce the heat and simmer the potatoes until very tender, about 30 minutes. (You can also cook the potatoes in a pressure cooker for about 5 minutes.)

Drain the potatoes and transfer them to a large mixing bowl. Add the butter, milk, and salt and pepper to taste. Use an electric mixer or a hand mixer to whip the potatoes to a smooth texture, about 5 minutes. You shouldn't see any lumps. If you do, keep mixing! Serve immediately.

# Beth's Hash-Brown Potato Casserole

Serves 8

There are as many versions of this casserole as there are southern cooks and church cookbooks. Beth's is a compilation of several. I like the potatoes shredded instead of cubed and not as much butter as some recipes have (don't worry, there's still plenty!).

- 2 pounds large red potatoes, peeled
- 2 cups sour cream
- 10 ounces Cheddar cheese, shredded
- 1 10-ounce can cream of mushroom soup
- 1 small onion, finely chopped
- 1 teaspoon salt
- ½ teaspoon pepper
- 2 cups crushed Ritz crackers
- ½ cup (1 stick) butter, melted

*From Beth:* If you're in a hurry, substitute a 2-pound bag of frozen hash browns, thawed, for the red potatoes.

Preheat the oven to 350°F. Grease a 9 x 13 x 2-inch casserole dish.

Use the large holes of a box grater or the grating blade of a food processor to shred the potatoes into a large bowl. Add the sour cream, cheese, soup, onion, salt, and pepper. Turn the mixture into the prepared baking dish and sprinkle with the crushed crackers. Pour the melted butter over the top of the casserole. Cover with foil and bake for 45 minutes, then uncover and bake for 20 minutes more, or until lightly browned on top.

# Grandma Lizzie's Cornbread Dressing

Cornbread dressing is my absolute favorite part of the Thanksgiving meal. In fact, I have been known to make this recipe in July because I just can't bear the thought of eating it only once a year! The recipe was never written down until Beth and I demanded that Mama show us how to make it. She came up with the ingredient amounts and demonstrated the mixing technique. (Hint: You've gotta get your hands in it!)

½  loaf white bread, cut into small cubes and toasted

½  medium onion, finely chopped

2  tablespoons butter or turkey fat (skimmed from the pan drippings)

1  pound Buttermilk Cornbread (page 154; about ¾ recipe)

¼  pound saltine crackers (about 35 crackers or 1 sleeve), crumbled

3  hard-boiled large eggs, peeled and chopped

4  cups turkey pan juices (page 104), chicken broth (page 40), or low-sodium canned broth

Salt and pepper to taste

Preheat the oven to 350°F. Grease a 9 x 13 x 2-inch baking dish.

Place the bread cubes on a large baking sheet and toast in the oven for 30 minutes, turning once after 15 minutes, until lightly brown. Set aside to cool. Raise the oven temperature to 450°F.

In a medium skillet, sauté the onion in the butter until translucent and softened but not browned, about 5 minutes. In a very large bowl, crumble the corn bread, toasted bread cubes, and cracker crumbs. Add the onion and eggs and toss with a fork until mixed. Add 3 cups of the broth and mix well, adding more as needed to make a very moist but not soupy dressing. Season with salt and pepper to taste. Bake in the prepared pan for 15 minutes, or until lightly browned.

# Sweet Potato Soufflé

This is a nice variation on regular sweet potatoes for a Thanksgiving side dish. It's almost a dessert, it's so sweet!

  5  medium sweet potatoes (about 9 ounces each)

  2  large eggs

  1  cup granulated sugar

 ½  cup (1 stick) butter, at room temperature

1½  teaspoons vanilla extract

 ½  cup milk

     Pinch of salt

Topping

  1  cup finely chopped pecans

  1  cup brown sugar, packed

 ⅓  cup all-purpose flour

 ¼  cup (½ stick) butter, softened

Preheat the oven to 400°F. Grease a 2½-quart baking dish with butter.

On a foil-covered baking sheet, bake the sweet potatoes for 1 hour, or until they are soft. When cool enough to handle, peel the potatoes, place the flesh in a large mixing bowl, and mash until very smooth. Add the eggs, sugar, butter, vanilla, milk, and salt. Combine well with an electric mixer or hand mixer. Turn the mixture into the baking dish.

In a medium bowl, stir together the pecans, brown sugar, flour, and butter until thoroughly combined. Spoon the mixture over the sweet potatoes, making an even layer. Bake the casserole for 30 minutes, or until slightly browned. Let the casserole sit for 5 minutes before serving.

# quick breads and muffins

I could never be on a diet that eliminated an entire food group, and bread always seems to get the ax first in the diet world! I truly believe that moderation—not giving up something you love altogether—is the key. And bread is something I really do love!

This section includes the basic bread, muffins, corn bread, and sweet bread recipes I rely on year in, year out. Every single one of them is equally good toasted for breakfast, served warm with a little butter for a midafternoon snack with a cup of coffee, or any time you're hungry! And if you're like me, you'll be tempted to ignore the whole moderation thing and eat the entire loaf of Ashley's Banana Bread at one sitting.

# Daddy's Biscuits

Biscuits are synonymous with southern cooking. If I had the time, I would have homemade biscuits at every single meal. They should be required in every household! When my niece Ashley was small, one of the things she liked best about going to Granddaddy and Grammy's house was breakfast. There was usually a conversation the night before about all the awesome things on the menu—bacon, grits, sausage, and, of course, homemade biscuits. Ashley would be up early to help make the biscuits, standing on a chair beside Granddaddy, wearing a big apron and covered with flour.

4   tablespoons vegetable shortening

2   cups self-rising flour (see Note)

¾   cup buttermilk, well shaken

Preheat the oven to 450°F. Lightly grease a baking sheet with non-stick cooking spray. Using a pastry blender or two table knives, cut the shortening into the flour until it resembles coarse meal. Use a fork to stir in the buttermilk to make a soft dough, or until the dough comes together and leaves the sides of the bowl. Continue stirring with the fork until all the flour is worked into the dough, then turn the dough out onto a lightly floured board and knead 3 or 4 times until smooth and manageable.

With your hands or a floured rolling pin, flatten the dough to a thickness of ½ inch. Cut the dough with a 2½-inch floured biscuit cutter. Place the rounds on the baking sheet 1 inch apart for crisp biscuits or almost touching for softer biscuits. Bake for 8 to 10 minutes, or until lightly browned.

Makes 12

*From Gwen:* I mix the dough from start to finish with my fingers. I taught Trisha's dad to use a fork because all the dough seemed to end up on his big hands and not in the pan!

*From Trisha:* Reroll dough scraps for an extra couple of biscuits.

Note: If you cannot find self-rising flour, substitute 2 cups all-purpose flour, 3 teaspoons baking powder, and ¼ teaspoon salt.

# Jack's Yeast Bread

Makes 2
1-pound loaves

*From Gwen:*
Jack used specially shaped tubes such as stars, rounds, and scallops for party sandwich bread.

This was Daddy's "I quit smoking" bread. When I was in high school, he stopped smoking for good. Being a man who was never still, he started looking for ways to occupy his hands other than smoking. He bought some of the first bread flour ever to hit the shelves in Monticello, Georgia, and started experimenting. He became known around town for his homemade bread, and often made loaves for bake sales and church suppers.

2 cups whole milk

3 tablespoons solid shortening

2 tablespoons sugar

2½ teaspoons salt

1½ tablespoons active dry yeast

¼ cup lukewarm water (80° to 85°F)

5–6 cups bread flour

¼ cup butter, melted

Scald the milk and add the solid shortening, sugar, and salt. Stir until the shortening is melted, and cool to lukewarm (80° to 85°F).

In a large, warm bowl, sprinkle the yeast over the lukewarm water. Wait 5 minutes and stir the yeast into the water. Add the cooled milk mixture. Stir in enough flour to make a very stiff dough. Turn the dough out onto a lightly floured board and knead about 10 minutes, or until it is smooth and satiny.

Place the dough in a warm, lightly buttered bowl. Turn the dough to coat it with butter. Cover the bowl with a cloth and allow the dough to rise in a warm place (80° to 85°F), free from drafts, until the dough has doubled in bulk, about 2 hours.

Using your fingers or your fist, punch down the dough to release the air and turn the dough over in the bowl so the smooth oiled side is on top. Cover the bowl and let rise again until almost doubled in bulk, about 30 minutes.

Turn the dough out onto a board and divide into 2 equal portions. Shape each portion into a ball, cover with a cloth, and allow to rest for 10 minutes. Shape each ball into a loaf and place the loaves into 2 greased loaf pans, 5½ x 9½ x 3½-inches.

Note: Water may be substituted for part or all of the milk. Bread made with milk has a browner crust.

Brush the tops of the loaves with melted butter, cover, and let rise until doubled in bulk, about 1 hour. Preheat the oven to 400°F. Bake for 40 to 45 minutes. Turn the loaves out on a rack to cool. The bread is done when it sounds hollow when lightly tapped on the sides or bottom.

*Daddy making yeast bread using Lizzie's bread tray.*

# Buttermilk Cornbread

Serves 8

This is great bread for any meal, but one of my favorite ways to eat it is crumbled up in a big bowl with really cold milk. Mmmm! Beth likes it cold with buttermilk. Now that's just wrong!

4 tablespoons corn oil or bacon drippings

3 cups self-rising cornmeal

2½–3 cups buttermilk, well shaken

Preheat the oven to 450°F.

Pour 2 tablespoons of the oil into a well-seasoned 9-inch cast-iron skillet (see Note) and place over medium-high heat. Put the corn-

meal in a large mixing bowl. Make a well in the cornmeal and add the remaining 2 tablespoons oil. With a fork, stir in enough of the buttermilk to make a batter that is thick but can be easily poured into the hot skillet. You may not need all 3 cups.

Carefully pour the batter into the skillet. The oil will come up around the edges. Use the back of a spoon to smooth this over the top of the batter. Continue to heat on the stovetop for 1 minute, and then transfer the skillet to the oven and bake the corn bread for 20 minutes, or until browned on top. Immediately turn the cornbread out onto a cooling rack to keep the crust crisp.

Note: Season a new cast-iron skillet by coating the inside with vegetable shortening (not butter) and heating the pan in a very hot oven (450°F) for 1 hour. Cool the skillet and wipe off any excess oil before using. To care for a seasoned skillet, wipe the interior after each use. Do not soak it in soapy water or put it in the dishwasher.

# Ashley's Banana Bread

My sister hates bananas. Imagine all of the yummy recipes that eliminates for her! Nonetheless, when my niece Ashley makes this banana bread, it's so good, even Beth will eat it. Maybe it has something to do with all that butter.

¾ cup (1½ sticks) butter

1½ cups sugar

2 large eggs

4 ripe bananas, mashed

1 teaspoon vanilla extract

2 cups sifted all-purpose flour

1 teaspoon baking soda

1 teaspoon salt

½ cup buttermilk, well shaken

1 cup chopped pecans

Preheat the oven to 350°F. Grease 2 9 x 5-inch loaf pans.

With an electric mixer, cream the butter and sugar together until light and fluffy. Add the eggs one at a time, beating well after each addition. Beat in the bananas and vanilla. Sift the flour together with the baking soda and salt and add to the banana mixture alternately with the buttermilk, beginning and ending with flour. Fold in the nuts.

Pour the batter into the loaf pans and bake for 55 minutes. Cool slightly in the pan before turning the loaves out onto wire racks to cool completely.

# Lemon Blueberry Bread

*From Beth:* Dusting the blueberries with flour before adding them to the batter keeps them from sinking to the bottom of the pan.

Every summer, my sister Beth fills her freezer with blueberries her family has picked. They eat as many as they can while the berries are in season, share some with friends and family, and then freeze the rest. This quick bread is good made with fresh or frozen blueberries, and Beth uses lemons from her own lemon tree, right in her backyard! (I'm jealous!)

1   cup fresh blueberries

1½   cups plus 2 tablespoons sifted all-purpose flour

⅓   cup butter, melted

1   cup granulated sugar

3   tablespoons fresh lemon juice

2   large eggs

1   teaspoon baking powder

1   teaspoon salt

½   cup milk

2   tablespoons grated lemon zest

½   cup chopped pecans

Glaze

2   tablespoons fresh lemon juice

¼   cup confectioners' sugar

Preheat oven to 350°F. Grease a 4 x 8 x 2-inch loaf pan.

In a medium bowl, toss the blueberries in 2 tablespoons flour and set aside. In the bowl of an electric mixer, beat together the butter, granulated sugar, 3 tablespoons lemon juice, and eggs. Sift together 1½ cups flour, the baking powder, and the salt. Add the flour and milk alternately to the butter mixture, beginning and ending with flour. Fold in the lemon zest, pecans, and blueberries. Pour the batter into the pan and bake for 1 hour and 10 minutes; a toothpick inserted in the center of the loaf should come out clean. Cool for 10 minutes in the pan, then turn out onto a wire rack.

Make the glaze by stirring together 2 tablespoons lemon juice with the confectioners' sugar until completely smooth. Drizzle over the top of the loaf while it is still warm, allowing the glaze to drip down the sides. Serve the loaf warm or at room temperature.

# Blueberry Muffins

These are the best muffins of all time! My friend Lisa brings me quarts of fresh frozen blueberries every year, and I make these yummy muffins until the blueberries run out. Of course, either fresh or frozen blueberries will work in these muffins. This is a classic choice for breakfast; serve with a fresh cup of coffee.

|   |   |
|---|---|
| 2 | cups all-purpose flour |
| ¾ | cup sugar |
| 1 | tablespoon baking powder |
| ½ | teaspoon salt |
| ½ | teaspoon ground cinnamon |
| ½ | cup (1 stick) butter, melted |
| ½ | cup milk |
| 2 | large eggs, beaten |
| ½ | teaspoon vanilla extract |
| 1½ | cups fresh blueberries |

Preheat the oven to 350°F. Place paper liners in an 18-cup mini-muffin pan.

Sift the flour with the sugar, baking powder, salt, and cinnamon into a large bowl. Make a well in the center of the flour mixture. Add the melted butter, milk, eggs, and vanilla, and stir just enough to moisten the flour. Gently fold in the blueberries.

Spoon the batter into the lined muffin pan. Bake for 25 minutes, or until a toothpick inserted in a muffin comes out clean.

# Pecan-Pie Muffins

These muffins are rich and chewy, but they are also a bit delicate, so be sure to use paper liners in the muffin tins and spray them with nonstick spray; otherwise, they will crumble when you peel off the liners. This recipe also makes great mini-muffins; just shorten the baking time by 5 minutes.

Makes 9

- 1   cup chopped pecans
- 1   cup brown sugar, packed
- ½   cup all-purpose flour
- 2   large eggs
- ⅔   cup (1⅓ sticks) butter, melted

Preheat the oven to 350°F. Place paper liners in 9 muffin cups and spray with nonstick cooking spray.

In a large bowl, combine the pecans, sugar, and flour. Make a well in the center of the mixture.

In a separate bowl, beat the eggs until foamy. Add the melted butter and stir to combine. Pour the egg mixture into the well in the dry ingredients, stirring just until moistened.

Spoon the batter into the cups, filling each two-thirds full. Bake the muffins for 20 minutes, or until a toothpick comes out clean when inserted in a muffin. Remove the muffins from the pans immediately and cool on wire racks.

# cakes, pies, and puddings

I try to reserve my desserts for home-baked items so I can truly enjoy the flavors and can appreciate the hands that made them. When it's my hands that have done the baking, I'm always excited that I was able to make something that tasted so good!

I think one of the big reasons people don't cook much anymore is the misguided notion that it takes too much time and it's just too hard. If you learn one thing in this cookbook, I hope it is that good home-cooked food can be quick and easy. The cakes in this book range from super-easy, just throw it in the pan (Pineapple Upside-Down Cake) to good luck with that (Lizzie's Old-Fashioned Cocoa Cake with Caramel Frosting). If you're tackling one of the more difficult recipes, set aside a couple of hours to make it in advance, and rely on the quicker recipes or the quick substitution ideas for days when you don't have a lot of time to spend in the kitchen. The banana pudding recipe goes from start to finish literally in about 15 minutes!

Pies are a great dessert to make ahead because they store well for a day or two. I make a couple of pecan pies a few days before Thanksgiving every year. It's one less thing I have to think about on that hectic day, and it makes for a wonderful dessert whether served cold or warmed up in the microwave for a few seconds.

# Sour Cream Coffee Cake

Serves 12

Beth makes this cake every time it's her turn to take refreshments for her Sunday School class. It's made in a bundt pan, so it looks beautiful, and the sour cream gives it great flavor and a moist texture. Those little tunnels of brown sugar and nuts are a nice surprise. People always ask her for the recipe.

*From Gwen:*
Be sure to begin the layering with batter. Putting the streusel mixture first produces a sticky cake that is difficult to remove from the pan.

1 cup (2 sticks) butter, room temperature

2 cups granulated sugar

2 large eggs

2 cups all-purpose flour

1 teaspoon baking powder

½ teaspoon salt

1 cup sour cream

1 teaspoon vanilla extract

## Streusel Mixture

½ cup light brown sugar, packed

1½ teaspoons ground cinnamon

½ cup finely chopped pecans

## Glaze

1 cup confectioners' sugar

1½ tablespoons milk

½ teaspoon vanilla extract

Preheat the oven to 350°F. Grease and flour a 10-inch tube or bundt pan.

Use an electric mixer to cream the butter and granulated sugar together until fluffy. Add the eggs one at a time, beating well after each addition. Sift together the flour, baking powder, and salt. Add the flour to the butter mixture in thirds, alternating each addition of flour with the addition of half the sour cream. Stir in the vanilla.

In a separate bowl, combine the brown sugar, cinnamon, and the pecans.

Pour one-third of the batter into the prepared pan. Sprinkle with half the streusel mixture. Pour another third of the batter into the pan and sprinkle with the remaining streusel mixture. Scrape the remaining batter into the pan and smooth the top. Bake for 1 hour, or until a toothpick inserted in the center comes out clean. Allow the cake to cool in the pan for 10 minutes. Remove the cake from the pan and cool on a wire rack.

When the cake is completely cooled, stir the glaze ingredients together in a small bowl until smooth. Drizzle over the cooled cake.

# Kyle's Lemon Pound Cake

Serves 12

From Beth:
This cake is also good drizzled with Fresh Strawberry Sauce (page 180).

My nephew Kyle requests this cake every year on his birthday. You know that if this is a twelve-year-old boy's favorite cake, it's gotta be good!

- 3 cups all-purpose flour
- ½ teaspoon baking soda
- ½ teaspoon baking powder
- ¾ teaspoon salt
- ½ cup (1 stick) butter
- ½ cup vegetable shortening
- 2 cups sugar
- 4 large eggs
- 1 teaspoon vanilla extract
- 2 teaspoons freshly squeezed lemon juice
- 1 teaspoon finely grated lemon zest
- 1 cup buttermilk, well shaken

Preheat the oven to 350°F. Grease and flour a 10-inch tube pan.

Sift the flour together with the baking soda, baking powder, and salt. Set aside. In a large mixing bowl, beat the butter and shortening together until creamy, about 2 minutes. Add the sugar and beat an additional 5 minutes.

Add the eggs one at a time, beating only until the yolks disappear into the batter. Add the vanilla, lemon juice, and zest.

Add the flour mixture alternately with the buttermilk, beginning and ending with flour. Scrape the sides of the mixing bowl and beat only until well blended. Pour into the prepared pan and bake for 1 hour and 10 minutes. Cool slightly, then turn the cake out of the pan while it is still warm. Cool completely on a wire rack.

# Just-Married Pound Cake

My wedding to Garth was such a wonderful day! We wanted it to be a small, private event, and it was, made possible by the help of our friends and families. Everybody was happy to pitch in and help—everybody except my mom, that is, when I asked her to make the wedding cake! I know, it sounds crazy, but I knew she could do it. My mom taught school for twenty-five years, but there was a period in her life (when she had me, to be exact) when she needed to be home. To earn extra money for the family, she began baking and selling cakes for birthday parties and weddings. She resumed her teaching career when I started first grade and retired in 1991 to run my fan club. (She has since retired from that too, and has gone back to being just Mom.)

She came out to Oklahoma the week before the wedding to make a wedding cake that I think turned out to be much bigger than she had been picturing, but it was simply stunning. She gave me the bride and groom decoration from her own wedding day, June 19, 1960, and it literally made the cake. My parents were very happily married for forty-five years, and the only thing that could have made my wedding day better would have been to have Daddy there. I think he was, though. He probably wouldn't have had any wedding cake, but he would have enjoyed the fried chicken and the barbecue!

My finished wedding cake took four electric mixers to make, but we've included the regular pound cake recipe here.

*Gwen and Jack Yearwood at their wedding, June 19, 1960.*

1½  cups (3 sticks) Blue Bonnet margarine, room temperature

1  1-pound box confectioners' sugar, box reserved

6  large eggs, room temperature

1  pound sifted cake flour

1  teaspoon vanilla extract

Preheat the oven to 300°F. Grease and flour a 9-inch tube pan.

Using a heavy-duty mixer, cream the margarine and sugar until the mixture is very light and fluffy, about 5 minutes.

One at a time, break the eggs into a small bowl, then add one at a time to the batter, beating only as long as it takes to break another egg into the small bowl between additions. Scrape down the sides of the mixing bowl.

Measure the sifted flour into the empty confectioners' sugar box, filling it to the top. Add the flour to the sugar and egg mixture, stirring gently on low speed. Scrape the sides of the mixing bowl. Add the vanilla and mix again.

Pour the batter into the prepared pan and bake for 1 hour, or until the center is set. Check for doneness by touching the surface lightly with your fingertip or by inserting a toothpick in the center; it should come out clean.

Cool the cake in the pan for 10 minutes, then run a thin knife or spatula between the cake and the pan to loosen the edges and invert the cake onto a wire rack.

*From Gwen:*
*I can't believe I made this cake!*

*Garth's and my wedding cake from December 10, 2005.*

# White Cream Decorator Frosting

Using solid shortening instead of butter results in a pure white frosting that you can tint any color you like.

- ¾ cup solid white vegetable shortening, such as Crisco
- 1 pound confectioners' sugar
  Pinch of salt
- 4–5 tablespoons very warm water
- 1½ teaspoons clear vanilla extract (see Note)

Using an electric mixer, cream the shortening in a large bowl. Add the sugar gradually, blending well, and beat until fluffy. Beat in the salt, and then add the water by the tablespoon, beating continuously and adding just enough to achieve a smooth, spreadable consistency. Add the vanilla and beat on high until very fluffy. This frosting can be transferred to a pastry bag fitted with decorator tips for decorating cakes.

Note: If you can't find clear vanilla extract, you can use regular vanilla extract, but your icing won't be white. The regular extract will add a cream color to the icing.

# Buttercream Frosting

This recipe is basically the same as the White Cream Decorator Frosting except that, because you're not worried about the icing staying white, you can use milk and regular vanilla extract.

- ¾ cup (1½ sticks) butter, room temperature
- 1 pound confectioners' sugar
- 4–5 tablespoons light cream or milk
- 1½ teaspoons vanilla extract

With an electric mixer, cream the butter and sugar together until smooth. Add the milk by the tablespoon, beating well after each addition and adding just enough liquid to make a smooth, spreadable icing. Add the vanilla and continue to beat the icing on high speed until it is very light and fluffy, about 5 minutes. Makes enough to frost the top and sides of 1 9-inch pound cake.

*From Gwen:* Add food colorings of your choice for decorating cakes and cookies.

# Chocolate Pound Cake

Serves 12

I like a good plain pound cake, but I also like it when I can find a way to make it a little bit different or special. Chocolate pound cake is so simple and so good. This cake is excellent served at room temperature or heated for 15 seconds in the microwave and topped with a scoop of vanilla ice cream.

- 3 cups all-purpose flour
- ½ teaspoon baking powder
- ½ teaspoon salt
- ½ cup cocoa
- 1 cup (2 sticks) butter, room temperature
- ½ cup vegetable shortening
- 3 cups sugar
- 5 large eggs, room temperature
- 1 cup milk
- 2 teaspoons vanilla extract

Preheat the oven to 350°F. Grease and flour a 10-inch tube pan.

Sift the flour, baking powder, salt, and cocoa together 3 times. Set aside.

With an electric mixer, cream the butter, shortening, and sugar until fluffy.

Add the eggs one at a time, beating well after each addition.

Add the flour mixture and the milk alternately, beginning and ending with flour. Add the vanilla.

Pour the batter into the prepared pan and bake for 1 hour. Check for doneness by inserting a toothpick into the cake. It should come out clean. Cool the cake in the pan for 30 minutes before turning it out onto a wire rack to cool completely.

# German Chocolate Cake with Coconut Frosting

Serves 12

Every February, when Garth's birthday rolls around, I make this beautiful and delicious cake for him. Last fall, he made some sad statement like, "Only three more months until you make me that awesome German chocolate cake again!" I made the cake the next day. (I know, I'm a sucker.) I double the frosting recipe to frost the entire cake, because my husband likes extra frosting, but one recipe will frost the tops of the layers and do the trick just fine—unless you're Garth, of course!

If you have some left over, the frosting is also good spread on a graham cracker or on brownies (page 198). Okay, it's also good right off a spoon!

*From Gwen:* Refrigerate the cake after it's frosted. Before serving, touch up any frosting that may have run down the sides.

- 4 ounces sweet dark chocolate (see Shopping Hint, page 173)
- 1 cup (2 sticks) butter, at room temperature
- ¼ cup warm milk
- 2½ cups sifted cake flour
- 1 teaspoon baking soda
- ½ teaspoon salt
- 5 medium egg whites
- 2 cups sugar
- 5 medium egg yolks, at room temperature
- 1 teaspoon vanilla extract
- ¾ cup buttermilk, well shaken

continued . . .

Coconut Frosting

| | |
|---|---|
| 1 | cup sugar |
| 4 | medium egg yolks |
| 1 | cup evaporated milk |
| ½ | cup (1 stick) butter |
| 1 | teaspoon vanilla extract |
| 10 | ounces fresh or frozen and thawed grated coconut |
| 1½ | cups finely ground pecans, walnuts, or almonds |

Prepare the chocolate by melting it in the top of a double boiler, stirring until it is smooth. Add ¼ cup ( ½ stick) of the butter and stir until it is melted and blended. Add ¼ cup of warm milk and stir until smooth. Set the chocolate aside to cool.

Preheat the oven to 350°F.

Line the bottoms only of 3 9-inch cake pans with circles of parchment paper, or grease each pan bottom only with solid shortening and dust lightly with flour. Sift together the sifted and measured flour, baking soda, and salt.

Whip the egg whites until stiff using the wire beater of the mixer. Transfer the beaten whites to a separate bowl and set aside.

In the mixer bowl, cream the remaining 1½ sticks of butter and sugar together until fluffy. Add the egg yolks one at a time, beating well after each addition (see "From Trisha," opposite). Add the melted, cooled chocolate and the vanilla. Mix well.

With the mixer on very low, stir in the flour mixture alternately with the buttermilk. Do this by adding about a third of the flour and slowly stirring it in completely. Then add about half the buttermilk and stir it in. Continue adding flour and buttermilk in this manner, ending with flour. Scrape the sides and bottom of the bowl and stir again. With a long-handled spoon or spatula, fold and stir the beaten egg whites into the batter until the batter is smooth with no visible clumps of whites.

Divide the batter evenly between the prepared pans and bake for 30 to 40 minutes. Bake on the middle rack of the oven, allowing at least ¼-inch clearance between the pans and the oven walls. The cake will rise above the pan edges as it bakes but will not spill over and will settle back down as it continues to bake. The cake is done when it begins to pull away from the sides of the pans and springs back to a light touch. Cool layers in the pans for about 8 minutes.

Run a knife around the edges of each pan and turn the layers out onto wire racks that have been sprayed with cooking spray. Cool layers completely before frosting.

To make the frosting, combine the sugar, egg yolks, and evaporated milk in the top of a double boiler. Stir with a wire whisk until the yolks are fully incorporated. Add the butter. Place over simmering water and bring to a boil (see Note). Simmer for 12 to 15 minutes longer, stirring constantly, until the mixture thickens. Add the vanilla, coconut, and nuts. Cool.

To assemble the cake, place one layer on a cake stand and spread with frosting. Frost each layer completely, top and sides, as it is added to the cake.

*From Trisha:* Separated egg yolks will slide easily and individually from a small bowl if the bowl is rinsed with water first.

Note: You can also make the frosting in a regular saucepan, but be sure to stir it constantly, as it scorches quite easily. Also, you *must* use the finely grated fresh or frozen coconut, not canned or shredded, to be able to spread the frosting on the sides of the cake easily.

Shopping Hint: For those cooks who use a lot of sweet baking chocolate, the chocolate used in this recipe can be purchased in bulk online at www.cocoasupply.com. Choose La Equatoriale—Dark Chocolate Coverture. The cost, including postage, is half what you would probably pay in grocery stores. Share the large bar with your friends who bake.

# Lizzie's Old-Fashioned Cocoa Cake with Caramel Icing

Serves 12

*From Gwen:*
I have had more deliciously edible failures with this icing than with any other. I never make it the same way twice! As a young teacher in Dawson, Georgia, I boarded with Mrs. Mary Lou Alexander, who made a fabulous Caramel Icing. Her daughter, Kathy, has graciously shared the recipe.

So what's my birthday cake of choice? Chocolate cake with caramel icing. Yum! Most people have tried white cake with caramel icing, but my grandma Elizabeth Yearwood spread that amazing Caramel Icing on chocolate layers, and it was even more delicious. The cake recipe came from my grandma Paulk. I guess I could call this Two-Grandma Cake! Now my mom makes this cake for me every year. The Caramel Icing has a mind of its own, so you never really know what it's going to look like, but it doesn't matter to me. It always tastes amazing!

2 cups all-purpose flour

⅔ cup cocoa

1¼ teaspoons baking soda

¼ teaspoon baking powder

1 teaspoon salt

⅔ cup (1⅓ sticks) butter

1⅔ cups sugar

3 large eggs

½ teaspoon vanilla extract

1⅓ cups water

## Caramel Icing

4 cups sugar

1 cup milk

1 stick (½ cup) butter

⅛ teaspoon baking soda

1 teaspoon vanilla

Preheat the oven to 350°F. Grease and lightly flour 2 9-inch cake pans.

Sift together the flour, cocoa, baking soda and powder, and salt, and set aside. With an electric mixer, cream the butter and sugar until fluffy, about 5 minutes. Add the eggs and vanilla and beat on high speed for 3 minutes. Add the flour mixture alternately with 1⅓ cups water, beginning and ending with flour.

Divide the batter evenly between the pans and bake for 30 to 35 minutes. Turn the layers out onto racks that have been sprayed with cooking spray.

Mix 3 cups of the sugar and the milk in a heavy 3-quart saucepan. Bring slowly to a boil and keep it hot. Caramelize remaining cup of sugar in an iron skillet. Do this by cooking over medium-high heat and stirring and scraping the pan with a flat-edged spatula as the sugar melts. Continue to cook until the syrup turns to medium or dark brown in color. This occurs at about 320°F to 350°F on a candy thermometer. Do not scorch the syrup. Stream the syrup into the boiling sugar and milk mixture and cook to the soft ball stage, about 238°F. Add the butter, soda, and vanilla.

Pour the hot mixture into the metal bowl of an electric mixer and beat as it cools until the icing is creamy, 15 to 20 minutes. Spread on the cake layers while the icing is still warm. If it becomes too stiff, add a few drops of hot water.

Note: Makes more than enough to frost 2 9-inch cake layers. Leftover frosting can be stored in the refrigerator for up to 2 weeks, rewarmed, and used to frost brownies or cupcakes.

*Beth and me with Beth's piano birthday cake made by Gwen.*

# Pineapple Upside-Down Cake

I'm always looking for fun recipes to make with our girls, hoping they will grow up to love cooking as much as I do. This cake is fun because they can't believe you put all the pretty decorations on the bottom of the pan and the cake still turns out to be gorgeous!

| | |
|---|---|
| 3 | tablespoons butter |
| ½ | cup light brown sugar, packed |
| 9 | canned pineapple slices in juice, drained |
| 5 | maraschino cherries |
| 1½ | cups sifted all-purpose flour |
| 2 | teaspoons baking powder |
| ¼ | teaspoon salt |
| ⅓ | cup solid vegetable shortening |
| ⅔ | cup granulated sugar |
| 1 | large egg |
| ¾ | teaspoon vanilla extract |
| ⅔ | cup milk |

Preheat the oven to 350°F.

Place the butter in an 8 x 8 x 2-inch square pan and put it in the oven to melt. When the butter is melted, carefully remove the pan from the oven and sprinkle the brown sugar over the butter. Arrange the pineapple rings on top of the sugar in a single layer, making 3 rows. Cut the maraschino cherries in half and place 1 half in the center of each pineapple ring, cut side up. Set the pan aside.

Sift the flour, baking powder, and salt, then sift once more. Set aside.

Using an electric mixer, cream the shortening and the granulated sugar together until light and fluffy. Add the egg and beat until fully combined. Add the vanilla. Blend in the flour mixture alternately with the milk, beginning and ending with flour. Stir only enough after each addition to combine.

Pour the batter carefully into the pineapple-lined pan. Bake for 40 minutes and test for doneness by inserting a toothpick in the center or pressing the cake lightly with a fingertip; if the impression springs back, the cake is done. Run a knife around the edges of the pan and place a serving dish on top. Invert the cake onto the serving plate. Leave the pan inverted over the cake for several minutes to allow the syrup to soak into the cake.

*From Trisha:* You may have to cut the pineapple rings a little bit to make them smaller, so all nine fit in the pan.

# Iced Italian Cream Cake

We seem to place a lot of emphasis on birthday cakes in my family. We like for everyone to have his or her favorite cake, but more than that, we like the variety of awesome sweets we get to eat throughout the year! This cake was once Beth's birthday cake of choice—or so Mom thought until she learned that Beth actually preferred the chocolate caramel cake I always ask for. At first, I thought she was just trying to copy me (it's a sister thing!), but then I realized that if it's her favorite cake, too, that's twice a year for me!

This is great tasting, very pretty, and very easy. It deserves to be a first choice, too.

- 2 cups all-purpose flour
- 1 teaspoon baking soda
- ½ cup (1 stick) unsalted butter
- ½ cup vegetable shortening
- 2 cups sugar
- 5 large eggs, separated
- 1 cup buttermilk, well shaken
- 1 teaspoon vanilla extract
- ½ cup chopped pecans
- 1 cup sweetened shredded coconut

## Italian Cream Frosting

- 8 ounces cream cheese, room temperature
- 4 tablespoons (½ stick) butter, room temperature
- 1 pound confectioners' sugar
- 1 teaspoon vanilla extract
- ½ cup chopped nuts

Preheat the oven to 350°F. Grease and lightly flour 3 9-inch cake pans.

Sift the flour and soda together and set aside.

With an electric mixer, cream the butter and shortening with the sugar until fluffy, about 5 minutes. Add the egg yolks one at a time, beating well between each addition. With the mixer on medium speed, add the flour and buttermilk alternately, beginning and ending with buttermilk. Add the vanilla, coconut, and nuts, and stir well to incorporate.

In a separate bowl with clean beaters, whip the egg whites to stiff peaks. Gently fold the beaten egg whites into the batter, just until blended.

Pour the batter into the prepared pans and bake for 25 minutes. Test for doneness by touching the top of the cake with your finger. The cake is done if it bounces back up. Cool the layers on wire racks sprayed with cooking spray to prevent sticking.

With an electric mixer, beat the cream cheese with the butter on the high speed until fluffy. Reduce the speed to medium and blend in the sugar and vanilla. Beat well until the frosting is smooth.

When the cake is completely cool, spread the frosting between the layers and on the sides and top of the cake. Sprinkle with the nuts.

*Trisha and Beth with Lizzie's chocolate cake with caramel icing and iced Italian cream cake for their birthdays in September 1982.*

# Joe's "Say Cheese" Cheesecake with Fresh Strawberry Sauce

Serves 8 to 10

It has become a tradition in my house that I make everyone's favorite dessert on his or her birthday. Garth's favorite is German Chocolate Cake, Taylor's is Banana Pudding, and so on. When it came time for my friend Joe's birthday, his wife, Kim, let me know that *his* favorite was cheesecake. "No problem," I said, as I started thinking about that awesome cheesecake in a box I was going to make (I have to admit that it's my favorite). "He loves the old-style New York cheesecake," she explained. Umm . . . no problem? But I was committed, so I did what I always do: call my family for help. Beth hooked me up with several cheesecake recipes, and this is the one I like best. It made me a big hit on Joe's birthday.

*From Beth:* The strawberry sauce is good served on pound cake or angel food cake, too.

Note: The water bath prevents the cheesecake from cracking as it bakes.

## Crust
1½  cups fine graham cracker crumbs

¼  cup sugar

¼  cup ( ½ stick) butter, melted

## Filling
32  ounces (4 8-ounce packages) cream cheese

2  cups sour cream

4  large eggs

1¼  cups sugar

2½  tablespoons cornstarch

2  teaspoons vanilla extract

## Fresh Strawberry Sauce
1¼  cups fresh strawberries

¼  cup sugar

1½  teaspoons grated lime zest

Preheat the oven to 375°F. Spray the bottom of 10-inch springform pan with cooking spray, line the bottom with a round of parchment paper, and spray the paper with cooking spray. Place the pan on a sheet of heavy-duty aluminum foil and bring the foil up to enclose the seam between the bottom and sides.

To make the crust, stir together the graham cracker crumbs, sugar, and butter in a mixing bowl until the crumbs are coated. Press the mixture firmly into the bottom of the pan and up the sides. Set aside.

In a large bowl, beat the cream cheese with the sour cream. Add the eggs, one at a time, beating well after each addition. Add the sugar, cornstarch, and vanilla, and beat until smooth.

Pour the batter into the prepared crust. Place the foil-wrapped pan in a larger pan placed on the oven rack. Carefully pour ½-inch warm water into the larger pan (see Note). Bake for 1 hour. Turn off the oven and open the door. Let the cheesecake stand in the opened oven for 1 hour. Refrigerate the cheesecake for 2 hours or overnight before removing from the pan.

To make the sauce, process all ingredients in a food processor or blender until they are smooth. Chill for at least 1 hour. (This sauce is best if served cold from the refrigerator.)

# Basic Pastry

Makes 2
9-inch pie crusts

There are some really good ready-to-use piecrusts on the market these days. My favorite is Mrs. Smith's deep-dish frozen pie shells. Still, if you have time, it's always better to make your own! This pie shell can be used for recipes that call for baked or unbaked crusts.

- 2 cups sifted all-purpose flour
- 1 teaspoon salt
- ⅔ cup chilled solid shortening

    About 6 tablespoons ice water

Sift the flour and the salt together into a cold medium bowl. Cut in ⅓ cup of the shortening with two knives or a pastry blender until the mixture resembles cornmeal. Cut in the remaining ⅓ cup shortening until the mixture gathers into small pea-sized pieces. Sprinkle the ice water, 1 tablespoon at a time, over a small portion of the mixture. Use a fork to press the mixture together, making a small ball of dough. Sprinkle another tablespoon of water over another dry portion of the flour and press it together. Continue moistening small portions of the dry mixture until all of the flour is moistened. Use only enough water to make the dough stick together. It should not be wet or slippery. Press all the moistened portions together gently and quickly with your fingers. Do not knead. The less the dough is handled, the more tender and flaky the pastry will be. Cover and chill the dough.

On a lightly floured board or canvas, roll out half of the dough into a circle ⅛ inch thick and about 2 inches larger than the pie pan. Fold the circle in half to fit it loosely into the pie pan. Trim the excess dough with scissors, leaving about 1 inch of the pastry over the edge of the pan to be folded under to form a standing, fluted rim.

For a prebaked crust, press foil gently into the pan over the pastry and prick the bottom with the times of a fork to prevent air bubbles from forming during baking. Fill with pie weights or dried beans. Bake at 350°F for 15 to 20 minutes, or until lighter golden.

# Sweet Potato Pie

Sweet Potato Pie is always served at Thanksgiving at my house. I used to think there wasn't much of a difference between Sweet Potato Pie and Pumpkin Pie, but this recipe made me change my mind. It's just sweet enough, and it's so smooth and creamy. Hmmm . . . I need to think of more holidays to make this for, so I can eat it more often!

1½   cups puréed sweet potatoes, canned or home-baked (page 147)

1   cup sugar

2   large eggs

¼   cup (½ stick) butter, softened

¼   cup milk

¼   teaspoon ground cinnamon

¼   teaspoon ground nutmeg

   Pinch of salt

1   teaspoon vanilla extract

2   unbaked 9-inch pie shells, homemade (page 182) or purchased

Preheat the oven to 300°F.

In the bowl of an electric mixer, combine the potatoes, ½ cup sugar, and the eggs, butter, milk, cinnamon, nutmeg, salt, and vanilla. Beat until thoroughly blended and smooth. Divide evenly between the pie shells. Sprinkle ¼ cup sugar over each pie. Allow the pies to stand for 15 minutes before baking to allow the sugar to melt. Bake the pies for 1 hour, or until a toothpick inserted in the center comes out clean. Cool them before serving.

Makes 2
9-inch pies;
serves 16 to 20

*From Gwen:*
A sweet potato never tasted so good! The added sugar on top gives just the right finishing crunch.

# Pecan Pie

Every Georgia girl has a trusted pecan pie recipe if she knows what's good for her! This one came from a great family friend in Monticello named Betty Maxwell.

- 1 cup light brown sugar, packed
- ½ cup granulated sugar
- 2 large eggs
- ½ cup (1 stick) butter, melted
- 1½ teaspoons vanilla extract
- 2 tablespoons milk
- 1 tablespoon all-purpose flour
- 1 cup chopped pecans
- 1 9-inch deep-dish pie shell, unbaked, or homemade pastry (page 182)
- 1 cup pecan halves

Preheat the oven to 325°F.

To make the filling, beat the sugars with the eggs in an electric mixer until creamy, about 5 minutes. Add the melted butter, vanilla, milk, flour, and chopped pecans. Pour the mixture into the shell. Arrange the pecan halves on top of the pie in a circular pattern.

Bake the pie for 55 minutes. Check for doneness by shaking the pan slightly. The pie should be firm, with only a slight jiggle in the center. It will set more as it cools. Serve warm, topped with vanilla ice cream, or at room temperature with a dollop of whipped cream.

# French Coconut Pie

You can make the homemade pastry recipe if you like, but if you start with a purchased pie crust, this is a really quick and easy dessert. Be sure to use grated fresh or frozen coconut for ease in slicing.

*From Gwen:*
The coconut rises to the top to form a crunchy topping.

1½  cups sugar

1  tablespoon all-purpose flour

½  cup (1 stick) butter, melted

3  large eggs

½  cup buttermilk, well shaken

1  teaspoon vanilla extract

2  cups grated coconut, fresh or frozen

1  deep-dish unbaked 9-inch pie shell, homemade (page 182) or purchased

Preheat the oven to 350°F.

In the bowl of an electric mixer, beat the sugar and flour with the melted butter. Add the eggs one at a time, mixing well after each. Add the buttermilk and vanilla and combine again. Stir in the coconut.

Pour the filling into the prepared pie shell. Bake for 45 to 50 minutes, or until lightly brown and the center of the pie doesn't jiggle when shaken lightly. A toothpick inserted into the center of the pie should come out moist but not covered with custard. The coconut will rise to form a top crust during baking. Set the pie in the pan on a wire rack and cool completely before serving.

# Butterscotch Pie

When my brother-in-law John turned fifty, my sister, Beth, wanted to make a really special dessert for him. She remembered his mentioning a favorite butterscotch pie his mother, Blanche, used to make and this recipe came from her. It was a big hit on his birthday.

1 cup light brown sugar, packed

3 tablespoons butter

4 tablespoons heavy cream

2 cups milk

3 tablespoons cornstarch

3 large eggs, separated

½ teaspoon vanilla extract

Pinch of salt

¼ cup granulated sugar

1 9-inch pie crust, homemade (page 182) or purchased, prebaked as directed

Preheat the oven to 350°F.

In a medium saucepan, stir together the brown sugar, butter, and cream. Cook over medium heat until the sugar dissolves and the mixture comes to a full boil, becoming thick and brown, about 5 minutes.

In a measuring cup, mix the milk, cornstarch, egg yolks, and vanilla together. Add to the sugar mixture, stirring constantly, and cook until thick, about 3 minutes. Pour the filling into the prebaked pie crust.

Make the meringue by beating the egg whites with a pinch of salt until they begin to get stiff. Add the granulated sugar and continue beating until the whites are stiff and hold peaks. Spread the meringue on top of the pie, taking care to spread it to the edges of the crust. Bake until light brown.

# Blackberry Cobbler

Serves 10

After moving to Oklahoma in 2002, I discovered an abundance of wild blackberries growing on our farm. Channeling my best Martha Stewart, I decided I *had* to pick these berries myself and prepare the perfect blackberry cobbler for my family. (This is also where I learned about the abundance of chiggers in Oklahoma, something we call red bugs in Georgia. They apparently love to feast on unsuspecting berry pickers.) After talking a couple of my girlfriends into going blackberry picking with me, I had an ample supply of beautiful blackberries. When I called my mom, the goddess of all things culinary, to ask for Grandma Paulk's blackberry cobbler recipe, I got the familiar reply: "Well, actually there is no real recipe." Ahhh! My notes from that day go something like this:

Berries in water
Sugar
Bring to a boil
Flour
Shortening
Milk

You get the picture. The cobbler actually came out great, and I was proud of my handpicked berries, but truth be told, it was the first and last time I picked the berries wild. Store-bought berries at your local grocery or farmer's market are usually plumper and sweeter than wild berries. If you use wild berries, you will probably need to add more sugar.

*From Trisha:*
The last time I made this, I didn't have time to make homemade pastry, so I tried store-bought refrigerated roll-out pastry shells and cut them into strips. It worked great!

continued . . .

¾  cup sugar

2  cups plus 1 tablespoon self-rising flour (see Note)

2  cups fresh blackberries

¼  cup ( ½ stick) butter, cold, cut into small pieces

½–⅔  cup milk

   Vanilla ice cream for serving

Preheat the oven to 450°F. Butter a 1-quart casserole dish or baking pan.

In a medium saucepan combine the sugar, 1 tablespoon of the flour, berries, and 1 cup water. Bring to a boil, reduce the heat, and simmer for 2 minutes, then remove from the heat and set aside.

In a medium bowl, use a pastry blender or two knives to cut the butter into the remaining 2 cups flour. Stir in just enough milk to make a soft dough that pulls away from the sides of the bowl. Turn the dough out on a lightly floured board and pat into a square. Use a rolling pin to roll it to ½ inch thick. Cut the dough into 2-inch-wide strips.

Pour 1 cup of the blackberry mixture into the bottom of the pan. Arrange half of the dough strips on top of the blackberry mix, placing them close together. Bake until brown, about 12 minutes, then remove from the oven and pour the remaining berry mixture over the baked strips. Arrange another layer of dough strips on top and bake for 12 more minutes, or until brown. Serve warm with ice cream.

Note: If you don't have self-rising flour, substitute 2 cups all-purpose flour mixed with 3 teaspoons baking powder and ¼ teaspoon salt.

# Easy Peach Cobbler

Serves 8

*From Trisha:*
This forms its own top crust while it bakes.

Note: If you don't have self-rising flour, substitute 1 cup all-purpose flour mixed with 1½ teaspoons baking powder and ⅛ teaspoon salt.

You can't be considered a serious southern cook if you don't know how to make peach cobbler. Canned or frozen fruit works better in some recipes than fresh, and this is a perfect example. I recommend any brand of canned freestone peaches because they are tender and tasty. This dessert is easy to make and it tastes delicious, especially with a huge dollop of Home-Churned Ice Cream (page 212) on top.

- 2   15-ounce cans sliced peaches in syrup
- ½   cup (1 stick) butter
- 1   cup self-rising flour (see Note)
- 1   cup sugar
- 1   cup milk

Preheat the oven to 350°F. Drain 1 can of peaches; reserve the syrup from the other.

Place the butter in a 9 x 12-inch ovenproof baking dish. Heat the butter in the oven until it's melted. In a medium bowl, mix the flour and sugar. Stir in the milk and the reserved syrup. Carefully remove the baking dish from the oven and pour the batter over the melted butter. Arrange the peaches over the batter. Bake for 1 hour. The cobbler is done when the batter rises around the peaches and the crust is thick and golden brown. Serve warm with vanilla ice cream.

*From Gwen:*
Two types of peaches, freestone and clingstone, are just what the terms suggest. The flesh of a ripe freestone variety pulls easily away from the pit or stone, while the clingstone flesh, well, clings! Go online to www.lanepacking.com for all the scoop on Georgia peaches.

# Bret's Banana Pudding, Aunt T Style

Serves 1 hungry nephew

My nephew Bret is allergic to eggs, which always presents a challenge when it comes to dessert. The bigger challenge is that Bret loves banana pudding. When a seven-year-old boy who is very cute asks why everyone else is having banana pudding while he is not, Aunt Trisha has to think quickly, and because my regular recipe calls for four eggs, I have to get really creative. This banana pudding recipe came about on the spot, and Bret isn't the only one who loves it!

- 6 vanilla wafers
- 1 medium banana, sliced
- ½ cup nondairy topping, such as Cool Whip

On a dessert plate, make a layer of vanilla wafers and sliced bananas. Top with Cool Whip and serve!

*Bret eating "his" banana pudding.*

# Banana Pudding

Serves 8

*From Gwen:*
Wait, if you can, to allow the wafers to become soft before serving.

We should rename this recipe Goldilocks Pudding! My mother's notes say she made several attempts at my dad's favorite dessert before coming up with this particular version—not too hard, not too soft. It has become a mainstay in my home, too. Garth prefers the pudding without the meringue, so I usually make two versions, one with and one without. Either way, it's a homey, satisfying finish to any meal.

|       |                              |
| ----: | ---------------------------- |
| 4     | large eggs                   |
| ¾     | cup sugar                    |
| 3     | tablespoons all-purpose flour |
| ½     | teaspoon salt                |
| 2     | cups milk                    |
| ½     | teaspoon vanilla extract     |
| 30–40 | vanilla wafers               |
| 5–6   | medium ripe bananas          |
|       | Pinch of salt                |

Separate the yolks from the whites of 3 eggs. Set aside the whites. In the top of a double boiler, whisk together ½ cup of the sugar, the flour, and the salt. Stir in the whole egg and the 3 yolks, and then stir in the milk.

Cook uncovered, stirring often, for about 10 minutes, or until the mixture thickens. Remove from the heat and stir in the vanilla.

Preheat the oven to 425°F.

Spread a thin layer of pudding in a 1½-quart casserole dish. Arrange a layer of vanilla wafers on top of the pudding. Thinly slice the bananas crosswise, about ⅛ inch thick, and arrange a layer of banana slices over the wafers. Spread one-third of the remaining pudding over the bananas and continue layering wafers, bananas, and pudding, ending with pudding.

To make the meringue, beat the reserved egg whites with a pinch of salt until they are stiff. Gradually beat in the remaining ¼ cup sugar and continue beating until the whites will not slide out of the mixing bowl when it is tilted. Spread the meringue over the pudding with a spatula, making a few decorative peaks on top, and bake for 5 minutes, or until the meringue is lightly browned.

# cookies, candy, and ice cream

I've always claimed that I'm not much of a sweets person, that I prefer salty dishes, but I guess it would be more accurate to say I am not a big fan of store-bought sweets. If I'm going to eat something sweet, I would rather hold out for homemade brownies or cookies than waste my calories on something out of a box. And with the invention of electric ice-cream churns, making homemade ice cream has become a piece of cake! (Did I really just say that?)

I love to give homemade baked goods as gifts at Christmas. It says you think enough of the recipient to make something with your own two hands just for them. Cookies, candy, and fudge are relatively easy, inexpensive ways to give that gift. Of course, once the smell of baking chocolate chip cookies starts to waft through my house, I have a hard time giving anything away. Sometimes you need to give that gift to yourself, too!

Most of these recipes say to store leftovers in an airtight container for up to two weeks. Keep in mind that this was an educated guess. I would personally like to meet someone who has leftover cookies in their home for two weeks! My crowd can make a dozen cookies disappear in a matter of seconds.

# Brownies

Makes 16
brownies

From Gwen:
I always double
this recipe and
bake it in a
9 x 13 x 2-inch
pan.

I love these brownies plain, but Garth likes them frosted, so I usually make some Coconut Frosting (page 172) on the side just for him. The unsweetened baking chocolate keeps the brownies from being too sweet. I know, sweets are supposed to be sweet, but trust me, these are just right!

- 2 ounces unsweetened baking chocolate
- ⅓ cup solid vegetable shortening, such as Crisco
- 2 large eggs
- 1 cup sugar
- ⅔ cup all-purpose flour
- ½ teaspoon baking powder
- ½ teaspoon salt
- 1 cup chopped pecans
- 1 teaspoon vanilla extract

Preheat the oven to 350°F. Grease the bottom of an 8 x 8 x 2-inch pan.

Melt the chocolate and shortening together over simmering water or in the microwave. Cool slightly. In a mixing bowl, beat the eggs well. Add the sugar and combine thoroughly, then stir in the chocolate mixture.

Sift the flour together with the baking powder and salt, then stir into the chocolate mixture. Stir in the nuts and vanilla.

Spread the batter evenly in the prepared pan. Bake for 25 to 30 minutes, or until a toothpick inserted in the center comes out clean. Cool in the pan for 5 minutes, then cut into 2-inch squares. These are good warm or cold.

# Chewy Chocolate Chip Cookies

Makes 3 to
4 dozen

I started making these cookies in the eighth grade, and they just might be responsible for my love of cooking. It wasn't just that they are gooey and awesome, which they are; it was also that people complimented me on my cooking skills, and that gave me confidence. It later worked out in the singing thing, too! Exactly how chewy these cookies are depends on how big you make them. I make mine a little bigger than the recipe calls for because I like them soft in the middle. They are best served with a really cold glass of milk . . . or more cookies!

⅔  cup (1⅓ sticks) butter, room temperature

¾  cup granulated sugar

¼  cup dark brown sugar, packed

1  large egg, room temperature

1  teaspoon vanilla extract

1¾  cups sifted all-purpose flour

½  teaspoon baking soda

½  teaspoon salt

1  cup (1 6-ounce package) semisweet chocolate chips

Place the oven rack in the center of the oven and preheat the oven to 375°F.

Using the electric mixer, beat the butter, sugars, egg, and vanilla together until smooth.

Sift the flour, baking soda, and salt together and, with the beater running, slowly add to the butter mixture. Stir in the chocolate chips.

Drop the batter by teaspoonfuls about 2 inches apart on an ungreased cookie sheet. Bake for 8 to 10 minutes, or until lightly browned. Carefully remove the cookies to a wire rack to cool. Store in an air-tight container.

# Snickerdoodles

Makes 4 to 5 dozen

One of our girls doesn't like chocolate! Hard to believe if you're a chocolate lover like me, but I'm always looking for a chocolate alternative for dessert around my house. Fortunately, this was Beth's specialty growing up, and I've stolen her recipe for my own.

½ cup salted butter

½ cup vegetable shortening

1½ cups plus 2 tablespoons sugar

2 medium eggs

2¾ cups all-purpose flour

2 teaspoons cream of tartar

1 teaspoon baking soda

¼ teaspoon salt

2 teaspoons ground cinnamon

Preheat the oven to 400°F. In a large bowl, combine the butter, shortening, 1½ cups sugar, and the eggs and mix thoroughly. Sift together the flour, cream of tartar, baking soda, and salt, and stir into the shortening mixture.

In a small bowl, stir together the remaining 2 tablespoons sugar with the cinnamon. Shape the dough into 1½-inch balls and roll each ball in the cinnamon sugar. Arrange the dough balls 2 inches apart on an ungreased cookie sheet. Bake 8 to 10 minutes. Transfer the cookies to wire racks for cooling. Store in an airtight container.

# Cinnamon Cookies

The original recipe for these cinnamon cookies is written on an index card in my sister Beth's earliest cursive handwriting, and it is probably the first recipe I remember her making when we were girls. She still makes them every Halloween.

Makes 2 dozen

 2  cups all-purpose flour

 1  teaspoon baking soda

 ½  teaspoon salt

 1  teaspoon ground cinnamon

 1  teaspoon ground cloves

 1  teaspoon ground ginger

 ¾  cup solid vegetable shortening, such as Crisco

1½  cups sugar

 ¼  cup molasses

 1  large egg

Preheat the oven to 350°F.

Onto a large piece of waxed paper, sift together the flour, baking soda, salt, cinnamon, cloves, and ginger. In a large mixing bowl, cream the shortening and 1 cup of the sugar. Add the flour mixture to the sugar mixture and combine. Mix in the molasses and the egg. Cover the dough in plastic wrap and chill for 1 hour, or until firm. Roll the dough into 1-inch balls, and then roll balls in the remaining sugar before placing on an ungreased cookie sheet, 1 to 1½ inches apart. Bake for 20 minutes. Transfer the cookies to a wire rack to cool. Store in an airtight container.

# Gingerbread Cookies

Makes 5 dozen

Note: Keep the bowl and the decorator tips covered with a moist cloth to prevent the icing from hardening prematurely.

I have always liked the smell of gingerbread cookies baking. It reminds me of my favorite holiday, Christmas, but I bake these cookies year round. My sister is the gingerbread house queen. I have made just one gingerbread house in my life—I'm not really patient enough to do the job justice!

- 1  cup vegetable shortening
- 1  cup sugar
- 1  large egg
- 1  cup molasses
- 2  tablespoons cider vinegar
- 4–5  cups sifted all-purpose flour
- 1½  teaspoons baking soda
- ½  teaspoon salt
- 3  teaspoons ground ginger
- 1  teaspoon ground cinnamon
- 1  teaspoon ground cloves

Using an electric mixer, cream the shortening and sugar together until light and fluffy. Add the egg, molasses, and vinegar and beat on high speed to blend thoroughly. Sift together 4 cups of the flour and the baking soda, salt, ginger, cinnamon, and cloves. Add the dry ingredients to the creamed shortening and sugar and mix to make a firm, manageable dough, adding more flour if needed. Wrap the dough in plastic and refrigerate for 3 hours or until firm.

Preheat the oven to 375°F. Lightly grease 1 or 2 baking sheets.

Spray a rolling pin with cooking spray and lightly flour your work surface. Roll the dough to ⅛-inch thickness and cut it into desired shapes with a knife or cookie cutters. (You can reroll the scraps to make a few more cookies.) Place the cookies 1 inch apart on the prepared baking sheet and bake for 5 to 6 minutes.

Cool the cookies for 2 minutes on the cookie sheet before removing to a wire rack to cool completely.

## Royal Icing

  3   egg whites, room temperature, or equivalent meringue powder

2½   cups sifted confectioners' sugar

¼   teaspoon cream of tartar

Beat the egg whites and ⅓ cup of the sugar with a wire whisk or the whisk attachment on your mixer. Add another ⅓ cup sugar and the cream of tartar and beat 10 minutes longer. Add the remaining sugar and beat until the mixture is smooth and thick. The icing can be tinted as desired with food coloring.

> Note: To make gingerbread house sections, spray the back of a jelly roll pan and a rolling pin with cooking spray. Roll out the dough to ⅛-inch thickness and place on the back of the jelly roll pan. Cut out the desired shapes for the walls and roof, then remove the trimmings (you can save and reroll these scraps for cookies or additional house embellishments) and bake for 5 to 6 minutes. Cool for 2 minutes on the pan before carefully removing to a cooling rack. Cool completely before assembling the gingerbread house. Use Royal Icing (see recipe above) to glue the gingerbread house together and to decorate the cookies.

*Trisha's gingerbread house from 1982.*

*Bret Bernard eating a gingerbread house.*

# Crescent Cookies

Makes 2 dozen

*From Gwen:*
You may know these as Wedding Cookies or Melting Moments.

The tradition of making homemade treats for gifts is still alive and well in the South. In the early to mid-1990s, I worked on videos and photo shoots in Nashville with a girl named Maria Smoot. She is responsible for some of the most beautiful hairstyles in country music. I found a tin of these cookies in my mailbox one Christmas with a sweet note from Maria. What was even sweeter was that she included the recipe.

- 1 cup (2 sticks) salted butter, room temperature
- 1 cup confectioners' sugar
- ⅛ teaspoon salt
- 2 teaspoons vanilla extract
- 2¼ cups sifted all-purpose flour
- ½ cup finely chopped pecans

Preheat the oven to 325°F.

In the bowl of an electric mixer, cream together the butter, ¼ cup of the sugar, the salt, and the vanilla until light and fluffy. Beat in the flour, and then stir in the pecans by hand.

Shape the dough into 1-inch balls. Roll each ball slightly and form into a half-moon crescent. Arrange the shaped cookies 2 inches apart on lightly greased cookie sheets. Bake for 15 minutes, or until the edges are slightly browned but the tops are still pale. Transfer the cookies to a rack to cool.

Put the remaining ¾ cup sugar in a shallow bowl. Roll the cooled cookies in the sugar, coating liberally. Store in an airtight container.

# Mari's Oatmeal Cookies

Beth's friend Mari sent these cookies with her on a family trip to Rosemary Beach, Florida, several summers ago. It was the first time my entire family had vacationed with Garth and the girls. I think these cookies started to quickly disappear shortly after Garth arrived!

1   cup (2 sticks) salted butter, room temperature

1   cup brown sugar, packed

1   cup granulated sugar

2   large eggs

1   teaspoon vanilla extract

2   cups sifted all-purpose flour

1   teaspoon baking soda

1   teaspoon baking powder

¼   teaspoon salt

2   cups old-fashioned oatmeal, such as Quaker

1   cup chopped pecans

1   cup grated coconut

Preheat the oven to 375°F.

In an electric mixer, cream the butter and the sugars. Add the eggs and vanilla and beat well. Sift together the flour, baking soda, baking powder, and salt, and add to the butter mixture. Add the oatmeal, nuts, and coconut.

Drop the dough by teaspoonfuls onto an ungreased baking sheet 2 inches apart. Bake for 10 minutes, or until light brown. Cool on the baking sheet for 2 minutes before transferring to a wire rack to cool completely. The cookies will be chewy.

# Skillet Almond Shortbread

Who ever heard of baking a dessert in a cast-iron skillet? You have now! The heavy pan ensures that the shortbread cooks evenly to a beautiful pale color top and bottom.

1¾  cups sugar

¾  cup (1½ sticks) butter, melted

2  large eggs

1½  cups all-purpose flour

½  teaspoon salt

1  teaspoon almond extract

½  cup sliced almonds with skins

*From Beth:*
My friend Phyllis brought this to our girls-only beach trip last year. It became an instant hit. It's a great leftover . . . if there's any left over!

Preheat the oven to 350°F. Line a 10-inch cast-iron skillet with aluminum foil and spray the foil with cooking spray. Alternatively, place a circle of parchment paper in the bottom of the skillet, then lightly grease or oil the paper.

In a large mixing bowl, stir 1½ cups of the sugar into the melted butter. Beat in the eggs one at a time. Sift the flour and salt onto the batter. Add the flavoring and stir well. Pour the batter into the skillet. Top with the sliced almonds and the remaining ¼ cup sugar. Bake for 35 minutes, or until slightly brown on top. Cool the shortbread in the skillet. When cool, use the foil to lift the shortbread from the skillet; remove the foil before serving. If you have used the parchment liner instead, run a sharp knife around the sides of the shortbread and invert the pan to remove it; peel off the parchment paper.

# Nutty Orange Biscotti

*From Trisha:*
I usually leave the fancy recipes to my sister, and this is one of hers, but it's easy to make. They look so fancy on the plate, and sound so cool, though, that people will think you worked really hard to make them.

Don't be surprised at how sticky this dough is as you're trying to shape it into a log for the first baking! After it comes out of the oven, it's easy to cut into biscotti slices. Cooking the slices slowly on both sides gives it that nice biscotti crunch.

- 4 large eggs
- 1 cup sugar
- 1½ tablespoons grated orange zest
- 2 tablespoons vegetable oil
- ½ teaspoon vanilla extract
- ½ teaspoon orange juice
- 1 teaspoon almond extract
- 3⅓ cups all-purpose flour
- 2 teaspoons baking powder
- 1 cup chopped almonds or nuts of your choice

Preheat the oven to 325°F.

In a large bowl, beat the eggs and sugar together at high speed with an electric mixer for 5 minutes, or until foamy. Add the orange zest, oil, vanilla, orange juice, and almond extract, beating until blended. Sift the flour and baking powder together and add to the sugar mixture, beating well. Fold in the almonds by hand. Cover the dough in the mixing bowl and place in the freezer for 30 minutes or in the refrigerator 2 hours until firm.

Divide the dough in half. Shape each portion into a 5 x 8-inch log on a lightly greased baking sheet. Bake for 25 minutes or until firm. Cool the dough logs on the baking sheet for 5 minutes, then transfer to wire racks to cool completely.

Using a serrated knife, cut each log diagonally into ½-inch slices. Return the biscotti to the greased baking sheets and bake for 15 minutes. Turn the cookies over and bake for 15 more minutes. Cool on wire racks.

# Home-Churned Ice Cream

Makes
3½ quarts

When we were children, we never made homemade ice cream unless we had company. I'm not sure if it was because we were being sociable or if it was because we needed help with the old hand churn. After working that hard, you definitely deserved a big bowl of ice cream! Daddy always added fresh peaches to this recipe because he loved homemade peach ice cream. Feel free to experiment with a fruit *you* love. I usually make it plain, then put out bowls of peaches, strawberries, bananas, nuts, and chocolate syrup so my guests can top it as they please.

- 2 recipes Boiled Custard, chilled (page 215)
- 1 pint fresh fruit, such as fresh Georgia peaches, peeled, pitted, and mashed
- 6 cups whole milk
- 20 pounds crushed ice
- 3 pounds rock salt

Wash the can, lid, and dasher of a tall 1-gallon electric or hand-cranked ice cream churn with hot soapy water. Rinse with cool water. In a bowl, mix the custard with the fruit. Set the dasher into the freezer can and pour in the fruit and custard. Add milk to within 3 inches of the top of the can or to the fill line marked on your freezer can. Put the lid on the can and place it in the freezer pail, making sure to center the can on the raised can rest in the bottom. Put several handfuls of ice around the can to hold it upright. Attach the motor or hand crank.

Start the motor of an electric churn and begin packing the space around the can with ice and salt, starting with about 4 inches ice and then adding about 4 ounces (½ cup) rock salt. Continue adding ice

continued . . .

and salt in this manner until the ice reaches the top but does not cover the top of the can. Add 1 cup cold water to help the ice begin to melt. The freezer pail should be placed in a large pan or sink so the salt water that drains out does not damage surfaces. Make sure the drainage hole stays open.

Freezing takes 20 to 30 minutes. Add more ice and salt as needed. An electric churn will stop when the ice cream is frozen. If the motor stalls too soon, unplug it and check to be sure no ice is caught between the bottom of the can and the freezer. Do this by using your hands to force the can to turn and then restart the churn. A hand churn takes about the same amount of time; you will know it is frozen when the churn becomes very difficult to turn.

Wipe away any ice and salt from the lid of the can and carefully

remove the lid. Pushing down on the can, carefully pull out the dasher, scraping any clinging ice cream back into the can. At this stage, the ice cream is soft. Put the provided cork stopper into the hole in the lid and replace the lid.

Harden the ice cream by adding more ice and salt to the freezer bucket, completely covering the can and securely corked lid. Cover the freezer with a heavy towel or newspaper layers and store the churn in a cool place until ready to serve. If you are not serving the ice cream within 1 hour, remove the towel and pack more ice and salt in the freezer pail. Dispose of the salt water in an area away from grass or plants. Scrub and rinse the pail thoroughly to avoid rust.

# Boiled Custard

Boiled custard is a southern tradition that has been used for centuries in recipes like banana pudding, pies, and homemade ice cream. It adds the richness and flavor of a pastry cream to every recipe it's used in, but it's not as thick.

Makes 2½ cups

2   cups whole milk

6   tablespoons sugar

1   tablespoon cornstarch or 2 tablespoons all-purpose flour
    Pinch of salt

2   large eggs

½   teaspoon vanilla extract

*From Gwen:* Don't be turned off by the term *custard.* This is delicious served cold.

Heat 1½ cups of the milk in a double boiler until a skim forms (just before boiling) on the top of the milk.

Sift together the sugar, cornstarch, and salt in a mixing bowl. Stir in the remaining ½ cup milk.

Beat the eggs in a small bowl. Whisking constantly, slowly stream ¼ cup hot milk into the eggs.

Slowly pour the egg-milk mixture back into the double boiler, whisking constantly to prevent lumps. Stir in the sugar mixture and continue cooking the custard until it thickens, about 15 minutes, stirring constantly (see Note). Stir in the vanilla.

Note: Combining hot milk and eggs is a delicate process, and lumps may appear even if you are very careful. If lumps do appear, strain the custard through a fine sieve.

# Blanche's Easy Ice Cream

Makes 1 gallon

*From Gwen:*
Beth and John requested this for their wedding rehearsal dinner in 1985.

I'm including this recipe from my sister's mother-in-law, Blanche (Whew! That's a mouthful!), because it is so easy, skips the time-consuming custard-making process of the previous recipe, and tastes awesome! Try both recipes and see which one you like best.

2   5 ½-ounce packages vanilla instant pudding/pie filling mix

3   cups sugar

8   cups whole milk

2   13-ounce cans evaporated milk

Combine the pudding mix and the sugar in a large bowl. Slowly stir in the milk. Continue stirring until the mixture is smooth. Pour the ice cream mixture into the 1-gallon canister of an electric ice cream freezer. Add milk if necessary to reach the fill line marked on the canister, leaving at least 3 inches of headspace. Follow the instructions for making Home-Churned Ice Cream (page 212).

# Caramel Candy

This candy is a Christmas memory for me. Beth and I can hardly wait for it to cool every year so we can slice it up and wrap it. We always eat as much as we wrap (or more), so truthfully, I don't really know how much the recipe makes!

Makes 6 to 7 dozen 1-inch cubes

*From Gwen:* The recipe in my file is written on the back of a mimeographed copy. Does anyone even remember the mimeograph machine? We retired teachers sure do.

| | |
|---|---|
| ¾ | cup (1½ sticks) butter |
| 1 | cup light brown sugar |
| 1 | cup granulated sugar |
| 1 | cup dark corn syrup |
| 2 | cups (1 pint) heavy cream |
| 2 | cups chopped pecans |
| 1 | teaspoon vanilla extract |

Generously grease a 9 x 12 x 2-inch pan using ¼ cup (½ stick) of the butter.

In a large saucepan, mix the brown sugar, granulated sugar, corn syrup, and 1 cup of the cream. Heat until the mixture begins to boil. Slowly stream the remaining 1 cup cream into the mixture, stirring while it's boiling. Attach a candy thermometer to the pan and cook the mixture over medium heat until it reaches 244°F. Remove the pan from the heat and add the remaining ½ cup butter, the chopped pecans, and the vanilla. Pour the candy into the buttered pan.

Cool the candy in the refrigerator until it is just firm but not hard, about 1 hour. Cut into 1-inch squares. Cut waxed paper into 4-inch squares and wrap each piece of candy individually. Store in the refrigerator. Remove the candy from the refrigerator and allow it to soften slightly before serving. The wrapped candy's flavor is improved by aging in the refrigerator for 2 weeks.

# Peanut Brittle

Georgia produces more peanuts than peaches—maybe it should be called the peanut state! This is one great way to use them. Daddy loved peanut brittle, and he made this all the time when I was growing up.

1 teaspoon vanilla extract

1 teaspoon baking soda

1 teaspoon salt

1 cup (2 sticks) butter

3 cups sugar

1 cup light corn syrup

3 cups shelled raw peanuts

Measure the vanilla into a small bowl and set aside. Combine the baking soda and salt in another small bowl and set aside. Butter 2 jelly roll pans or cookie sheets with sides liberally with the butter, using ½ stick butter on each one. Set aside.

Combine the sugar, corn syrup, and ½ cup water in a large saucepan. Bring the mixture to a boil, attach a candy thermometer, and cook over medium-high heat until the syrup spins a thread when poured from a spoon or reaches 240°F on the thermometer. Stir in the peanuts and continue cooking and stirring until the candy becomes golden brown or reaches 300°F. Remove from the heat immediately and quickly add the remaining 1 stick butter and the vanilla, baking soda, and salt. Stir only until the butter melts, then quickly pour the brittle onto the cookie sheets, spreading the mixture thinly. When the brittle has completely cooled, break the candy into pieces and store in a tightly covered container.

# Colleen's Chocolate Fudge

Garth's mom was famous for her fudge, and I feel honored to include her recipe in this cookbook. I think that one of her secrets was the old, deep cast-iron skillet she used to make it in. I know the peanut butter makes it really smooth!

Makes 24 pieces

*From Trisha:* Use whole milk in this fudge to make it extra creamy.

½   cup (1 stick) butter

3   cups sugar

⅔   cup cocoa

1   teaspoon salt

1½  cups milk

½   cup smooth peanut butter

1   cup chopped pecans

2   teaspoons vanilla extract

Coat an 8 x 8-inch pan or platter with 4 tablespoons of butter. In a medium saucepan, stir together the sugar, cocoa, and salt. Stir in the milk. Bring the mixture to a rolling boil and reduce the heat to medium-low. Attach a candy thermometer to the saucepan and continue to simmer for 25 to 30 minutes, or until the mixture reaches 240°F or a drop of the mixture forms a soft ball when dropped into cold water. Remove the pan from the heat, stir in 4 tablespoons butter, the peanut butter, the pecans, and the vanilla. Pour the fudge out onto the buttered pan or platter. Let the fudge cool on the platter for 20 minutes, then cut it into bite-size pieces.

# thanks

Wow! Putting together a cookbook entails so much more than just finding some recipes you like and sticking them in a notebook! To everyone at Clarkson Potter, especially Pam Krauss, for helping make this dream into a beautiful reality (and for teaching me all the cool publishing lingo!), and Jennifer Beal Davis, thank you for designing this lovely book. Kate Tyler, Sydney Webber, Jane Treuhaft, Patricia Bozza, Joan Denman, Merri Ann Morrell, and Lauren Shakely: Your talents are greatly appreciated! Kathleen Fleury, thank you for always keeping me in the loop, and closing the gap between New York and Oklahoma! Special thanks to Ken Levitan and Vector Management for making it all happen.

I never knew a photograph of food could make me so hungry! Ben Fink, thank you for making our simple food look so divine. I knew I loved you the minute you said we could eat the food right after we photographed it! Special thanks to Jeff Kavanaugh, Philippa Brathwaite, and Susan Sugarman for photographing, styling, and preparing everything necessary for these photos. Thank you to Russ Harrington for shooting the cover. Melissa Perry, thank you for cooking every one of these recipes and reminding me every day that directions in my head needed to be written down on paper! Thanks to Debra Wingo, Mary Beth Felts, Claudia Fowler, and Sheri McCoy-Haynes for hair, makeup, wardrobe, and helping decorate tables and eat food!

Thank you to the people of Monticello, Georgia, who gave their time, location (thanks for letting us use your pond, Joanne Jordan!), a place to stay (thanks Mr. Chick and Mrs. Mary Ellen Wilson, and the Monticello Motel!), setting up picnic tables and getting the house ready (Kathryn and James Sauls, and George Deraney), and Sherry Partenza for the catfish!

Thank you to the friends and family who contributed recipes and stories for this cookbook: Margaret Akins, Jan Anderson, Blanche Bernard, the Bernard family, the Brooks family, Leslie Cromer, the Geissler family, Jarrah Herter, Herb and Glenda Hickey, Kathy Alexander Hicks, Liz Huckeba, Betty Hutson, the LeFlore family, Betty Maxwell, Wilson and Beth Paulk, Julianne Perry, Phyllis Pritchett, Jodi Roberts, Venita Sandifer, Gail Shoup, Donald and Patti Shuford, Mari Smith, the Smittle Family, Maria Smoot, Violet Steinke, and Jean Williamson.

Lastly, a big thank-you to my mom, Gwen, and my sister, Beth. What an adventure! We did it, and it's finally here! I love you both so much and am so proud that we got to do this together.

# index

# home cooking WITH
# trisha yearwood

## stories & recipes to share with family & friends

*with* Gwen Yearwood & Beth Yearwood Bernard
*foreword by* Garth Brooks

Clarkson Potter/Publishers
New York

# dedication

There are those we've lost along the way who continue to live on in the sharing of these recipes and the telling of these stories. I can almost hear Garth's mom, Colleen, whispering in my ear, "The secret's the cinnamon!" when I'm making her cabbage rolls. Every time I make chocolate pie, I will see Ben Tillman smiling at me when I walk into the Tillman House and ask for fried chicken. I'll smile knowing that Miss Betty got to sign a few autographs along the way because of the success of her recipes in the first cookbook. And always, there is my daddy, humbly "apologizing" for some of the best meals I ever tasted, yet I know he feels proud seeing the people he loves the most represented in these pages. This book is dedicated to all those we love who aren't with us anymore but whose lives, stories, laughter, and good food are represented here.

We love you, always.
–Gwen, Beth, and Patricia

# contents

# foreword

The greatest thing that can happen to an artist is to have someone come up to you and tell you how one of your songs has changed his or her life for the better. As an artist, you enjoy this experience so much. There is nothing in music that could please you more . . . until you see it happen to your spouse. Talk about pride! To see people's faces light up as they are telling Trisha how a song moved them to become more than what they were, to take chances, to take responsibility . . . to take control. That is what communicating and communicating well is all about. Now take that one step further. I cannot count the times I have seen someone approach Trisha with his or her cookbook in hand to either share a story or ask a question—and they always ask Trisha for her signature inside the cover. I have watched her tirelessly sign, exchange recipe tips, laugh, and swap stories over the first cookbook. If you have ever met Miss Yearwood and talked to her about family traditions and meals, then you will understand what I am about to say. I can't tell which one she enjoys more: cooking or singing! She does both with a love unequaled. As her husband, I am very proud of all of her accomplishments, and I am very happy for her success. But I find myself being even happier for her because she loves what she does. And I think that is the secret to her success in music and in cooking. The greatest compliment you can give a cook is to ask for more, and that is all I hear as I stand by and listen to people talk to Trisha. For those people and for myself, I am very happy to introduce a second helping of heartfelt recipes from our family to yours.

Garth Brooks

# introduction

Never in my wildest dreams did I think I'd be sitting here writing
an introduction to a second cookbook! Mom, Beth, and I were so
overwhelmed and thrilled at the response to *Georgia Cooking in an
Oklahoma Kitchen*. What a sweet surprise! We enjoyed getting to
meet so many of you out on the road, and exchanging recipes and
stories. I was happy to find out that our way of life was shared by
many of you in all parts of the country, not just the south! What
I learned from you was that you liked our family stories because
they reminded you of your own lives, and that you liked our recipes
because they were easy to prepare and didn't have a lot of fancy,
hard-to-find ingredients. We decided to stick to the saying "If it
ain't broke, don't fix it!"

We have a wonderful extended family, full of cousins, aunts,
uncles, and friends who were kind enough to contribute recipes. For
instance, it was from those family members and friends that we found
my grandmother Elizabeth Yearwood's infamous Coconut Cake with
Coconut Lemon Glaze recipe, which she used to make for my daddy.

Since we've received a lot of recipes that are traditions in our
extended family but are new to us, we've been doing a lot of testing.
We didn't want to include anything in this book that we hadn't

made ourselves and didn't absolutely *love*. This has worked out well for our family members and friends, who have really benefited from our testing—and gained a few pounds to boot!

Some of these newer recipes already feel like old favorites. I make things like Crockpot Macaroni and Cheese, Baked Bean Casserole, and Asparagus Bundles so often now that they feel like dishes I've been making all my life. The Key Lime Cake recipe that I got from family friend Angela Spivey has become the new dessert hit at my house.

One of the best things about putting together this collection has been discovering new recipes. We all tend to stick to what we know, and I'm usually a bit wary about trying out something new on my family, but this cookbook has made me brave! It's a real treat for me to get to introduce some "new" old recipes to my family, like my grandma Lizzie Paulk's Old-Fashioned Strawberry Shortcake, and fresh ideas for breakfast, such as Apple Dumplings and Country Quiche.

I have always associated really good food with really good company. If you're with people you love, and you're having fun and loving life, great food is almost like another guest at the table. You laugh, talk, and savor a good appetizer together. Or you assign your friends the job of chopping up the vegetables while you fire up the grill. It's really all about being together, and enjoying life surrounded by people you love and food you can share!

Anyone can cook at home, but that doesn't necessarily make it home cooking. There's a lot of love in these pages that comes from generations of Yearwoods, Paulks, Bernards, Brooks, and beyond. *That's* home cooking. I'm proud to share this collection of recipes and stories with you.

# helpful hints

- If you have a slow cooker, now commonly referred to as a crockpot, that is over ten years old, chances are it has a liner that isn't removable. Think about buying a new crockpot with a removable liner for easy cleanup. The liner is also great if you want to remove the pot to serve at the table.

- Never put hot water in a cold glass or ceramic pot or pitcher. If you're making tea, be sure to put some cold water into your cold pitcher before adding hot steeped tea. The same goes for cold to hot. Never put a hot ceramic or glass bowl into the sink and fill it with cold water. You can easily crack a nice pan or pitcher (or your new removable crockpot liner) this way. Let the pot cool completely before rinsing.

- Take the time to grate your own cheese instead of buying preshredded for use in a recipe. The agents sometimes used to keep commercially grated cheese from clumping give the cheese a waxy taste and a rough texture. Always read the label to look for additives to cheese.

- Cake Release made by Wilton is a product I've discovered that you can use instead of cooking spray or greasing and flouring your pans. It works great in all pans, but is especially good in Bundt pans and helps the cakes to release easily.
- When icing a cake, use a decorating turntable for easy turning. Cake-decorating turntables are fairly inexpensive (some under $10) and can be easily found at craft stores or online.
- Invest in an inexpensive offset spatula for frosting cakes and cookies. The slight bend makes icing a breeze.
- When baking a pie in a disposable metal pie plate, cut away the pan's outer rim with scissors to release the pie. This makes it much easier to cut slices of pie, and eliminates digging in the pan to get all the crust.
- Beater Blade makes a blade for stand mixers that has a rubber scraper on it. It basically works like a spatula and keeps your mixing bowl scraped while it turns. It works best in smooth cake batters.

# breakfast

The saying is that breakfast is the most important meal of the day. People who think they aren't breakfast eaters should take a look at these dishes before they say no. Whether you like something light or hearty, sweet or salty, something that feeds a crowd or just one, there's a dish here for you. Breakfast was always a weekend treat for my sister and me as we grew up. Daddy didn't have to get up early and be at work on the weekends, so he would usually make us a huge breakfast that included bacon, sausage, eggs, grits, and homemade biscuits.

I'm a big believer that cooking for someone else is an act of love. We serve breakfast in bed to our moms on Mother's Day, our dads on Father's Day, or as a special treat for a birthday or anniversary, but you don't have to wait for a special occasion to show people you love them. Make every day special with these satisfying dishes.

# mama's homemade waffles
## with hot maple syrup

Pancakes and waffles were special morning treats at our house. As you might imagine, breakfast in a home where both parents worked and the children were running off to school every day was more often than not a quick piece of peanut butter toast or a bagel. We usually saved the big breakfasts for the weekends, and I remember waking up on Saturday mornings to the smell of something homemade cooking. Pancakes were a sweet breakfast surprise. Even today when I make them, I feel like it's a special occasion! We usually use one of our favorite store-bought syrups, but this Hot Maple Syrup from our cousin, SuSan Yearwood, is easy to make and also tastes great over Blueberry Pancakes (page 22). Just make sure to watch the syrup carefully once it starts to boil, reducing the heat as necessary to prevent it from boiling over. MAKES 6 WAFFLES

WAFFLES

2 cups sifted all-purpose flour

3 teaspoons baking powder

½ teaspoon salt

2 large eggs, separated

1½ cups milk

3 tablespoons unsalted butter, melted

Hot Maple Syrup (recipe follows)

Sift together the flour, baking powder, and salt.

Beat the egg whites until stiff. Set aside.

Beat the egg yolks. Add the milk and butter. Add the flour mixture, stirring until just blended. Fold in the beaten egg whites. Bake in a hot waffle maker that has been sprayed with cooking spray for about 5 minutes, until golden brown. Serve immediately with Hot Maple Syrup (page 20), melted butter, honey, or jam.

FROM GWEN: This batter works great in a Belgian waffle maker, too.

FROM BETH: Folding in the beaten whites makes these waffles really crisp.

# hot maple syrup   MAKES 4 CUPS

3 cups granulated sugar

2 cups light brown sugar

2 tablespoons dark corn syrup

2 cups water

2 teaspoons maple flavoring

2 teaspoons vanilla extract

1 teaspoon almond extract

Mix the sugars, syrup, water, maple flavoring, and extracts in a medium saucepan and cook over medium-high heat until the sugars dissolve. Bring the mixture to a boil, then reduce the heat to medium and simmer for 10 minutes, stirring occasionally, as the syrup reaches the correct consistency. Serve warm over pancakes or waffles. Store any leftover syrup in the refrigerator for up to 2 weeks.

Change it up by making bacon waffles. Cut bacon to fit each waffle grid. Close the cover and bake for 1 minute before adding waffle batter. Scramble some eggs and you have a complete breakfast.

# blueberry pancakes

Like me, my nephew Kyle loves anything made with blueberries, and he also loves breakfast for supper, a tradition we have perfected here in Oklahoma. There really isn't any rule about when breakfast should be served. If we feel like having eggs and bacon for supper, we do it! Serve these pancakes topped with Hot Maple Syrup (page 20). SERVES 4 TO 6

1¾ cups all-purpose flour

2 tablespoons sugar

1 teaspoon baking powder

½ teaspoon baking soda

½ teaspoon salt

2 large eggs

1 cup milk

1 cup sour cream

¼ cup (½ stick) butter, melted

½ teaspoon vanilla extract

½ teaspoon lemon zest

1½ cups fresh or frozen blueberries

Sift the flour, sugar, baking powder, baking soda, and salt into a large mixing bowl. In a separate large bowl, lightly whisk the eggs. Add the milk, sour cream, melted butter, and vanilla, whisking to blend. Make a well in the dry ingredients and pour the egg mixture into it. Whisk the ingredients together just until blended. Fold the lemon zest and blueberries into the batter.

Heat a large skillet over medium heat or use an electric skillet on a medium setting. Use cooking spray or pour in vegetable oil to lightly coat the surface of the skillet. For each pancake, pour about ¼ cup of the batter into the hot skillet. Cook 3 or 4 pancakes at a time, depending on the size of the skillet. If the batter seems too thick, thin it with a little milk (1 to 2 tablespoons). When bubbles begin to form and "pop" on the pancake's surface (about 1 minute) and the outer edge looks done, flip it over and cook briefly (about 30 seconds) on the other side.

# garth's breakfast bowl

Garth likes to cook breakfast. It's wonderful to sleep in and wake up to the smell of bacon cooking. Don't be too jealous, but he always has a fresh pot of coffee already made, too! He created this breakfast bowl because he wanted something really hearty. He's the first person I ever met who puts pasta with eggs and bacon, but it works, and it tastes great! If you're really hungry, all the better if you're going to eat one of these breakfast bowls. Don't worry if you can't finish it; Garth will come along later and "clean up"! SERVES 4

2 tablespoons butter

8 large eggs

1 16-ounce bag frozen hash browns or Tater Tots, thawed

1 pound pork sausage

1 pound bacon

1 9-ounce package cheese and roasted garlic tortellini

10 ounces sharp Cheddar cheese, grated (about 2½ cups)

In a large skillet, melt the butter and scramble the eggs.

In a separate large skillet, cook the hash browns according to package directions. In a third large skillet, break up the sausage with a wooden spoon and cook until browned. Drain off the excess fat. Transfer the sausage to a bowl. Cook the bacon in the same skillet. Drain on paper towels and set aside. Cook the tortellini according to the package directions. Layer a large bowl with hash browns, sausage, bacon, tortellini, eggs, and cheese.

Any potato will do. Garth's even been known to use french fries! I sometimes fry an egg sunny side up and pile it on top of Garth's bowl. He likes the way the yolk oozes into the dish.

# country quiche

The first time I had quiche was in a quaint little café in Nashville. I loved it, and thought it was really fancy. You know how they say, "Real men don't eat quiche." Well, I don't even know who "they" are, but I'll bet you any real man would eat this quiche. It's full of all things good and very hearty. I turned Garth loose on this recipe and he suggested the tortellini. It made it even better. SERVES 16

1 pound ground pork sausage with sage

6 large eggs

1 teaspoon baking powder

20 grape tomatoes, sliced in half

10 ounces sharp Cheddar cheese, grated (about 2½ cups)

Salt and pepper

2 9-inch unbaked frozen pie shells

Preheat the oven to 350°F.

In a large skillet, cook the sausage until done, then drain off the excess fat and set aside.

Whisk the eggs, baking powder, and tomatoes together. Add the cooked sausage and the cheese to the egg mixture and stir together with a large spoon. Add salt and pepper to taste. Divide the mixture in half and pour into the unbaked pie shells. Bake for 30 minutes, or until the filling is set.

> FROM GARTH: I boil some cheese tortellini and add it into the quiche before baking.

Set the frozen pie shells out to thaw a bit while you're preparing the quiche.

# hawaiian fresh fruit salad

My family was lucky enough to go to Hawaii a few years ago for vacation. It was an incredible experience. Mama and I would wake up every morning looking forward to breakfast because the fruit was just amazing. I would eat fruit for breakfast every day if it tasted like those Hawaiian pineapples. Our cousin Lydia lives in Hawaii and gave us this recipe. She's lucky to be able to choose a variety of fresh fruit year-round.  SERVES 6

6 cups of your favorite fresh fruits, such as:

Bananas, peeled and sliced

Blueberries

Pineapple, cut into bite-size pieces

Blackberries

Raspberries

Mango, peeled and cubed

Strawberries, stems removed and berries cut into halves

Kiwi, peeled, sliced, and each slice cut in half

Oranges, peeled and cut into chunks

1/3 cup fresh lime juice

1½ tablespoons honey

¾ teaspoon ground ginger or minced fresh ginger

Mix the fruit in a large salad bowl. Mix the lime juice, honey, and ginger in a small bowl. Pour the dressing over the fruit, and stir. Serve immediately if you use bananas. (If you make the salad ahead of time, hold out the bananas until just before serving.)

Watermelon is my favorite fruit, so I add chunks of it to this salad when it's in season.

# apple dumplings

Quick and delicious! This is like having your own individual apple pie. My nephew Bret loves these served warm for breakfast.  SERVES 8

2 Granny Smith apples
1 cup water
1 cup sugar
½ cup (1 stick) butter
¼ teaspoon vanilla extract
8 canned buttermilk biscuits
4 teaspoons ground cinnamon

Preheat the oven to 375°F.

Peel, core, and slice the apples vertically into 8 slices each. Cover with water to keep the slices from turning brown.

In a medium saucepan, mix the water, ¾ cup of the sugar, the butter, and the vanilla. Bring the sugar mixture to a boil over medium heat.

Separate each biscuit into 2 layers. Wrap a biscuit layer around a slice of apple, stretching the biscuit slightly to overlap, and seal on the bottom. Place the wrapped slices, sealed side down, in a 9 × 12 × 2-inch casserole dish. Pour the hot sugar mixture over the apple slices. Mix the remaining ¼ cup sugar with the cinnamon and sprinkle the mixture over the tops of the wrapped apples. Bake for 35 minutes, or until golden brown.

# monkey bread muffins

Monkey bread is usually baked in a large tube pan and served by pulling off a "lump" of bread at a time. My niece Ashley tried this idea for making monkey bread in individual servings by downsizing the biscuit pieces and using our Hot Maple Syrup (page 20) in the mix. The muffins are a lot cuter and less messy! **SERVES 12**

1 12-ounce can biscuits (10 in each can)

3 tablespoons Hot Maple Syrup (page 20)

¼ cup (½ stick) butter, melted

⅔ cup sugar

1 tablespoon ground cinnamon

½ cup finely chopped pecans

NOTE: To make traditional monkey bread, grease all surfaces of a 10-inch tube pan. Drop the coated biscuit pieces evenly inside the tube pan. Pour the maple butter over the biscuits and bake at 350°F for 40 to 45 minutes. Let the bread stand for 5 minutes before turning out onto a cake plate. Pull off one lump at a time.

Preheat the oven to 375°F.

Place cupcake liners in 12 muffin cups. With kitchen shears, cut each biscuit into 4 pieces. In a small bowl, combine the maple syrup and melted butter. In a separate bowl, mix the sugar, cinnamon, and chopped pecans. Dip each biscuit piece into the maple butter, and roll in the sugar mixture. Place 3 or 4 coated pieces in each muffin cup, pressing to compact (see Note). Bake the muffins for 15 to 17 minutes. Allow to cool in the pan for 5 minutes before removing to wire racks. Serve warm.

# cinnamon rolls

My daddy used to make the most amazing cinnamon rolls. I always think of him when I smell them baking. This recipe comes from a friend of Beth's. The neighborhood kids would know to go to Vicki's house at the first sign of snow because her mom would have a fresh batch of cinnamon rolls for them. We only get a little snow here in Oklahoma every year, and Mama and Beth *never* get snow, so we officially decided that any day, rain or shine, is a good day for homemade cinnamon rolls! MAKES 2 DOZEN ROLLS

½ ounce (2 packages) active dry yeast

1 cup lukewarm (80–90°F) water

1 cup vegetable shortening, such as Crisco

¾ cup granulated sugar

1 cup boiling water

2 large eggs

6 cups self-rising flour

1 teaspoon salt

½ cup cinnamon sugar

1 cup (2 sticks) butter

2 teaspoons milk

1 16-ounce box confectioners' sugar

FROM GWEN: Make your own cinnamon sugar by mixing 2 teaspoons of ground cinnamon with ½ cup granulated sugar.

Butter the bottoms of four 9-inch round pans.

In a small bowl, dissolve the yeast in the lukewarm water. In a separate bowl, add the vegetable shortening and sugar to the boiling water. Set this mixture aside to cool slightly. In a large mixing bowl, beat the eggs and mix with the flour and salt. Add the dissolved yeast and the vegetable shortening–sugar mixture to the flour mixture. Mix until thoroughly combined. Cover the dough in the bowl with a clean towel and let it rise for 2 hours.

On a lightly floured surface, roll out the dough to a 19 × 14-inch rectangle and sprinkle with some of the cinnamon sugar. Slice 1 stick of butter into small pieces and dot all over the cinnamon sugar. Roll up the dough like a jellyroll and cut into 1-inch slices, using a heavy cotton thread or floss. Place the rolls in the prepared pans, cover, and allow them to rise for 2 hours.

Near the end of the rising time, preheat the oven to 350°F. While the oven preheats, melt the remaining stick of butter and add the milk and confectioners' sugar, mixing until smooth. Bake the rolls for 13 to 15 minutes, or until very light brown. Drizzle the icing over the rolls while they're hot.

# beignets

I always say that I am not really a "sweets" person. The truth is I am more of a sweets snob. I like desserts, but only if they're homemade. One of my weaknesses, though, is doughnuts. I could live at Krispy Kreme and be happy. They give you a little hat to wear, they let you watch the doughnuts coming off the line, they smother them with glaze, and then they give you one, right off the assembly line. I immediately buy at least a dozen. These beignets are a little taste of Krispy Kreme heaven at home. All you need is a small baker's hat! MAKES 5 DOZEN BEIGNETS

¼ ounce (1 package) active dry yeast

1½ cups warm water (105°F)

½ cup granulated sugar

1 teaspoon salt

2 large eggs

1 cup evaporated milk

7 cups all-purpose flour, sifted

¼ cup vegetable shortening, such as Crisco

8 cups peanut oil

Confectioners' sugar for sprinkling

In the bowl of an electric mixer, sprinkle the yeast over the warm water. Stir to dissolve. Add the sugar, salt, eggs, and milk. Beat until blended. Add 4 cups of the flour by big spoonfuls. Beat until smooth. Add the shortening, and then beat in the remaining 3 cups flour. Cover the bowl with plastic wrap and chill in the refrigerator for 3 hours.

In a large electric fryer, preheat the oil to 360°F.

On a lightly floured surface, roll out the dough to a ⅛-inch thickness. Cut the dough into 2½-inch squares. Deep-fry each square in the hot oil for 2 to 3 minutes, or until lightly browned on each side. Drain on paper towels. Sprinkle heavily with confectioners' sugar.

> FROM GWEN: Deep-fry in batches of about 12 at a time.

> FROM BETH: Depending on the size of your electric fryer, it may take more or less than 8 cups of oil. Just pour the oil as deep as you can into your fryer.

# snacks and appetizers

As I recall, we didn't do a lot of snacking in my family when I was growing up. Breakfast was either something on the fly or a big weekend bonanza. Lunch was from the school lunchroom. The lunch ladies at Piedmont Academy, where I went to school from first through twelfth grades, were amazing cooks, so lunch was always worth waiting for. Most children today aren't that jazzed about eating in their school cafeterias, but we had it made. Even the hamburgers were handmade right there in the school kitchen!

As an adult, I find myself making more dips and appetizers, sometimes in place of a meal. We have our friends and their children over on most weekends, and of course for special occasions like the World Series or the Super Bowl. Sometimes I'll make an entrée or Garth will grill steaks, and we'll ask them to bring sides—but more often than not, I'll say, "Let's just have snacks for everybody!" These snacks and appetizers are some of our must-haves.

# corn salsa

I love fresh vegetables—especially in the summer. We always had a garden at home, and there just isn't anything quite like a homegrown tomato. This recipe pairs corn with garden-fresh tomatoes, jalapeño peppers, and cilantro. The resulting salsa is mouth-wateringly good and very easy to make. I serve it at summer birthday parties and on Super Bowl Sunday. SERVES 20

1 15-ounce can yellow corn, drained

1 15-ounce can white corn, drained

1 4-ounce can chopped green chiles, drained

1 2½-ounce can sliced black olives, drained

4 green onions, minced

2 medium tomatoes, finely chopped

2 jalapeño peppers, seeded and chopped

3 tablespoons white vinegar

⅓ cup olive oil

½ teaspoon salt

1 tablespoon finely chopped fresh cilantro

Tortilla chips, for dipping

Mix the corn, chiles, olives, onions, tomatoes, jalapeños, vinegar, oil, and salt in a medium bowl and chill in the refrigerator for at least 1 hour. Just before serving, add the cilantro. Serve with your favorite tortilla chips.

Substitute Fritos Scoops for plain tortilla chips. More salsa per bite!

# watermelon salsa

Who says you need tomatoes to make salsa? Phyllis Pritchett of Martin, Tennessee, shared this recipe for a delicious summer salsa made with watermelon! This seemingly odd mix of ingredients makes an amazing appetizer. Add any fruit you like. I add diced mango sometimes for color and flavor. MAKES 3 CUPS

1½ teaspoons lime zest (from about 1 lime)

¼ cup fresh lime juice (from about 3 limes)

1 tablespoon sugar

¾ teaspoon pepper

3 cups seeded and finely chopped watermelon

1 cucumber, peeled, seeded, and diced

1 jalapeño pepper, seeded and minced

1 small red onion, finely chopped

8 fresh basil leaves, finely chopped

½ teaspoon garlic salt

Tortilla or pita chips

Stir together the lime zest, lime juice, sugar, and pepper. Add the watermelon, cucumber, jalapeño, onion, and basil and toss gently. Chill the salsa until ready to serve and add the garlic salt just before serving. Serve with tortilla chips or pita chips.

*I like it spicy, so I use 2 jalapeños instead of 1!*

# charleston cheese dip

Cheese seems to be a staple in many southern dishes. I was on tour a few years ago and had a show in Charleston. When I got to my hotel room, the staff had left me a lovely basket of goodies. Usually, amenities baskets are full of things like fruit and candy. This basket was accompanied by a tray of homemade cheese dip and crackers. It was perfect for this Georgia gal! **SERVES 10**

½ cup mayonnaise

1 8-ounce package cream cheese, softened

1 cup grated sharp Cheddar cheese (about 4 ounces)

½ cup grated Monterey Jack cheese (about 2 ounces)

2 green onions, finely chopped

Dash of cayenne pepper

8 Ritz or butter crackers, crushed

8 slices bacon, cooked and crumbled

Preheat the oven to 350°F.

In a medium bowl, mix the mayonnaise, cream cheese, Cheddar cheese, Monterey Jack cheese, green onions, and cayenne pepper. Transfer the mixture to a shallow baking dish, such as a 9-inch pie pan. Top the mixture with the cracker crumbs and bake for 15 minutes, or until heated through. Remove the pan from the oven and top with the bacon. Serve immediately with corn chips, crackers, or bagel chips.

# hot corn dip

I made this dip recently for "Girls' Night In." Every now and then a group of my girl-friends and I get together and watch our favorite television show, or watch chick flicks–insert your favorite movie here. My favorite tearjerker chick flicks are *Steel Magnolias*, *Return to Me*, and *Message in a Bottle*. We keep this dip warming in a slow cooker and snack on it all evening. Corn chips make this dip divine!  SERVES 12

2 11-ounce cans Mexican corn, drained

2 4½-ounce cans chopped green chiles, drained

2 cups grated Monterey Jack cheese (about 8 ounces)

¾ cup grated Parmesan cheese

1 cup mayonnaise

Corn chips, for dipping

Preheat the oven to 350°F. Grease a 9 × 13 × 2-inch casserole dish.

In a medium bowl, mix the corn, chiles, cheeses, and mayonnaise until fully combined. Spread the mixture in the prepared casserole dish and bake, uncovered, for 30 to 40 minutes, or until bubbly around the edges. Serve the dip warm from the oven with corn chips.

# spicy edamame dip

When I was a young girl, we had a big garden every year. I didn't know how good I had it until I moved to the big city of Nashville and ate my first canned vegetable! Aside from our personal garden, my daddy planted a big field each year with soybeans, which he sold at harvest. I never really understood why we grew something we didn't eat. I ended up loving soybeans. If I had known about this tasty dip back then, I doubt my daddy would have had many soybeans to sell! SERVES 12

4 large garlic cloves, unpeeled

16 ounces shelled edamame beans (about 2 cups)

1 teaspoon salt

½ teaspoon cayenne pepper

¼ teaspoon ground cumin

4 tablespoons olive oil

¼ cup fresh lime juice

¼ cup finely chopped fresh cilantro

Pita chips, for dipping

In a medium skillet over medium heat, roast the garlic, turning frequently, until softened, about 15 minutes. Remove from the heat, cool, and then slip off the skins. Set aside.

Bring about 8 cups of water to a boil in a saucepan and drop in the beans. Bring back to a boil and cook for 5 minutes. Reserve ¾ cup of the cooking water before draining. Drain the beans and cool.

Transfer the garlic into a blender and chop coarsely. Add the beans, salt, cayenne pepper, and cumin. Process in the blender, adding the reserved water a little at a time until smooth. (You may not need to add all of the water.) Add the olive oil, lime juice, and cilantro. Pulse to combine. Use pita chips for dipping.

# cheese boat

This appetizer was shared with us by a South Georgia pastor's wife, Vicki Martin. She got it from a church hostess in Hawkinsville, Georgia, years before. The bread "boat" is a cute way to serve this warm cheesy appetizer. SERVES 10

1 loaf French or Italian bread

10 ounces sharp Cheddar cheese, grated (about 2½ cups)

3 2-ounce packages corned beef, such as Carl Buddig, finely chopped

½ bell pepper, cored, seeded, and finely chopped

½ teaspoon hot sauce, such as Tabasco

½ teaspoon chili powder

2 8-ounce packages cream cheese, room temperature

1 medium tomato, finely chopped

1 bunch green onions, finely chopped

Large corn chips

Preheat the oven to 350°F.

Cut an oval in the top of the loaf of bread, scooping out the bread in the center and making a "bread boat." Place the bread on a cookie sheet.

In a large bowl, mix the cheese, beef, bell pepper, hot sauce, chili powder, cream cheese, tomato, and green onions until fully combined. Spoon the mixture into the hollow center of the bread loaf. Bake for 30 minutes, until bubbling, and serve warm with corn chips.

# jalapeño bites

My mom loves spicy dishes, and this recipe for a jalapeño pepper snack is one of her favorites. I've had deep-fried Cheddar jalapeño poppers at restaurants, but these cheesy bites use cream cheese and Parmesan for a different flavor. I really can't be left alone with these! MAKES 36 BITES

1 8-ounce package cream cheese, softened

8 ounces Parmesan cheese, grated (about 2 cups)

4 tablespoons seeded and chopped jalapeño peppers

1 large egg, beaten

3 cups dry plain bread crumbs

Preheat the oven to 350°F.

Mix the cream cheese, Parmesan cheese, jalapeños, and egg to form a paste. Shape into balls using about $\frac{1}{2}$ tablespoon of paste for each. Roll the balls in the bread crumbs. Place on an ungreased baking sheet and bake for 10 to 15 minutes, until golden brown. Serve warm.

Handle hot chiles like jalapeño, habanero, or cayenne with care. Always wash your hands after handling. They may cause chemical burns to sensitive skin. If you've ever handled a hot chile and then scratched your eyes, you know what I'm talking about!

# warren's chicken bites

My cousin Warren brought these little tidbits to a family reunion. He's a hunter and used dove breasts in his recipe. I'm embarrassed to say that I don't care for dove or quail. I'm even more embarrassed to tell you that after a big bird hunt, Mama would fry up everything Daddy brought home and I would eat Vienna sausages! I use chicken here, but I'm thinking . . . Warren's Vienna bites! Hmmm . . . MAKES 8 BITE-SIZE SERVINGS

4 chicken tenders, flattened and cut in half

1 3-ounce package cream cheese, softened

2 teaspoons seeded and finely chopped jalapeño pepper

8 bacon slices

Top each piece of chicken with ½ teaspoon cream cheese and ¼ teaspoon jalapeño. Roll up each filling-covered chicken piece and wrap with 1 slice of bacon, securing with a toothpick. Grill for 8 to 10 minutes on an indoor grill. Or, if you are using an outdoor grill, turn the pieces once during grilling.

FROM GWEN: Substitute dove breast, dark meat chicken, or turkey for the chicken tenders, if you like.

Warren brought these bites, made with dove breast, to the Paulk family reunion.

# six-week pickles

Louise Aiken, a ninety-four-year-old family friend, has her own garden and grows her own cucumbers. She gave Mama three jars of these pickles at Christmas, one for each of us. They went fast! Louise was given the recipe by a Monticello, Georgia, friend, Nona Wilson. The time spent on these pickles is mostly just waiting. MAKES 6 PINTS

6 pounds cucumbers
(about 16 medium),
1½ inches in diameter

2 quarts white vinegar

4 pounds sugar

4 scant drops cinnamon oil

4 scant drops clove oil

FROM GWEN: Louise buys cinnamon oil and clove oil at the local drugstore. Since the recipe calls for only a few drops, the tiny bottles last forever and she just shares hers with me.

Wash the cucumbers thoroughly. Pack the whole cucumbers in a 1-gallon widemouthed glass jar. Do not trim the ends of the cucumbers. Fill the jar with enough vinegar to cover the cucumbers. Cover and set aside at room temperature for 6 weeks.

After 6 weeks, drain the cucumbers in a colander. Do not rinse the cucumbers. Trim the cucumber ends and slice into ⅛- to ¼-inch slices.

Put a layer of cucumber slices back into the glass jar and layer with the sugar. Repeat the layering process until you've used all of the cucumber slices and sugar. Add the cinnamon and clove oil. The jar will be about three-fourths full. Shake the jar at least four times during the day or stir with a wooden spoon to distribute the sugar and oils. The vinegar on the cucumbers will dissolve the sugar. Set aside for 2 or 3 days to allow the sugar to dissolve and the oil flavors to develop. Transfer the pickles to pint jars for storage.

*Most pickle recipes include endless soaking in lime and rinsing. This one is super-easy.*

# sweet tea

This was the first thing I remember making at home as a child. Sweet tea is the staple of every good southern meal. I like it warm, right after it's made, but most people love it cold and over ice. I had been making this tea for many years before I realized I was making it wrong. My sister was watching me make it one day and said, "Whoa! You're putting way too much sugar in that!" I guess the original Yearwood recipe calls for ¾ cup sugar. Too late to turn back now! This really should be called Sweet Sweet Tea.   MAKES 1 GALLON

4 large, family-size tea bags
16 cups water
1½ cups sugar

Fill a teakettle or saucepan with enough water to completely cover the tea bags, about 2 cups. Bring to a boil and remove from the heat. Let the tea stand for 10 minutes. Put the sugar into a gallon pitcher and add 1 cup of cold water. Stir to mix slightly. Pour the hot tea into the sugar mixture and stir until the sugar is dissolved. Stir in the remaining 13 cups of cold water to fill the pitcher.

*If using a glass pitcher, mix the sugar with 1 cup cold water before adding the hot tea to prevent the pitcher from cracking.*

# red candy apples

You have to be pretty confident in your dental work to eat these! Beth lost her first tooth while eating a candy apple. What a sweet treat for the tooth fairy! Candy apples always remind me of Halloween carnivals, so we usually come home after trick-or-treating (yes, I still dress up!) and make these with our friends and all of the children. I'm not sure who eats more, the kids or the adults. MAKES 8 CANDY APPLES

Chopped peanuts or pecans

8 firm apples, such as Jonathan or Fuji

8 popsicle sticks

2 cups sugar

½ cup water

1 cup light corn syrup

1 2-ounce box Red Hots cinnamon candy

Few drops of red food coloring

FROM GWEN: Substitute 1 drop of cinnamon oil or peppermint oil for the Red Hots candy.

Bring a medium pot of water to a boil. Grease a cookie sheet with cooking spray. Set aside.

Put the chopped nuts in a shallow bowl. Set aside. Wash the apples thoroughly. Remove the stems from the apples and insert a stick into the center of the bottom of each apple. To remove any wax that may coat the apples, dip each apple quickly in the boiling water. Drain and dry the apple.

In a medium saucepan, bring the sugar, ½ cup water, and syrup to a boil. Cook to 250°F, or until the syrup spins a thread when poured from the edge of a cooking spoon. Pour in the candy pieces and continue cooking to 285°F. Remove from the heat and add the food coloring to achieve the desired shade of red.

Dip the apples quickly in the hot mixture, twisting as you dip to cover the entire apple. Roll the apples in the nuts, coating the bottom half of each apple. Place on the greased cookie sheet and allow the coating to cool and harden. (The syrup can be reheated if it cools too much during the dipping process.)

*Opposite, left:* Me and Beth, Halloween 1967. Mama made our costumes!

# soups and salads

When I think about ordering soup and a salad at a restaurant, I am usually in the mood for a light lunch or dinner. There are some great summer salads in this chapter, but there are also hearty soups, chilis, and salads that will really fill you up! Many things here can be served as meals right by themselves.

I usually crave soup on a cold or rainy day, but I am guilty of making soup in late summer, before it's quite cold enough, because I just can't wait until the first chilly day!

The salads are great starters, wonderful entrées, and perfect accompaniments to a sandwich.

# chicken soup

We had never heard of Gold Medal Wondra flour before seeing it in the ingredients list for this amazing soup, and we figured we'd never find it in our local grocery stores. But Beth found it on the shelf at Harvey's grocery store in Tifton, Georgia! It is a very fine flour that dissolves quickly so you don't end up with lumps in your gravy or soup. It's pretty awesome. Who knew? This recipe comes from our cousin Donna Paulk, who started making this soup when her very young grandsons didn't like baby food. SERVES 10

Salt and pepper

4 whole chicken breasts, bone in and with skin

2 medium bell peppers, cored, seeded, and chopped

2 medium onions, chopped

1 cup chopped celery

1 48-ounce can chicken broth

3 medium red potatoes, chopped

1 16-ounce package frozen mixed vegetables

1 cup tricolor rotini pasta, uncooked

1 cup small carrots, cut lengthwise into fourths

3 tablespoons Wondra or all-purpose flour

2 cups (16 ounces) heavy whipping cream

¼ cup (½ stick) butter

Sprinkle salt and pepper on each chicken breast and place in an 8- to 10-quart stockpot. Add the bell peppers, onions, and celery, then pour the chicken broth over all. Bring to a boil. Reduce the heat to a simmer and cook the chicken for 40 to 50 minutes, or until done.

Transfer the chicken to a bowl. Allow to cool slightly. Remove the bones and skin and discard. Shred the chicken and put back into the pot. Add the potatoes and cook for 12 to 15 minutes. Add the mixed vegetables and cook for 12 to 15 minutes more. Add the pasta and carrots, and cook for 7 minutes more. In a quart glass measuring cup, mix the flour into ¼ cup water until smooth. Pour in the cream, then add to the soup mixture along with the butter. Cook for 10 more minutes. Allow to stand for at least 15 minutes before serving.

FROM BETH: If you can't find this magic flour at your local grocer, use all-purpose flour and make sure to whisk out any lumps. Of course, you can always take a road trip to Tifton, the Turfgrass capital of the South!

# rainy day chicken and rice soup

Everybody craves soup on cold, wintry days. I love this rainy-day soup, even in the summer. Most soups have rice, potatoes, or pasta, but rarely all three. Maybe we should nickname this "exercise" soup since it's loaded with carbohydrates. I like to have a big bowl of this over cornbread, then take a nap, but that's just me. SERVES 8

4 boneless, skinless chicken breast halves

5 chicken bouillon cubes

1 small onion, finely chopped

2 tablespoons dried parsley

½ teaspoon pepper

8 cups water

6 carrots, peeled and sliced

4 medium potatoes, peeled and cubed

6 ounces fettuccine noodles

1 12-ounce brick American cheese, cubed (about 3 cups)

¾ cup instant rice, uncooked

In a large stockpot, boil the chicken, bouillon cubes, onion, parsley, and pepper in the water until fully cooked, about 30 minutes. Remove the chicken from the broth and strain the broth into a large bowl. Discard the onion mixture. Allow the chicken to cool. Cut into cubes.

Measure the broth and add enough water to make 8 cups of liquid in the large stockpot. Bring the broth to a boil. Add the carrots and potatoes, and cook for 20 minutes, or until the potatoes are done. Add the noodles and cook for 10 minutes more. Remove the pot from the heat and add the cheese and rice. Stir the mixture and let it stand for 10 minutes before serving.

# tennessee jambalaya

This hearty kielbasa sausage stew comes from Beth's Tennessee pal Colleen Cates. Cajun jambalaya recipes call for any meat that walks, crawls, swims, or flies! We decided this dish is the Tennessee version of Louisiana jambalaya, sans seafood! Serve over rice.

SERVES 6

4 slices bacon

1 to 1½ pounds kielbasa sausage, thinly sliced

1½ teaspoons onion powder

2 15.5-ounce cans black beans with juice

2 8-ounce cans tomato sauce

1 4-ounce can green chiles

2 medium carrots, shredded

½ teaspoon Italian seasoning

⅛ teaspoon pepper

In a large stockpot, cook the bacon until crisp and set aside. Cook the sausage in the bacon drippings until lightly browned. Stir in the onion powder, black beans, tomato sauce, chiles, carrots, and seasonings. Bring the stew to a boil, then reduce the heat and simmer, covered, for 45 minutes. Stir occasionally. Crumble the bacon and sprinkle on top of the stew before serving. Serve over rice.

# fancy chili

Everybody has his or her own favorite chili recipe. I've never had one that I could really call mine until now. I make this nonstop during the winter. It not only tastes great but is also pretty in the bowl, with the colorful peppers and carrots. That's why I call it Fancy Chili. This chili is awesome served over Sour Cream Cornbread (page 144). SERVES 4

1 tablespoon olive oil

2 garlic cloves, minced

½ cup chopped green onion

½ pound lean ground beef

2 tablespoons hot chili powder

1 28-ounce can fire-roasted diced tomatoes

1 15-ounce can black beans, rinsed and drained

1 medium bell pepper, cored, seeded, and diced

4 carrots, peeled and grated

½ teaspoon brown sugar

Pinch of salt

In a large saucepan, heat the oil over medium heat. Add the garlic and green onion, and cook for about 1 minute. Add the ground beef and cook until browned, about 5 minutes. Stir in the chili powder until fully combined. Add the tomatoes, beans, bell pepper, carrots, brown sugar, and salt. Bring the mixture to a boil, then reduce the heat to low. Cover and simmer the chili for 15 minutes.

FROM BETH: This chili is really good with ground turkey breast substituted for the ground beef.

Save some of the green onion for a garnish, if you like. I serve my chili over rice with a dollop of sour cream. What's a dollop, anyway?

# lettuce wedge with blue cheese dressing

I was an adult before I acquired a taste for blue cheese, but I love the strong flavor of it, and nothing beats homemade salad dressing. This creamy dressing served over the lettuce wedge is simple, yet satisfying. SERVES 8

Juice of 1 large lemon

1 cup mayonnaise

1 cup buttermilk

½ cup sour cream

1½ teaspoons garlic powder

1½ teaspoons onion powder

6 ounces blue cheese, crumbled (about 1½ cups)

2 heads iceberg lettuce

10 slices bacon, cooked and crumbled

1 medium tomato, finely diced

In a medium mixing bowl, combine the lemon juice, mayonnaise, buttermilk, sour cream, garlic powder, and onion powder. Whisk the mixture together until smooth. Add the cheese and mix just until blended. Chill in an airtight container in the refrigerator for at least 2 hours before serving (makes 2½ cups).

Core and quarter each head of lettuce and divide among 4 salad plates.

Serve a generous dollop over each lettuce wedge and top with bacon and tomato.

Leftover dressing can be stored in an airtight container in the refrigerator for up to 2 weeks.

# strawberry salad

In late February or early March, it's strawberry time in Georgia. We look for every opportunity to put a strawberry in something—from appetizers to desserts. Fresh sliced strawberries in this cool garden salad have made it a favorite at our house. What a tasty way to get your fruit and veggies! SERVES 4 TO 6

1 package ramen noodles, crushed, flavor packet discarded

¼ cup sunflower seeds

¼ cup sliced almonds

¼ cup (½ stick) butter, melted

1 head romaine lettuce, washed and dried

1 5-ounce bag baby spinach

1 pint strawberries, hulled and thinly sliced

1 cup grated Parmesan cheese

¾ cup sugar

½ cup red wine vinegar

2 garlic cloves, minced

½ teaspoon salt

½ teaspoon paprika

¾ cup vegetable oil

Preheat the oven to 350°F.

In a small bowl, mix the ramen noodles, sunflower seeds, almonds, and melted butter. Transfer to a baking sheet and toast in the oven, stirring occasionally, until browned, about 10 minutes. Remove from the oven and set aside to cool.

Tear the lettuce and combine with the spinach, strawberries, and Parmesan cheese in a large salad bowl.

Dissolve the sugar in the vinegar. Combine the garlic, salt, paprika, and oil, and then add to the sugar-vinegar mixture. Mix well and store in the refrigerator until ready to serve.

Just before serving, sprinkle the crunchy topping over the salad greens and toss the salad with enough dressing to coat the greens.

FROM BETH: To save time, this salad can be made *without* the crunchy topping. It will still be delicious.

# cornbread salad with french dressing

Cornbread served at every meal is a southern thing. I was surprised the first time I traveled west of the Mississippi to find out that not everybody serves cornbread with every meal! Here, putting the bread in the salad makes it really hearty. Add the homemade dressing, and you don't need anything else, except maybe a glass of Sweet Tea (page 54)!

SERVES 6

SALAD

6 cups torn romaine lettuce pieces

2 cups crumbled Sour Cream Cornbread (page 144)

4 medium tomatoes, chopped

1 small green bell pepper, finely chopped

1 medium sweet onion, such as Vidalia, finely chopped

French Dressing (recipe below)

9 slices bacon, cooked and crumbled

Layer the ingredients in a large salad bowl, beginning with the lettuce, then adding the cornbread, tomatoes, bell pepper, and onion. Let stand in the refrigerator for 3 hours.

When ready to serve, pour the dressing over the salad and sprinkle the bacon on top.

# french dressing   MAKES 3 CUPS

½ cup apple cider vinegar

½ cup water

1 cup sugar

1 teaspoon salt

1 tablespoon paprika

1 tablespoon grated onion

1 tablespoon yellow mustard

1 cup vegetable oil

Put the vinegar, water, sugar, salt, paprika, onion, mustard, and oil in a blender and process until well blended. Chill in the refrigerator.

# ty's thai salad

I had this salad at California Pizza Kitchen when I was in Los Angeles with Garth for a series of concerts he did to benefit the victims of the southern California wildfires in 2008. I loved this salad so much that I decided to try to re-create it at home. I still order their salad every time I'm in Los Angeles, and I think this one comes pretty close to the original! SERVES 12

1 head napa cabbage, shredded

1 head red cabbage, shredded

2 boneless, skinless chicken breasts, cooked, chilled, and thinly sliced

1 large cucumber, julienned

1 10-ounce bag shelled edamame, cooked

2 carrots, peeled and grated

4 green onions, finely diced

Sweet Lime-Cilantro Dressing (recipe below)

1 avocado, peeled and finely sliced

In a large serving bowl, toss the cabbages, chicken, cucumber, edamame, carrots, and green onions. Top each serving with 2 tablespoons of Sweet Lime-Cilantro dressing and 2 slices of avocado, for garnish.

*Just before serving, I add crispy wontons, a few dry-roasted peanuts, and a dash of peanut sauce.*

## sweet lime-cilantro dressing   MAKES 2 CUPS

2 cups olive oil

Juice of 2 limes

2 garlic cloves, minced

1½ cups finely chopped fresh cilantro

1 cup sugar

½ teaspoon salt

½ teaspoon pepper

Put the oil, lime juice, garlic, cilantro, sugar, salt, and pepper in a large blender and blend until smooth.

# marinated vegetable salad

The salad is usually the last thing you prepare before serving a meal, so you're working on it when you may feel rushed to get the food on the table. This colorful salad is prepared ahead and marinated overnight so it's ready to serve when you are. SERVES 8 TO 10

1 cup red wine vinegar

1 cup sugar

½ cup olive oil

1 teaspoon salt

16 ounces frozen or fresh shelled green peas, cooked 3 minutes and drained

16 ounces cut green beans, frozen or fresh, cooked 3 minutes and drained

2 small sweet onions, thinly sliced

1 2-ounce jar chopped pimiento

1 red bell pepper, cored, seeded, and chopped

1½ cups thinly chopped celery

Bring the vinegar and sugar to a boil in a medium saucepan. Add the oil and salt and set aside to cool. Add the peas, beans, onions, pimiento, bell pepper, and celery. Transfer the mixture to a bowl, cover with plastic wrap, and marinate in the refrigerator for 24 hours. Drain and serve.

FROM GWEN: You may substitute canned peas and beans.

# uncle marshall's ham salad

My uncle Marshall was a truck driver. He drove a big blue Peterbilt truck and kept his cigarettes rolled up in his shirtsleeve. I thought he was the coolest guy on the planet. I never dreamed he could cook! He's gone now, but his granddaughter, Christy, used to watch him make this salad, and she shared his recipe with me. When I make the salad, I still picture him outside working on his truck. Real men cook! SERVES 6

3 cups ground or finely diced fully cooked ham (about 14 ounces)

1 teaspoon finely chopped sweet Vidalia onion

2 teaspoons sweet pickle relish

½ cup mayonnaise

1 tablespoon yellow mustard

Combine the ham, onion, relish, mayonnaise, and mustard. Serve on crackers or in a sandwich.

Grandaddy Paulk standing beside Uncle Marshall's Peterbilt truck, 1974.

My uncle Marshall Edward Paulk was a truck driver.

# chicken poppy seed salad

Everybody loves the basic, tried-and-true chicken salad recipe that I make, but I had this chunky chicken salad at the Paulk family reunion in Willacoochee, Georgia, this past spring and I fell in love with it. The recipe comes from Lindsey Rundorff, who is the great-granddaughter of my great-aunt Cora Paulk, my mama's aunt. Draw that one on your family tree! Aunt Cora was all of four feet eleven inches tall, one of the sweetest ladies you could ever know, and a real pistol. She lived to be ninety-six years old. She'd be tickled pink to know she ended up in a cookbook! SERVES 12

2½ pounds boneless, skinless chicken breasts

4 celery stalks, finely chopped

4 cups seedless grapes, halved

2 cups slivered almonds

2 cups mayonnaise

¼ teaspoon salt

¼ teaspoon pepper

2 tablespoons poppy seeds

2 tablespoons dried dill

Boil the chicken in a large pot filled with water until done, about 45 minutes. Drain the chicken and set aside to cool. Once the chicken is cooled, dice into small pieces and place in a large mixing bowl. Add the celery, grapes, almonds, mayonnaise, salt, pepper, poppy seeds, and dill. Mix until the salad is fully combined. Store in the refrigerator.

I add mandarin oranges if I have them in the pantry, just for fun.

# shamrock salad

This is a favorite of my mom's. Grandma Yearwood served this at the first meal my mom had with the Yearwood family after she met my dad. Daddy was an only child, so it must have been pretty intimidating to sit with just Mrs. Elizabeth and Mr. Bo for dinner! The fact that my mom is a really good cook, too, was an icebreaker for them, and I think it was the first thing they liked about her—besides the fact that Daddy was obviously crazy about her! SERVES 10

1 3-ounce package lime-flavored gelatin

1 cup boiling water

2/3 cup evaporated milk

1 9-ounce can crushed pineapple with juice

1 tablespoon fresh lemon juice

1 12-ounce container cottage cheese

1/2 cup finely chopped celery

1/2 cup mayonnaise

1/2 cup finely chopped pecans

10 lettuce leaves

10 lime slices, for garnish

In a medium bowl, stir the gelatin into the boiling water. When the gelatin is completely dissolved, stir in the evaporated milk, pineapple, lemon juice, cottage cheese, celery, mayonnaise, and pecans. Pour the mixture into a 1½-quart square clear glass dish. Chill overnight, or until firm. Cut the chilled salad into squares and serve on lettuce leaves. Garnish with twisted lime slices.

Elizabeth Winslett Yearwood, 1950s.

# beef and pork

I am a meat-and-potatoes girl! I adhere to the
latest recommendations that say we *should* eat lean red meat,
just not every day of the week. I think that's all the more
reason to make sure that when you do eat red meat, it's something special. You can choose lean meats for all of these
recipes and they will still taste rich and hearty!

I grew up loving pork. You can definitely tell in this collection of recipes that I love bacon! I tend to avoid ribs because
they're usually so hard to eat, but my cousin Fred's Barbecued
Pork Ribs (page 97) are fall-off-the-bone good.

# uncle wilson's stuffed bell peppers

My uncle Wilson is just one of those people. You know, the guy who always has a smile and a kind word for you. I have so many memories of him, throughout my life, laughing, smiling, and cooking great food. He made his debut in our first cookbook, and the Vidalia Onion Association even put him on their Web site. I'm not sure if he's too famous now to take my calls, but I'm sure glad he's still sharing recipes, like this one, with me. These peppers are one of his specialties. I do love his cooking, almost as much as I love him!

SERVES 6

6 large red or green bell peppers

2½ cups long-grain white rice (or rice of your choice)

2 pounds lean ground beef

½ medium-size sweet onion, such as Vidalia, diced

2 garlic cloves, finely chopped

1 14.5-ounce can diced tomatoes, with their juices

1 10-ounce can Rotel diced tomatoes and green chilies

16 ounces sharp Cheddar cheese, grated (about 4 cups)

½ teaspoon pepper

1 teaspoon salt

Preheat the oven to 400°F.

Cut the bell peppers in half, top to bottom. Remove the seeds and the ribs. Set aside. In a medium saucepan, cook the rice according to package directions. In a medium skillet, brown the ground beef, onion, and garlic. Drain the meat. In a medium saucepan, bring the tomatoes to a boil, then reduce the heat and simmer for 5 minutes. Remove from the heat. In a large bowl, combine the ground beef, rice, tomatoes, pepper, and salt and mix until blended.

In a 9 × 13 × 2-inch pan, place the bell peppers skin side down. Evenly divide the beef mixture among the pepper halves. Cover the pan with aluminum foil and bake for 40 minutes. Remove the foil and sprinkle the cheese on the top. Return the pan to the oven, uncovered, for about 5 minutes, until the cheese melts.

FROM GWEN: Before using, wilt the pepper halves in boiling water for about 5 minutes. This will reduce the cooking time from 40 minutes to 15.

A Fourth of July "must-have" at the annual gathering of family and friends. The secret? Aunt Beth helps him!

# colleen's cabbage rolls

My mother always told me it's a no-win situation to try to cook things for your husband "just like his mama used to make." I agree with her, but I also believe taste is a strong sense that can evoke wonderful memories. This dish was among Garth's family's favorites made by his mother, Colleen. I doubt that my version, taken from her handwritten recipe, is as good as hers, but I think it makes Garth smile and remember his mom when I make it. Colleen always said the secret to this dish was the cinnamon! SERVES 6

½ pound lean ground beef

1 cup long-grain white rice, cooked

½ teaspoon salt

¼ teaspoon pepper

¼ teaspoon ground cinnamon

¼ teaspoon ground cloves

1 8-ounce can stewed tomatoes

2 heads green cabbage

9 cups water

2 tablespoons sugar

1 tablespoon lemon juice

1 tablespoon vinegar

2 bay leaves

1 12-ounce can tomato juice

Preheat the oven to 350°F.

In a large bowl, mix the beef, rice, salt, pepper, cinnamon, cloves, and tomatoes. Set aside.

Wash and core the cabbage. Bring a large stockpot filled with 8 cups of the water, the sugar, lemon juice, vinegar, and bay leaves to a boil. Blanch the cabbage in the boiling mixture for 5 minutes, or just until softened. Drain the cabbage, let it cool, then carefully peel 12 leaves from the cabbage.

Place ¼ cup of the beef and rice mixture onto each leaf. Fold in the sides of the leaf and wrap into a roll, enclosing all the filling. Place the cabbage rolls, seam side down, closely together in a 9 × 13 × 2-inch shallow baking pan.

In a small bowl, combine the tomato juice with the remaining 1 cup water and pour the mixture over the cabbage rolls. Cover the pan with aluminum foil and bake for 45 to 50 minutes, or until the meat is well done.

I use 2 heads of cabbage to get the 12 biggest leaves possible. If the outside of your cabbage has bright green leaves, discard them. They won't get as tender in cooking as the brighter leaves underneath.

# baked spaghetti

This dish meets all the requirements for the perfect potluck take-along. It's a crowd pleaser, it's big enough to feed a crowd—and it's easy to transport. Beth takes this to church suppers, but I just make it for Garth and the girls. We never have any leftovers!

SERVES 12

6 slices bacon

1 teaspoon minced garlic

1 cup chopped onion

1 cup chopped bell pepper

3 14.5-ounce cans diced tomatoes with liquid

1 2.25-ounce can sliced ripe black olives, drained

1–2 tablespoons dried oregano, according to taste

1 pound ground beef, browned and drained

12 ounces thin spaghetti, cooked and drained

2 cups grated Cheddar cheese (5 ounces)

1 10-ounce can cream of mushroom soup

¼ cup water

¼ cup grated Parmesan cheese

Preheat the oven to 350°F. Grease a 9 × 13 × 2-inch baking dish.

In a large skillet, cook the bacon until slightly crisp, then cut it into smaller pieces. Remove the bacon and sauté the garlic, onion, and bell pepper in the bacon drippings until tender. Add the tomatoes, olives, oregano, bacon, and the cooked beef. Simmer this mixture, uncovered, for 10 minutes. Place half of the spaghetti in the prepared pan. Top the spaghetti with half of the vegetable-beef mixture. Sprinkle this layer with 1 cup of Cheddar cheese. Repeat the layers. Mix the canned soup and water until smooth, and pour over the casserole. Sprinkle the top with Parmesan cheese. Bake, uncovered, for 30 to 35 minutes, or until heated through.

FROM BETH: This entrée is also good if you substitute mozzarella cheese for the Cheddar.

# cordelia's roast beef

Nothing smells better than a roast cooking in the oven—the Dutch oven, that is. This roast smells great all over the house as it slowly simmers in its own gravy. When my friend Mandy comes over for this meal, she loves the smell so much that she will go outside and come back in, just to get the full effect all over again! If there is any left over, use it to make hash (see recipe below). **SERVES 8**

2 tablespoons salt

1 3-pound eye of round beef roast

½ cup all-purpose flour

3 tablespoons vegetable oil

2 10-ounce cans French onion soup

1 10-ounce can golden mushroom soup

Rub the salt into the meat very well. Coat the meat with flour.

In a large cast-iron Dutch oven, heat the vegetable oil. Sear the roast on all sides. Transfer the seared roast to a platter and scrape the pan to loosen the drippings. Add the soups and 3 soup cans of water to the pan. Bring to a boil, then reduce the heat to a simmer, return the roast and its juices to the pan, cover, and cook for 3 hours, or until the meat is tender.

Slice and serve with the pan gravy.

# roast beef hash    MAKES 12 ½-CUP SERVINGS

2 cups roast beef drippings (cooking liquid)

4 tablespoons all-purpose flour

2 cups water

1 small onion, chopped

1 pound leftover beef roast, chopped or shredded

1 4-ounce can evaporated milk

Pour the drippings from cooking a roast into a measuring cup and let the fat rise to the surface. Skim off the fat, reserving 4 tablespoons in a saucepan and discarding the rest. (If the fat measures less than 4 tablespoons, add enough butter to make up the difference.) Measure the defatted pan juices; if you have less than 2 cups, add water to make 2 cups. Boil the pan juices, the 2 cups water, and the onion until the onion is clear. Add the beef and return to a boil. Remove from the heat and stir in the evaporated milk. Serve over rice, grits, or cornbread.

*I also like the hash over buttered toast with eggs.*

# slow-cooker pork loin

Before I found this recipe, my attempts at cooking pork loin usually began with high hopes and ended with dry, overcooked meat. The secret is the slow-cooking crockpot. Spices in the rub get a chance to really flavor the loin, and it doesn't dry out. In fact, it's so tender that it actually falls apart! SERVES 8

1 2½- to 3-pound pork loin

½ teaspoon garlic powder

¼ teaspoon ground ginger

1/8 teaspoon dried thyme

¼ teaspoon black pepper

1 tablespoon cooking oil

2 cups chicken broth

2 tablespoons lemon juice

3 teaspoons soy sauce

3 tablespoons cornstarch

Salt and pepper

Trim the visible fat from the loin. If necessary, cut the roast to fit into a 3½-, 4-, or 5-quart crockpot. In a small bowl, combine the garlic powder, ginger, thyme, and pepper. Rub the spice mixture over the entire surface of the loin. In a large skillet, heat the oil and brown the loin slowly on all sides. Drain off the fat. Transfer the loin to the crockpot. Combine the chicken broth, lemon juice, and soy sauce; pour over the loin. Cover and cook on a low-heat setting for 8 to 10 hours or on a high-heat setting for 4 to 5 hours. When the roast is done, transfer the meat to a serving platter and cover to keep it warm. To make the gravy, pour the juices from the crockpot into a glass measuring cup. Skim off the fat. Measure 2 cups of liquid, adding water to the juices, if necessary, to make 2 cups. Transfer the juices to a saucepan, reserving ½ cup. Stir the cornstarch into the reserved ½ cup of juice until dissolved, then stir into the juices in the saucepan. Heat, stirring frequently, until the gravy is thickened and bubbly, 5 to 7 minutes. Cook and stir 2 minutes more. Season the gravy to taste with salt and pepper. Slice the roast and serve it with the gravy.

# meatballs

In my busy life, I just don't have time to try complicated recipes. I think I always assumed homemade meatballs had to be really difficult and time-consuming. One day my friend Kim came over and showed me how to make these meatballs. They are so easy to make and so good! She likes to make the bigger ones, but I like the small bite-size ones. Simmer these meatballs in your favorite spaghetti sauce for 30 minutes.

MAKES 20 MEDIUM MEATBALLS OR 35 SMALL MEATBALLS; SERVES 10

2 pounds lean ground beef

½ pound ground pork

2 cups Italian-flavored
bread crumbs

4 medium eggs, lightly beaten

1 cup milk

½ cup fresh parsley,
finely chopped

2 garlic cloves, minced

1 medium onion, minced

Preheat the oven to 350°F.

In a large bowl or mixer, thoroughly mix the beef, pork, bread crumbs, eggs, milk, parsley, garlic, and onion. Chill in the refrigerator for 30 minutes. Shape into meatballs and place on a foil-lined shallow baking pan. Bake 30 minutes for medium- or 25 minutes for bite-size meatballs.

Stick toothpicks in these meatballs and serve them as an appetizer.

# cowboy lasagne

In my introduction to *Georgia Cooking in an Oklahoma Kitchen,* I mentioned that Garth had recently asked me about trying to create a heartier, meatier lasagne, and we started experimenting. Here's what we came up with. Remember those old commercials that said, "How do you handle a hungry man?" Well, here's how! SERVES 12

1 pound lean ground beef, chuck or round

1 pound sage-flavored sausage

1 medium onion, finely chopped

1 garlic clove, minced

2 tablespoons olive oil

1 pound sliced pepperoni

1 16-ounce can tomatoes, diced or stewed

1 12-ounce can tomato paste

2 cups water

2 teaspoons salt

½ teaspoon pepper

1 tablespoon dried oregano

16 ounces lasagna noodles

16 ounces ricotta cheese

16 ounces mozzarella cheese, shredded

1 cup grated Parmesan cheese

Preheat the oven to 350°F.

In a large, heavy skillet, lightly brown the ground beef, sausage, onion, and garlic in the oil. Be sure to keep the meat chunky, not finely separated, while cooking. Drain the meat. Add the pepperoni, tomatoes, tomato paste, water, salt, pepper, and oregano. Simmer, uncovered, for 30 minutes.

Cook and drain the lasagna noodles according to package directions.

In a 9 × 13 × 2-inch baking pan, spread 1 cup of the prepared sauce. Alternate layers of lasagna, sauce, ricotta, mozzarella, and Parmesan cheeses, ending with sauce, mozzarella, and Parmesan. Bake for 40 minutes, or until lightly browned and bubbling. Allow the dish to stand for 15 minutes before serving. Cut the lasagne into 3-inch squares and serve.

FROM BETH: My family likes cottage cheese in place of ricotta. It gives the lasagne even more texture.

Serves 12 regular people or 1 hungry cowboy and his wife!

# pork medallions

The combination of ginger and orange makes this a tasty recipe. The little medallions, garnished with orange slices, are pretty, too. The tenderloin cooks quickly. The only thing you have to remember is that you need to marinate the pork the night before you want to serve it.  SERVES 8

½ cup teriyaki marinade

¼ cup apple cider vinegar

2 tablespoons minced garlic

¼ cup ginger sauce

¼ cup orange juice

2 pork tenderloins, about 1 pound each

4 tablespoons olive oil

1 medium red onion, coarsely chopped

¼ cup teriyaki sauce

¼ cup V8 juice

¼ cup honey

¼ cup orange marmalade

2 oranges

Mix the teriyaki marinade, vinegar, garlic, ginger sauce, and orange juice. Pour this mixture over the tenderloins in a roasting pan. Cover and refrigerate overnight.

The next day, preheat the oven to 350°F.

Heat the olive oil in a heavy skillet. Remove the tenderloins from the marinade and put them, along with the chopped onion, in the hot oil. Sear the meat on all sides. Return the pork and onion to the marinade in the roasting pan. Cover loosely with foil and bake for 20 minutes.

Mix the teriyaki sauce, V8 juice, honey, and orange marmalade. When 20 minutes are up, remove the pork from the oven, remove the foil, and with a very sharp knife cut deep slits into the meat. Pour the honey sauce into these slits and over the meat. Slice the unpeeled oranges into ¼-inch crosswise pieces and arrange on the top and sides of the tenderloins. Return the meat to the oven and bake, uncovered, for an additional 15 minutes, or until the orange slices begin to curl. Remove the meat from the oven and let stand for 10 minutes before slicing into medallions. Transfer to a platter to serve.

# fred's barbecued pork ribs

My cousin Fred was the organizer of the first Paulk reunion in Willacoochee, Georgia, in 1993. He said from the beginning, "Ya'll come and I'll provide the meat. You can bring something if you want to but it's more important that you come." He's kept his promise by providing delicious pork ribs every time. His "special spray" makes these ribs flavorful. We recommend that you have your butcher cut each pork rib slab in half lengthwise and then into two-rib sections. They cook faster and are easier to handle and eat.

SERVES 10 TO 15

6 pounds meaty pork rib slabs

4 tablespoons seasoned salt (with onion and garlic)

4 tablespoons lemon pepper seasoning

1 cup lemon juice

1 cup apple cider vinegar

2 tablespoons Worcestershire sauce

Preheat an electric or gas grill to 250°F.

Rub all sides of the pork with the seasoned salt and lemon pepper seasoning. Put the rib sections on the grill. Prepare Fred's Special Spray by mixing the lemon juice, vinegar, and Worcestershire sauce. Put this mixture in a food-safe spray bottle. Spray the ribs with Fred's Special Spray. Cook the ribs until they are browned, about 1½ hours, spraying often with the sauce. Put the ribs in a 4-inch-deep stainless-steel pan with a lid. Spray the ribs once more and close the lid completely. Increase the grill temperature to 300°F and cook the covered ribs for 3 hours more.

*For the second cooking, you can substitute a baking bag for the covered pan and cook the ribs in a 300°F oven for 3 hours.*

Fred Paulk, 1957.

Fred Paulk playing the harmonica at the Paulk family reunion.

# chicken and fish

I love chicken and am always looking for a new way to serve it. Garth loves anything in a casserole, so you'll find that many of the recipes in this chapter are a meal in a dish. All of the fish we ate growing up came from our own pond, so I don't have any fancy fish recipes.

And growing up in middle Georgia made it difficult to get fresh seafood, so we usually saved our shrimp and crab eating for beach vacations. We finally learned to make our own Low-Country Boil (page 110) and we enjoy that every summer.

# chicken piccata

This dish is the result of a collaboration of two people who've never even met! Beth's neighbor Hope Kozma and Stone Workman, a friend in Monticello, Georgia, both make delicious chicken piccata, so we combined the best of theirs! If capers are not your thing, substitute frozen green peas for a tasty alternative. SERVES 4 TO 6

¼ cup olive oil

2 large eggs

½ cup all-purpose flour

½ cup grated Parmesan cheese

1 pound thinly sliced boneless, skinless chicken breasts

5 tablespoons butter

½ teaspoon minced garlic

1 cup chicken broth

1 3.5-ounce jar capers, rinsed and drained

1 tablespoon fresh lemon juice

1½ tablespoons white wine vinegar

2 tablespoons chopped fresh parsley

FROM BETH: If using regular boneless chicken breasts, flatten them with a meat mallet to uniform thickness.

Heat the olive oil on the stovetop in a large skillet over medium heat.

Beat the eggs in a shallow bowl. In a separate dish, mix the flour and Parmesan cheese. Dredge the chicken pieces in the eggs and then in the flour-cheese mixture.

Add 2 tablespoons of butter to the heated olive oil, and when the butter melts, add the floured chicken breasts. Cook for 3 to 4 minutes on each side, until browned. Transfer the chicken to a platter and set aside.

Add the remaining 3 tablespoons of butter and the garlic to the skillet drippings. Sauté the garlic for 30 seconds, being careful not to burn it. Add the chicken broth and capers to the skillet, stirring to mix. Cook the liquid for 3 to 5 minutes over medium-low heat, until reduced by half. Add the lemon juice and vinegar, and heat through. Return the chicken to the skillet, spooning some of the sauce over the chicken. Cover the skillet and cook for an additional 8 to 10 minutes over medium heat, until the sauce bubbles and the chicken is cooked through. Sprinkle with chopped parsley and serve.

*If the sauce is too tangy to you, substitute ½ cup white wine for the vinegar to get a milder flavor.*

# chicken pizza

After discovering a delicious chicken pizza on a family beach trip, we decided to create it at home. We love this recipe because it's so different from traditional pizza—not a tomato in sight. Now we can all enjoy it more than once a year! SERVES 12 TO 14

2 13.8-ounce cans premade pizza crust dough

4 tablespoons olive oil

2 teaspoons minced garlic

2 cups shredded mozzarella cheese (about 8 ounces)

2 cups shredded Cheddar cheese (about 8 ounces)

1 bell pepper, cored, seeded, and cut into strips

1 red onion, sliced vertically

3 boneless, skinless chicken breast halves, grilled and diced

6 slices bacon, cooked until crisp and crumbled

Preheat the oven to 350°F.

Roll the pizza dough out and fit onto two 15-inch pizza pans. Drizzle 1 tablespoon of olive oil and 1 teaspoon of garlic on each pizza crust, followed by ½ cup each of the mozzarella cheese and ½ cup of the Cheddar cheese. Scatter half of the bell pepper, sliced onion, chicken, and bacon on top of the cheeses. Sprinkle another ½ cup mozzarella cheese and ½ cup Cheddar cheese over each pizza and drizzle each pizza with 1 tablespoon more of olive oil. Bake the pizzas for 20 to 25 minutes, or until the crusts are lightly browned. Slice each pizza into 8 pieces.

Pizza doesn't have to be round! I make this pizza dough into a rectangle and cut it into squares to serve.

# linda's chicken and dressing

Our cousin Linda Paulk brought this chicken and dressing casserole to our family reunion, and I loved it. It combines all the things I love about my grandma Lizzie's cornbread dressing with the poultry all in one dish. Linda doesn't use a recipe, but she was kind enough to write one down for me! SERVES 12

1 hen, about 4 pounds (see Note)

Salt and pepper

1 8-inch pan prepared cornbread (about 1 pound)

32 saltine crackers, crumbled

10 slices white bread, torn into pieces

8 large eggs, boiled and chopped

2 tablespoons olive oil

1 medium onion, chopped

4 celery stalks, diced

NOTE: A hen is more flavorful, but if you can't find one, substitute a roasting chicken.

In a large pot with a lid, cover the hen with water and add 1 tablespoon salt and ½ teaspoon black pepper. Bring the water to a boil. Reduce the heat, cover, and simmer the hen until tender, about 1 hour and 30 minutes, or until the meat falls off the bone. Reserve the broth and meat separately and discard the bones.

In a very large bowl, crumble the cornbread, crackers, and bread crumbs. Add the chopped eggs. In a medium saucepan, heat the olive oil and cook the onion and celery until tender, about 7 minutes. Add ¼ cup of the reserved chicken broth and continue cooking until the vegetables are translucent, about 6 minutes. Add the onion and celery to the bread mixture. Add 2 cups of the broth and mix well using a sturdy spoon or your hands. Continue adding broth until the mixture is very moist, almost soupy. Put the dressing in a 9 × 13 × 2-inch casserole dish. Press chunks of boiled hen into the dressing, using about three fourths of the meat. Cover the casserole and refrigerate overnight.

The next day, preheat the oven to 350°F. Remove the casserole from the refrigerator and let stand at room temperature while the oven is heating. Bake for 45 minutes, or until heated through. The dressing should be moist. If it appears to dry out too much overnight, pour another cup of broth over it.

# chicken spinach lasagne

The mention of spinach in a recipe usually sends a few folks running from the dinner table, but in this twist on lasagne, one taste will have them asking for more. Beth's friends often gather in each others' homes for a weekend bring-a-dish, and when it's her turn to host, she usually makes this lasagne. Even the kids like it! You can put it together ahead of time and bake it just before dinner is to be served. It's great with some wild rice and a green salad. The spinach can just be your little secret! SERVES 12

1 10-ounce package frozen spinach, thawed and drained

2 boneless, skinless chicken breast halves, cooked and shredded

2 cups grated Cheddar cheese (5 ounces)

1 small onion, finely chopped

1 tablespoon cornstarch

½ teaspoon salt

¼ teaspoon black pepper

1 tablespoon soy sauce

1 10-ounce can cream of mushroom soup

1 8-ounce container sour cream

½ cup sliced fresh mushrooms

⅓ cup mayonnaise

8 ounces lasagna noodles, cooked according to package directions

1 cup grated Parmesan cheese

1 cup pecans, finely chopped

Preheat the oven to 350°F.

In a large bowl, combine the spinach, chicken, Cheddar cheese, onion, cornstarch, salt, pepper, soy sauce, soup, sour cream, mushrooms, and mayonnaise. Put a layer of noodles in the bottom of a greased 9 × 13 × 2-inch casserole dish. Spread half of the spinach mixture over the noodles. Put another layer of noodles over the mixture and cover with the remaining spinach mixture. Sprinkle the Parmesan cheese over the casserole. Then sprinkle the pecans on top. Bake for 1 hour. Let the casserole sit for 15 minutes before serving.

# pete's catfish

My eighty-eight-year-old cousin Pete Yearwood is an experienced fisher[...]
large catfish. My daddy, Jack, was an only child, so his few remaining re[...]
special to me. Pete reminds me a lot of my daddy, from the sparkle in his [...]
sense of humor. When my dad built our house in 1970, he found a fresh s[...]
woods. He built a pond out of that spring, and he would often take Beth a[...]
baited our hooks for us and removed them from our catches long after w[...]
enough to do it ourselves. We never caught a fish as big as Pete's, though[...]

**6 large catfish fillets**

**1 tablespoon
plus 1 teaspoon salt**

**1 cup cornmeal**

**2 tablespoons all-purpose flour**

**¼ teaspoon black pepper**

**2 quarts peanut oil**

Put the catfish in enough water to fully cover[...]
of salt, cover with plastic wrap, and soak ove[...]
refrigerator.

Mix the cornmeal, flour, 1 teaspoon salt, and[...]
plastic bag. Drain the water from the catfish[...]
to the bag with the cornmeal. Shake the bag[...]

Heat the oil[...]
Dutch over[...]
few pieces[...]
oil. Do not[...]
fish until g[...]
10 minutes[...]
with a slott[...]
warm in a[...]
the remain[...]

FROM GWEN: A steak from one of these fish is more than a serving. Pete says the key to a good piece of fish is in the way it's cut. He cuts 1-inch slices, crosswise, from the largest part of the fish, then fillets one side of the remaining tail portion and leaves the bone in the other side.

FROM BETH: Serve this fish with a side of Jalapeño Hushpuppies (page 152).

Pete holding a 45-pound flathead catfish that he cau[...]
eighty-seven years old! He was fishing in the Ocone[...]
Greensboro, Georgia, with a rod and reel. He had t[...]
this one!

# chicken and wild rice casserole

Including the fresh vegetables we grew in our summer garden, Beth and I were raised on basic foods: meat, potatoes, white rice, and gravy. That pretty much covers every meal you'd ever need. My mama was serving up the dishes that her mama, Lizzie, taught her to make. I think we were all slow to try new things, because we knew what we liked, and we didn't change things that much. This dish is the first "new" recipe I remember trying that had wild rice in it. I thought I was doing something crazy by eating wild rice! This dish has now become a regular at my dinner table. I love to take this casserole to parties or church suppers. **SERVES 10 TO 12**

**2 4½-ounce cans sliced
mushrooms, drained
(reserve juice), or
16 ounces sliced fresh
mushrooms**

**1 cup (2 sticks) butter**

**1 small onion, chopped**

**½ cup all-purpose flour**

**3 cups chicken broth**

**3 cups half-and-half**

**4 boneless, skinless chicken
breast halves, cooked
and diced**

**2 6-ounce boxes long-grain
and wild rice mix, such as
Uncle Ben's, cooked**

**1 cup slivered almonds, toasted
and coarsely chopped**

**½ cup sliced pimiento**

**4 tablespoons chopped
fresh parsley**

**1 teaspoon salt**

**½ teaspoon pepper**

Preheat the oven to 350°F. Grease a 9 × 13 × 2-inch casserole dish.

If you use fresh mushrooms, sauté them in a large skillet with 1 tablespoon of butter until tender, about 10 minutes. Drain and reserve the juice.

In a large skillet, sauté the onion in the remaining butter until tender. Stir in the flour, cooking for 2 to 3 minutes. Combine the mushroom juice with enough broth to make 3 cups of liquid. Slowly stir the juice-broth mixture into the onion mixture. Stir in the half-and-half. Cook until the mixture is thickened. Add the sautéed or canned mushrooms, the chicken, rice, toasted almonds, pimiento, parsley, salt, and pepper. Pour into the prepared casserole dish. Bake, uncovered, for 30 to 45 minutes, until most of the liquid is absorbed.

# saucy bass

My great-grandmother Mary Paulk had a large farm pond in Willaco[?] liked to paddle a boat out into the dark waters and fish for bream with grandaddy Paulk fished for bass with a rod and reel, often taking my for him. I'll bet they never cooked bass this way! SERVES 4

2 teaspoons salt

1½ pounds largemouth bass fillets (8 fillets total)

½ cup ketchup

½ cup mayonnaise

1 tablespoon yellow mustard

1 tablespoon Worcestershire sauce

¼ cup brown sugar

2 teaspoons apple cider vinegar

½ cup olive oil or salted butter, melted

½ cup chopped sweet onion

1 lemon, sliced

Preheat the oven to 300°F.

Line a 9 × 13 × 2-inch casserole dish with the bass and transfer it to the dish.

Make the basting sauce by mixing the ket[?] mustard, Worcestershire sauce, brown su[?] and onion. Pour the sauce over the bass a[?] 45 minutes, or until the meat flakes easily sauce over the fish at 20-minute intervals pancake turners, carefully remove the fis[?] garnish with lemon slices.

*Try substituting other fish, such as whole rainbow trout. Adjust the baking times by testing flakiness.*

My daddy proudly displaying his largemouth bass!     Mary Pa[?]

# low-country boil

The only thing I knew about Low-Country Boil before I tried it for myself was a scene from the movie *Steel Magnolias*, where Dolly Parton is serving it up at a county fair to Julia Roberts. (I should just say, Truvy is serving Shelby. All true Southerners know this movie by heart.) My family has always loved the beach, and this recipe makes me look forward to going. Of course, you don't have to have a beach to make it. The guys usually cook this outdoors over a gas flame, and by the time the crowd gathers, it's ready to eat. Don't expect any leftovers. SERVES 15 TO 20

1 8-ounce bottle concentrated Louisiana-style shrimp and crab boil seasoning, like Zatarain's Liquid

8 pounds medium red potatoes

5 medium sweet onions, such as Vidalia, peeled

5 pounds cured, smoked pork sausage links, cut into 3-inch pieces

16 8-inch ears of corn, cut in half

8 pounds raw medium shrimp

Fill a 10-gallon stockpot half full with water. Add the seasoning and bring to a rolling boil. Add the whole potatoes to the pot. Allow the water to return to a boil and cook for 5 minutes. Add the onions and sausage. Bring the water back to a boil and cook for 15 minutes. Add the corn, bring the water back to a boil, and cook for 10 minutes, or until the potatoes are done. Add the shrimp, bring the water back to a boil, and cook until the shrimp turn pink, about 3 minutes. Drain through a colander, discard the liquid, and serve on a large platter or on newspaper.

FROM BETH: Use whole potatoes. Cutting them before boiling will cause them to be mushy.

*It is easier to cook a large Low-Country Boil over a gas cooker outside.*

# sides

Obviously, I love to cook for my family and my friends. At first, they would ask if they could bring a side for dinner, and I would say no. I didn't want anybody else to have to spend time in the kitchen when I was more than happy to make the entire meal, top to bottom. I learned, though, that it feels good to bring something to the table. It brings everyone closer together if each has had a hand in preparing the meal. Now, if people ask if they can bring a side dish or if they can help in the kitchen, I say, "Yes!"

For example, I think our girls enjoy the Asparagus Bundles (page 127) more if they have helped cut the spears and wrap the bacon themselves. They can be proud that they were a part of preparing the meal, and they are learning that most of these sides are very easy to make. I hope their participation will encourage them to cook more when they are grown and out on their own. In the meantime, I'll tell you what's for supper, and you can bring one of these delicious sides to go with it!

# okra and tomatoes

If you only like okra fried, you may be surprised at this pretty combination dish. Choose small okra pods. They're the most tender. **SERVES 6 TO 8**

1 small onion, finely chopped

1 bell pepper, finely chopped

2 garlic cloves, minced

1 tablespoon butter

⅓ cup ketchup

½ cup grated carrot

1 teaspoon dried basil

2 large tomatoes, diced

1 10-ounce can tomatoes with chiles, such as Rotel brand

3 cups sliced fresh okra, in ½-inch pieces

In a medium skillet, sauté the onion, bell pepper, and garlic in the butter until tender. Add the ketchup, carrot, basil, and fresh and canned tomatoes, then cook 10 to 15 minutes more. Add the okra and continue cooking until the vegetables are tender, taking care not to overcook the okra. Serve over rice or as a side dish.

If you prefer a less spicy dish, dice 2 large, fresh tomatoes rather than the canned tomatoes with chiles.

# crunchy slaw

My memories of meals in my hometown of Monticello, Georgia, involve a lot of Styrofoam containers—at chicken barbecues at horse shows, pork barbecue fund-raisers for the Boy Scouts, fish fries at our family friends the Hickeys' farm, and lots more. Daddy cooked a lot of chicken, pork, and stew in those days and slaw was a required side dish on those plates. It was always a mayonnaise-based slaw, so I thought that was the only kind in existence. By the way, I'm sure there's some law about having mayonnaise—and butter, for that matter—in every dish that comes out of the state of Georgia. If there isn't, there should be! My sister, Beth, recently shared with me this tasty slaw recipe with lots of crunch and a sweet-and-sour dressing. SERVES 10 TO 12

### SALAD

1 head green cabbage, finely chopped

8 green onions, finely chopped

½ cup sliced almonds

½ cup sesame seeds

¼ cup (½ stick) butter

2 3-ounce packages ramen noodles, flavor packets discarded

### DRESSING

2 tablespoons sugar

½ cup vegetable oil

3 tablespoons red wine vinegar

1 teaspoon salt

½ teaspoon pepper

Mix the cabbage and green onions in a large bowl. In a small saucepan over medium heat, brown the almonds and sesame seeds in the butter.

Combine the dressing ingredients in a small bowl and stir well. Just before serving, add the sesame seeds, almonds, and crushed raw ramen noodles to the cabbage and green onions. Pour the dressing, a little at a time, over the salad mix, then toss.

# broccoli casserole

My mama was a schoolteacher for twenty-five years. She even taught me in the third grade! My best friend in elementary school was Julie Perry. Julie's mom taught the second grade, and Julie had already had her mom as a teacher, so she showed me the ropes. People always ask me if it was weird having my mama for a teacher and I always say yes. I never knew whether to call her "Miss Yearwood" or "Mama"! Julie and I were friends from the first grade all the way through high school graduation. We spent lots of time at each other's homes, working on school projects or having "spend the night" parties. I ate a lot of meals at Mr. Edwin and "Miss" Julianne's house. This recipe came from Mrs. Perry.

SERVES 8 TO 10

2 10-ounce packages frozen chopped broccoli, or 1 pound fresh broccoli florets

2 large eggs, beaten

1 cup mayonnaise

1 10-ounce can cream of mushroom soup

4 tablespoons grated sweet onion

10 ounces sharp Cheddar cheese, grated (about 2½ cups)

Salt and pepper

½ cup bread crumbs, crushed regular potato chips, or cheese cracker crumbs

Preheat the oven to 350°F. Butter a 9 × 13 × 2-inch casserole dish.

Cook the broccoli in water, drain, and set aside to cool.

In a large bowl, combine the broccoli, eggs, mayonnaise, soup, onion, and 2 cups of the grated cheese. Add salt and pepper and put into the prepared casserole dish. Bake for 30 minutes. Remove the casserole from the oven and sprinkle the surface with the cracker crumbs. Top with the remaining cheese. Return to the oven and bake until the crumbs brown slightly and the cheese melts, about 10 minutes.

# squash casserole

My sister, Beth, was always the squash eater in our family. Just the thought of the yellow stringy stuff could send me from the table. This is the recipe that changed it all for me. I have Garth to thank because he loves squash casserole, so I went in search of a recipe. Beth shared this one with me (of course). I tasted it just to be nice, and never looked back. I am now officially a squash eater! SERVES 8

2 pounds yellow summer squash, trimmed and sliced ¼ inch thick

½ small sweet onion, such as Vidalia, peeled and diced

1 teaspoon salt

1 large egg

½ cup mayonnaise

½ cup grated Cheddar cheese (about 2 ounces)

¼ teaspoon black pepper

½ cup butter crackers, such as Ritz, crushed (about 12 crackers)

Preheat the oven to 350°F. Butter a 2-quart casserole dish.

Place the sliced squash and the onion in a medium saucepan with about a cup of water and ½ teaspoon of the salt. Cover and cook over medium until the squash is tender, about 15 minutes. Drain and cool.

Put the squash into a bowl and beat with an electric mixer; the mixture should remain kind of chunky. Add the egg, mayonnaise, cheese, remaining ½ teaspoon salt, and the pepper and mix until combined. Pour the squash mixture into the prepared dish, top with the crumbs, and bake for 30 minutes.

The natural moisture content of a squash varies with the variety, and with growing conditions. Choose a yellow straight or crookneck summer squash, and drain the cooked squash thoroughly before combining it with the other ingredients.

# crockpot macaroni and cheese

There are a lot of recipes in this book that I cook every week. This is a dish that I would make every day, but I rarely do because I simply can't be alone with it! I love macaroni and cheese, and this recipe is the bomb. After the time is up, and you open the crockpot lid for the first time to see the cheese and butter just bubbling on the top, you will fall in love. Be prepared to eat the entire dish—and don't say I didn't warn you!  SERVES 12

8 ounces elbow macaroni, cooked

1 12-ounce can evaporated milk

1½ cups whole milk

2 large eggs, beaten

¼ cup (½ stick) butter, melted

1 teaspoon salt

Dash of pepper

2 10-ounce bricks sharp Cheddar cheese, grated (about 5 cups)

Dash of paprika

In a large 4-quart crockpot sprayed with cooking spray, mix the macaroni, milks, eggs, butter, salt, pepper, and all but ½ cup of the grated cheese. Sprinkle the reserved cheese over the top of the mixture and then sprinkle with paprika. Cook on low heat for 3 hours and 15 minutes. Turn off the crockpot, stir the mixture, and serve hot.

If you don't have a crockpot, grease a 9x13x2-inch pan with butter, add the mixture, and bake at 350°F for 50 minutes.

# vegetable pie

A friend of mine brought this pie to lunch one day, saying that she had just thrown in some vegetables that she had on hand. That's the great thing about this dish—you can vary the ingredients based on what you like or what you have in your garden or refrigerator! I recently rediscovered the recipe when we had an overabundance of yellow squash and zucchini, and it quickly became a summer specialty in my family. **SERVES 12**

1 tablespoon olive oil

1 garlic clove, minced

1 cup peeled and chopped
sweet onion,
such as Vidalia

1 large zucchini squash,
thinly sliced

1 large yellow squash,
thinly sliced

½ teaspoon salt

½ teaspoon pepper

1 cup mayonnaise

1½ cups grated mozzarella
cheese (about 6 ounces)

1½ cups grated Cheddar
cheese (about 6 ounces)

2 large tomatoes, peeled and
cut into ¼-inch slices

2 9-inch deep-dish pie shells,
prebaked as directed

1 8-ounce can water
chestnuts, drained

Preheat the oven to 325°F.

Heat the olive oil in a medium skillet over medium heat. When hot, add the garlic and sauté for 2 minutes; don't let it brown. Add the onion, zucchini squash, yellow squash, and half of the salt and pepper. Cook until the squash is tender, about 15 minutes. Divide the mixture in half.

Mix the mayonnaise and cheeses and set aside. Layer the sliced tomatoes in the bottom of the baked pie crusts. Sprinkle the tomatoes with the remaining salt and pepper. Layer the squash mixture on top of the tomatoes, then layer the water chestnuts. Top each pie with half of the mayonnaise and cheese mixture. Bake, uncovered, for 40 minutes. Allow the dish to stand for 15 minutes before cutting into wedges and serving.

# asparagus bundles

I went through my entire childhood thinking I hated asparagus. I remember telling my mom I didn't like it, and I remember her asking, "Have you ever even tried it?" I can feel heads nodding right now. Of course I never tried it! It was green. I was a kid. Need I say more? I was over thirty years old before I finally tried asparagus. I'm making up for lost time now. I love it any way that it's prepared. These bundles make it look almost too pretty to eat. SERVES 6

2 pounds fresh asparagus, ends trimmed

12 slices bacon

½ cup light brown sugar

½ cup (1 stick) butter

1 tablespoon soy sauce

½ teaspoon garlic salt

¼ teaspoon freshly ground pepper

Preheat the oven to 400°F.

Divide the asparagus spears into 12 bundles. Carefully wrap 1 piece of bacon around each bundle, starting about ½ inch from the bottom of the tips. Secure the bacon-wrapped spears with a toothpick. Lay the bundles in a low-sided casserole dish.

In a medium saucepan, combine the brown sugar, butter, soy sauce, garlic salt, and pepper. Bring the mixture to a boil. Pour the hot sugar mixture over the asparagus bundles. Transfer the dish to the oven and roast for 25 minutes, or until the spears have begun to wilt and the bacon looks fully cooked. Remove the toothpicks before serving.

# twice-baked potatoes

My mama used to make these for us when we were children. Potatoes fixed any way are my favorite vegetable, and this combines the idea of baked potatoes with mashed potatoes. You really can't go wrong. When I think about how I grew up, I feel very lucky. Our parents always ensured, even as our lives got busier, that we had time together as a family. Getting together every evening for supper was a way to share great food and talk about our day. SERVES 12

6 large baking potatoes

2 tablespoons olive oil

3 tablespoons milk

3 tablespoons butter

2 cups sour cream

10 ounces sharp Cheddar cheese, grated (about 2½ cups)

1 tablespoon garlic salt

Salt and pepper

6 slices bacon, cooked and crumbled

½ cup finely chopped green onion

Preheat the oven to 400°F.

Wash the potatoes and pierce them with a fork. Rub the potatoes with the olive oil and place them on a jellyroll pan or a large cookie sheet with a rim. Bake the potatoes for 45 minutes to an hour, or until done. Remove the potatoes from the oven and cut them in half lengthwise. Set aside. Reduce the temperature of the oven to 350°F.

When the potatoes are cool enough to handle, scoop out the potato flesh into a large electric mixing bowl. Add the milk, butter, sour cream, cheese, garlic salt, and salt and pepper to taste. Mix until creamy. Divide the mixture evenly and spoon it back into the potato shells. Return the potatoes to the oven for 15 minutes. Remove from the oven and garnish with the bacon and green onion.

I learned the hard way not to wrap the potatoes in foil before baking. It softens the shells and they will fall apart — not good! Baking them unwrapped makes the shells stronger for scooping out the potato flesh later.

# cabbage casserole

I love cabbage! I love it raw or steamed, in slaw–you name it. I grew up going to lots of church family night suppers and school fund-raisers. There was almost always some kind of cabbage dish at these events, but I don't remember ever having anything that tasted this good. There probably isn't a more decadent way to serve cabbage! It would be good with other vegetables, such as broccoli or asparagus. Try your favorite. SERVES 10

1 medium head green cabbage

½ cup water

6 slices bacon, cooked and crumbled

1 cup mayonnaise

8 ounces sharp Cheddar cheese, grated (about 2 cups)

1 10-ounce can cream of chicken soup

2 large eggs, beaten

1 teaspoon salt

½ teaspoon pepper

40 butter crackers, such as Ritz, crushed

¼ cup (½ stick) butter, melted

Preheat the oven to 350°F. Spray a 9 × 12 × 2-inch baking dish with cooking spray.

Cut the cabbage in half, then lay each half flat side down and cut each section into eighths. In a large saucepan over medium heat, add the chopped cabbage and the water, and steam the cabbage just until wilted, about 5 minutes. Set the pan off the heat. Drain the cabbage. Add the crumbled bacon, mayonnaise, cheese, soup, eggs, salt, and pepper and stir together until completely mixed. Pour the mixture into the prepared dish. In a small bowl, combine the cracker crumbs with the melted butter, then sprinkle over the top of the cabbage mixture. Bake for 30 minutes, or until lightly browned on top.

# potato casserole

Whenever I ask my children for menu suggestions, they always say mashed potatoes. I think they would eat mashed potatoes with anything! The only problem in our house is that nobody likes them cold, and on the rare occasion when we have leftovers, they usually sit in the refrigerator until I throw them out. In this recipe, the potatoes stay creamy and it's an easy dish to warm up in the microwave. You can even make it ahead of time and pop it into the oven at the last minute. SERVES 8

6 large russet potatoes

1 tablespoon salt

8 slices bacon

¼ cup (½ stick) butter

½ cup mayonnaise

½ cup sour cream

1 cup milk

8 ounces Cheddar cheese, grated (about 2 cups)

½ teaspoon garlic salt

½ teaspoon pepper

Preheat the oven to 400°F. Grease a 2-quart baking dish.

Peel the potatoes and cut them into 1-inch cubes. Place the potatoes and salt in a large saucepan with water to cover and bring to a boil. Reduce the heat and simmer the potatoes until very tender, about 30 minutes.

While the potatoes boil, cook the bacon in a medium skillet or in the microwave. Drain the bacon on paper towels and, when cool enough to handle, crumble it into small pieces. Set aside.

Drain the potatoes and transfer them to a large mixing bowl. Add the butter, mayonnaise, sour cream, milk, and half of the cheese to the potatoes. Add the garlic salt and pepper. Use an electric mixer to whip the potato mixture until thoroughly combined and spoon into the prepared baking dish. Sprinkle the crumbled bacon and the remaining cheese over the top and bake for 20 minutes, or until the cheese is melted and the casserole is heated through.

You can cook the potatoes faster if you use a pressure cooker. Cook the potatoes for about 5 minutes.

# baked bean casserole

I'm always saying, "Simple is better!" I have made simple baked beans as a side ever since I began cooking twenty years ago. This recipe came from Beth's friend Gail Shoup. The dish quickly became the new baked bean side at our house. It is hearty enough for a meal. Garth loves a smoked barbecue sauce that our friend Charlie Nichols makes and brings to him on a regular basis. Garth calls it Charlie-que Sauce! It's a secret recipe that Charlie got from his grandmother. I use Charlie-que Sauce in these beans because it's Garth's favorite, but any thick barbecue sauce will do. Maybe someday I'll get Charlie's secret recipe! SERVES 12

1½ pounds lean ground beef

1 small onion, finely chopped

1 bell pepper, cored, seeded, and finely chopped

2 16-ounce cans pork and beans

½ cup barbecue sauce

½ cup ketchup

2 tablespoons spicy brown mustard

2 tablespoons Worcestershire sauce

1 tablespoon soy sauce

4 tablespoons brown sugar

6 to 8 slices bacon, cooked and crumbled

Preheat the oven to 350°F. Spray a 9 × 13 × 2-inch casserole dish with cooking spray.

In a large saucepan, brown the ground beef, onion, and bell pepper. Add the pork and beans, barbecue sauce, ketchup, mustard, Worcestershire sauce, soy sauce, and brown sugar to the mixture. Simmer for 5 minutes. Transfer the mixture to the prepared casserole dish. Crumble the bacon over the top of the casserole. Cover the dish with aluminum foil and bake for 45 minutes. Remove the foil and continue to bake for an additional 10 minutes. Let the casserole stand for 10 minutes before serving.

These beans go great with Fred's Barbecued Pork Ribs (page 99).

# cranberry-orange relish

We've always served the traditional canned cranberry sauce (one of my nephew Kyle's favorite food groups) at Thanksgiving and Christmas, but a couple of years ago, Beth's friend Vicki Walker brought us this delicious mixture of fresh oranges, cranberries, and nuts. We still open a can for Kyle (and, let's be honest, for Aunt Trisha), but everybody else loves this stuff. Kyle and I are just old school.  **MAKES 2 CUPS**

1 12-ounce package fresh cranberries

2 oranges, peeled

1 cup sugar

½ cup pecans, finely chopped

Using a food processor, pulse the cranberries and oranges. Transfer the chopped fruit to a 1-quart bowl and add ½ cup of sugar, stirring to mix. Add more sugar to taste, as the sweetness of the oranges will vary. Add the chopped pecans and serve.

FROM GWEN: This relish will keep for up to 2 weeks in the refrigerator (if it doesn't disappear before then!).

# sweet potato pudding

I meet a lot of people who say they didn't think they liked sweet potatoes—until they tried them prepared in a different way from just baked and topped with butter and brown sugar. I happen to love sweet potatoes any way they're prepared, but this pudding is a good alternative for those who don't care for the potato plain. This has lots of flavor and is a great side dish for Thanksgiving.  SERVES 8

2½ pounds (about 3) medium sweet potatoes

½ cup (1 stick) butter, room temperature

2 large eggs

1 tablespoon self-rising cornmeal

1 cup sugar

½ cup milk

¼ teaspoon salt

1 teaspoon vanilla extract

1 cup pecan halves

½ cup packed brown sugar

*This dish can be topped with whipped cream and eaten for dessert!*

Preheat the oven to 400°F. Spray an 8-inch square baking dish with cooking spray.

On a foil-covered baking sheet, bake the sweet potatoes for 1 hour, or until they are soft. Remove and let cool. Reduce the heat of the oven to 325°F. When cool enough to handle, peel the

This was brought to the Paulk family reunion by my great aunt Ora's daughter, Pat Sizemore Foster.

FROM GWEN: The top of this pudding should be browned, but watch to make sure you don't burn the pecans.

potatoes, place the flesh in a large mixing bowl, add the butter, and mash until smooth. Add the eggs, one at a time, beating well after each addition. Add the cornmeal, sugar, milk, salt, and ½ teaspoon of the vanilla and beat until smooth. Pour the batter into the prepared baking dish. Arrange the pecan halves on top of the pudding and top with the brown sugar. Sprinkle the remaining ½ teaspoon vanilla by small droplets over the brown sugar. Bake for 45 minutes, or until the top is browned.

# homemade whipped cream  MAKES 3 OR 4 CUPS

2 cups (1 pint) whipping cream, chilled in the refrigerator

4 tablespoons sugar

Chill a large metal mixing bowl and the wire beater attachment in the freezer for about 20 minutes.

Pour the chilled cream into the cold mixing bowl and beat until it forms soft mounds, about 10 minutes. Reduce the mixer speed, stirring as you add the sugar by tablespoonfuls. Continue beating until the cream forms more defined peaks, about 5 minutes. The mixture should hold its shape when dropped from a spoon. Don't overbeat or you'll have sweetened butter!

FROM GWEN: Beating times and the amount produced may differ depending on the temperature of the bowl and the cream.

FROM GWEN: Leftover whipped cream will separate slightly when stored in the refrigerator, but may be whipped again.

# breads

A meal isn't complete without bread! I try to serve some sort of bread at every home-cooked meal. These rolls and breads are good on their own, or served crumbled up underneath a rich soup or chili. The sweet breads in this chapter are a welcome addition to a morning cup of coffee or served as a light dessert after supper.

# easiest muffins

For those of you who, like me, are a little intimidated by the idea of making biscuits from scratch, try these muffins. Somehow when you call them muffins, they sound easier! They're sometimes called 2-2-1 muffins or drop biscuits, but whatever you call them, they're quick and easy. These are great right out of the oven as is or served with soup on a cold winter day. This recipe came from family friend Mary Lou Jordan.   SERVES 12

1 cup (2 sticks) margarine, softened

1 cup sour cream

2 cups self-rising flour

Preheat the oven to 400°F. In an electric mixer, mix the margarine and sour cream. Add the flour and mix well. Drop large spoonfuls of the dough into a muffin pan that has been sprayed with cooking spray or lined with muffin cups. Bake for 25 minutes, or until the tops of the muffins are golden brown.

> FROM GWEN: For smaller muffins, use mini muffin pans and reduce the baking time to 15 minutes.

After adding the flour, add 1/2 cup grated Cheddar cheese and 1/4 teaspoon garlic powder for cheesy muffins.

# spoon rolls

My cousin on my daddy's side of the family Peggy Leach shared this really easy recipe. Mix the batter to keep in the refrigerator, and you can have hot rolls at a moment's notice.

MAKES 5 DOZEN MINI ROLLS

¼ ounce (1 packet) active dry yeast

2 cups warm (100°F) water

¾ cup (1½ sticks) butter, melted

¼ cup sugar

1 large egg

4 cups self-rising flour

Dissolve the yeast in the warm water. Mix the butter and sugar with an electric mixer. Beat in the egg. Add the yeast and mix well. Gradually stir in the flour, until smooth. Pour into a 2-quart, greased, airtight bowl. Store tightly covered in the refrigerator overnight.

The next day, preheat the oven to 350°F. Grease miniature muffin tins.

Spoon the dough into the muffin tins and bake the rolls for 18 to 20 minutes, or until browned.

FROM GWEN: The batter will rise in the refrigerator. Do not punch down. Just dip by large spoonfuls to fill muffin cups. Any remaining batter can be stored in the refrigerator for a couple more days.

FROM BETH: The batter may become thinner on the second day. Just stir it and add a bit more flour if needed.

# sour cream cornbread

We've been preparing and sharing many of the recipes in this book for generations, so it's a big deal when I find something new that I like. I *flipped* over this cornbread! I still make my basic cornbread, but when I'm making a winter soup or chili, I now make this hearty version to go along with it. It's also good right out of the oven, topped with a little butter. (Let's face it—what isn't?)  SERVES 8

1¼ cups self-rising buttermilk cornmeal mix

1 15-ounce can creamed corn

1 cup sour cream

¼ cup vegetable oil

3 large eggs

Preheat the oven to 450°F. Spray a well-seasoned 10-inch cast-iron skillet with cooking spray.

In a medium mixing bowl, combine the cornmeal mix, creamed corn, sour cream, oil, and eggs. Pour the mixture into the skillet and bake for 30 minutes, or until lightly brown.

*This cornbread is great served with Fancy Chili (page 64).*

# margaret's raisin bread

My fourth-grade teacher made this in 1-pound coffee cans as gifts for her children's teachers back in the '70s. I got her recipe for my mom. Mom still has it in her recipe file, handwritten by me. MAKES 3 MINI LOAVES

1 cup boiling water

1½ cups raisins

2 teaspoons baking soda

1½ cups all-purpose flour

1 cup sugar

¼ teaspoon salt

1 cup crushed bran flakes

1 large egg

¼ cup vegetable oil

NOTE: To bake in cans, heavily grease and flour the insides of three 16-ounce cans.

Preheat the oven to 350°F. Prepare three 6 × 3 × 2-inch miniature loaf pans by greasing them and lining the bottoms with parchment paper (see Note).

In a medium heatproof mixing bowl, pour the boiling water over the raisins and baking soda. Set aside to cool.

In a medium mixing bowl, sift together the flour, sugar, and salt. Stir in the bran flake crumbs. Lightly beat together the egg and oil, and stir into the flour mixture. Stir in the cooled raisins and water. Divide the batter evenly among the three pans. Bake for about 30 minutes, or until a toothpick inserted in the center comes out clean. Cool in the pans for about 10 minutes, then turn out onto racks for cooling.

FROM BETH: My children love to bake in a can!

# cranberry bread

I love sweet-tasting breads. They're a nice alternative to dessert. They're also a great addition to a salad or a substitution for morning toast. I love this bread for a late-afternoon snack, toasted, topped with a dab of butter, and served with a fresh cup of coffee. MAKES 1 LOAF

2 cups all-purpose flour

1½ teaspoons baking powder

½ teaspoon baking soda

½ teaspoon salt

1 cup sugar

2 teaspoons grated orange zest

½ cup fresh orange juice

¼ cup warm water

1 large egg

2 tablespoons butter, melted

1 cup walnuts, finely chopped

1 cup fresh cranberries, chopped

Preheat the oven to 350°F. Spray a 9 × 5-inch loaf pan with cooking spray.

Sift together the flour, baking powder, baking soda, salt, and sugar. In a large mixing bowl, combine the orange zest, orange juice, water, egg, and butter. Add the flour mixture to the egg mixture and mix until the ingredients are just blended. With a spatula, fold in the walnuts and cranberries. Pour the batter into the prepared pan. Bake for 1 hour. Cool in the pan for 10 minutes, then turn out onto a cooling rack.

My friend Melissa adds 8 ounces of white chocolate chips to this recipe. Yum!

# pat's pumpkin bread

Pat McCormack makes this pumpkin bread every Christmas. That's how I got my first taste of this awesome treat. She makes mini loaves in cute porcelain pans, wraps them in red and green cellophane, and gives them as gifts. The only problem is that she lives in California. Her daughter, Mandy, a good friend of mine, decided that we shouldn't wait to get these in the mail from her mom, so she made a batch this past Halloween for us to enjoy. By the way, Miss Pat, this doesn't get you out of making me some for Christmas.

MAKES 3 LOAVES

1 cup vegetable oil

3 cups sugar

4 large eggs

1 15-ounce can pumpkin

3½ cups all-purpose flour

½ teaspoon baking powder

2 teaspoons baking soda

1 teaspoon ground cinnamon

1 teaspoon ground allspice

1 teaspoon salt

1 teaspoon ground cloves

⅔ cup water

½ cup walnuts, finely chopped

Preheat the oven to 350°F. Spray three 9 × 5-inch loaf pans with cooking spray.

In an electric mixer, beat the oil, sugar, eggs, and pumpkin until smooth. Sift together the flour, baking powder, baking soda, cinnamon, allspice, salt, and cloves. Add the flour mixture and the water to the egg mixture, alternating flour and water and beginning and ending with the flour mixture. Fold in the walnuts. Pour into the loaf pans and bake for 1 hour and 10 minutes, or until a toothpick inserted into the center of each loaf comes out clean.

# zucchini bread

If you've ever planted a vegetable garden in the South, then you know that a few zucchini plants go a long way. Now, we love zucchini, but once you've eaten it steamed, fried, and sautéed, and you're still giving it away, it's nice to have a sweet alternative! This quickbread recipe combines the humble zucchini with cinnamon, coconut, and even maraschino cherries. There's more than one way to eat your veggies. MAKES 2 LOAVES

3 cups all-purpose flour

1 teaspoon salt

1 teaspoon baking soda

1 teaspoon baking powder

1 teaspoon ground cinnamon

3 large eggs, beaten

1 cup vegetable oil

2 cups sugar

3 cups grated zucchini

½ cup frozen grated coconut, thawed

½ cup walnuts, chopped

¼ cup maraschino cherries

Preheat the oven to 325°F. Grease two 5 × 9-inch loaf pans with cooking spray.

In a mixing bowl, sift together the flour, salt, baking soda, baking powder, and cinnamon. Mix the beaten eggs, oil, and sugar and add to the flour mixture. Stir in the grated zucchini, coconut, nuts, and cherries. Pour the batter into the loaf pans and bake for 1 hour; a toothpick inserted into the center of the loaf should come out clean. Cool for 10 minutes before removing the loaves from the pans. Turn the breads out onto wire racks to cool completely.

# broccoli cornbread

At some southern restaurants, you'll always be given a choice of biscuits or cornbread. It's a no-brainer for me. I like biscuits, but I *love* cornbread, so the more varieties I can come up with, the better. My mom's neighbor Elizabeth Davis shared a pan of this with us. She and I are several years apart in age, but our families were neighbors growing up, and sometimes we would give her a ride to school in the mornings. Elizabeth's a grown woman now with children of her own, but to me she'll always be that little eight-year-old girl riding to school with us! SERVES 8

3 tablespoons corn oil

1½ cups self-rising buttermilk cornbread mix

½ cup chopped sweet onion, such as Vidalia

10 ounces pepper Jack cheese, grated (about 2½ cups)

8 ounces (2 cups) fresh broccoli florets, chopped

½ teaspoon black pepper

1 jalapeño pepper, seeded and chopped

1 cup sour cream

¾ cup buttermilk

2 tablespoons butter, melted

Preheat the oven to 350°F.

Put the corn oil in a 9-inch heavy cast-iron skillet that has been well seasoned to prevent sticking (see Note).

In a large bowl, mix the cornbread mix, onion, cheese, broccoli, black pepper, and jalapeño pepper. Stir in the sour cream, buttermilk, and melted butter to make a thick batter.

Heat the oil in the skillet and spoon in the batter, pressing it evenly to the edge. Oil will come up around the edges of the skillet. Spread this oil over the top of the batter to make the bread brown. Bake for 45 minutes. Cool in the pan for 10 minutes, then carefully loosen the edges and bottom with an egg turner. Put the bread on a rack to cool.

NOTE: This bread is very soft and may stick to a skillet that is not well seasoned. If this happens, cut the bread out of the skillet in serving portions.

FROM BETH: Four thinly sliced yellow squash may be substituted for the broccoli.

# jalapeño hushpuppies

Jalapeños are one of my favorite things to use to spice up a recipe. Fresh jalapeños are the best and have less sodium than canned—but canned works, too! The corn makes these hushpuppies really moist. If you're cooking up a "mess" of fish, try these alongside Pete's Catfish (page 109). MAKES ABOUT 36

1½ quarts peanut oil

1½ cups self-rising cornmeal

1 cup self-rising flour

½ cup chopped onion

1 7-ounce can diced jalapeño peppers, drained, or ¾ cup fresh jalapeños, seeded and finely diced

1 15-ounce can creamed corn

2 large eggs, lightly beaten

Salt

Heat the oil to 350°F in a deep fryer or Dutch oven.

In a 1-quart mixing bowl, stir the cornmeal, flour, onion, jalapeño, corn, and eggs until blended. Allow to stand for 5 minutes.

Drop the batter by teaspoonfuls into the hot oil. Don't overcrowd; leave room for the hushpuppies to be turned. Cook the hushpuppies to a golden brown, about 3 minutes. Remove from the oil with a slotted spoon and drain on paper towels. Keep the cooked hushpuppies warm in the oven while cooking the rest of the batter. Lightly salt to taste before serving.

# blanche's miniature cherry muffins

Blanche Bernard is Beth's mother-in-law. This is the first recipe that Blanche gave Beth after Beth and John married. (She also gave the mini-muffin tins that Beth still uses twenty-four years later to bake them.) My nine-year-old nephew Bret had these for the first time recently and said, "Cherries have never really been my pleasure, but these muffins are good!" The boy has a way with words! MAKES 36 TO 40 MUFFINS

¼ cup butter, room temperature

½ cup brown sugar

½ cup granulated sugar

2 eggs yolks, well beaten

1 cup all-purpose flour

¼ teaspoon baking powder

1 10-ounce jar maraschino cherries, drained, juices reserved

2 egg whites, stiffly beaten

½ cup chopped pecans

Powdered sugar for dusting

Preheat the oven to 400°F. Grease the cups of 2 mini-muffin tins and set aside. Cream the butter and brown and granulated sugars. Add the beaten egg yolks, flour, baking powder and 2 tablespoons of the cherry juice, blending well. Fold in the egg whites. Sprinkle ¼ teaspoon of chopped nuts in the bottom of each muffin cup. Spoon in 1 teaspoon of batter, then place half a cherry in the center of the batter. Drop another teaspoon of batter on top. Sprinkle a few chopped nuts on top of each muffin. Bake for 10 minutes, then remove from the tins and dust with powdered sugar while hot.

FROM BETH: Using a measuring spoon to measure the batter will keep the muffin cups from running over. They are good with or without the powdered sugar coating.

# cakes and pies

Most people have dessert as the sweet reward after a satisfying supper. I tend to save dessert for an afternoon snack with coffee, so that I can be hungry for it and then savor every bite.

There's something for everyone in this chapter. Our daughter August isn't a chocolate fan (insert audible gasp here!). I usually make an alternative for her when I'm baking a chocolate dessert. From Key Lime Cake (page 161) to Magic Lemon Meringue Pie (page 187), there are lots of choices for those who don't like to wallow in chocolate, like most of us!

# fresh apple cake

I was intrigued by this recipe because I couldn't imagine how it would turn out. The Bundt pan makes it really pretty, so it's a nice cake to take to a party or family gathering. The cinnamon and walnuts give it a spicy, holiday flavor. SERVES 10 TO 12

### CAKE

2 cups sugar

3 large eggs

1½ cups vegetable oil

½ cup orange juice, regular or fresh

3 cups all-purpose flour

½ teaspoon salt

1 teaspoon baking soda

½ teaspoon ground cinnamon

1 teaspoon vanilla extract

1 cup walnuts, finely chopped

2½ cups peeled, cored, and finely diced sweet apples (about 4 medium apples)

### GLAZE

6 tablespoons (¾ stick) butter

¾ cup sugar

½ teaspoon baking soda

⅓ cup buttermilk

Preheat the oven to 325°F. Thoroughly grease a 10-inch Bundt pan with Crisco and lightly flour it.

With an electric mixer, beat the sugar, eggs, and oil until smooth. Add the orange juice and mix well. Sift together the flour, salt, baking soda, and cinnamon. Add the flour mixture to the sugar mixture and beat well. Add the vanilla. Stir in the walnuts and apples, until blended. Pour the batter into the pan. Bake for 1 hour and 30 minutes. Remove the cake from the oven, let it cool in the pan for 15 minutes, then turn out onto a cake plate.

For the glaze, combine the butter, sugar, baking soda, and buttermilk in a large saucepan and bring to a boil. Boil the mixture for 5 to 10 minutes, until it thickens slightly and begins to turn light brown. Take off the heat. Using a toothpick, punch 15 or 20 holes in the top of the cake and pour the glaze over the cake. Let the cake set and cool before serving. Store the cake in an airtight cake carrier in the refrigerator for up to 2 weeks.

FROM GWEN: Cakes baked in Bundt pans tend to stick, so liberally grease and flour your pan for a perfect cake.

# lizzie's strawberry cake

I always think homemade has to mean strictly from scratch, so I tried every way I could think of to make this strawberry cake without using a cake mix! I even used a homemade white cake in place of the mix. It tasted good, but not any better than this recipe. When I found my grandmother Lizzie Paulk's original recipe from the 1930s, and saw it had a cake mix in it, I thought to myself, "Well, that makes it okay!" If you love strawberries as much as I do, you're in for a real treat.  SERVES 12

CAKE

1 standard box plain white cake mix

1 3-ounce box strawberry-flavored gelatin

⅔ cup vegetable oil

½ cup frozen sliced strawberries in syrup, thawed

½ cup water

4 large eggs

ICING

½ cup (1 stick) butter, room temperature

1 cup confectioners' sugar

1 cup frozen sliced strawberries in syrup, thawed

Preheat the oven to 350°F. Spray a 9 × 13 × 2-inch baking pan with cooking spray.

With an electric mixer, beat the cake mix, gelatin, oil, strawberries, and water until fully combined. Add the eggs, one at a time, beating well after each addition. Pour the batter into the prepared pan and gently smooth the top. Bake for 40 minutes, or until a toothpick inserted in the center of the cake comes out clean. Let cool in the pan.

In a blender or food processor, puree the butter, sugar, and strawberries for the glaze until smooth. Poke holes in the cake with a toothpick, then pour the icing over the cake, allowing some of it to seep into the cake. The more strawberry syrup you add, the thinner your icing will become. Store this cake, covered, in the refrigerator for up to 2 weeks.

Serve this cake right out of the pan!

# key lime cake

We had a big birthday party for my daddy when he turned seventy. He was a pretty humble guy and was embarrassed that so much attention was being focused on him, but he ultimately loved visiting with all of his friends, some he hadn't seen in a long time. Over two hundred friends and family signed the guest book that night; that's a testament to the man. I think of him when I make this cake because we served it that night. I miss my daddy, but there are always things to remind me of how much fun we had as a family.

SERVES 12

### CAKE

1 3-ounce package lime-flavored gelatin

1⅓ cups granulated sugar

2 cups sifted all-purpose flour

½ teaspoon salt

1 teaspoon baking powder

1 teaspoon baking soda

5 large eggs, slightly beaten

1½ cups vegetable oil

¾ cup orange juice

1 tablespoon lemon juice

½ teaspoon vanilla extract

½ cup Key lime juice (from about 25 small Key limes or 4 large regular limes)

½ cup confectioners' sugar

Preheat the oven to 350°F. Grease and flour three 9-inch round cake pans.

In a large mixing bowl, mix the gelatin, sugar, flour, salt, baking powder, and baking soda. Stir to mix well. Add the eggs, oil, orange juice, lemon juice, and vanilla. Divide the batter evenly among the 3 pans and bake for 35 to 40 minutes. Test for doneness by lightly touching the tops of the layers or inserting a toothpick. Cool the layers in the pans for 5 minutes, then turn them out onto racks.

While the layers are still hot, mix the lime juice and confectioners' sugar and pour it over the layers on the racks. You can pierce the layers with a fork to allow the glaze to soak in better. Allow the layers to cool completely as you prepare the icing.

*recipe continues*

FROM BETH: This is a very moist cake. It can also be baked in a 9 x 12 x 2-inch pan to be easily served in squares.

FROM GWEN: This recipe comes from family friend Angela Spivey. She uses whichever variety of lime is available in the local grocery.

## CREAM CHEESE ICING

½ cup (1 stick) butter, room temperature

1 8-ounce package cream cheese, room temperature

1 1-pound box confectioners' sugar

Cream the butter and cream cheese. Beat in the confectioners' sugar until the mixture is smooth and easy to spread. Spread the icing between the layers and on the top and sides of the cake.

The cream cheese icing is optional. This cake is beautiful and tastes great with just the glaze poured over it.

Key limes can be hard to find. Substitute regular lime juice for Key lime juice without sacrificing flavor.

# cold-oven pound cake

My dad's aunt Marie had eight children to rear during the Great Depression. Starting a cake in a cold oven was just one way to save on fuel at a time when every penny counted. Times have changed, but I like to make this cake the way Great-Aunt Marie did, and try to imagine what it must have been like to be a mother to eight children. Maybe I'll just preheat the oven! SERVES 15

1 cup (2 sticks) butter, room temperature

3 cups sugar

6 large eggs, room temperature

3 cups all-purpose flour, sifted

1 cup heavy whipping cream

1 teaspoon vanilla extract

Do not preheat the oven. Grease and flour the bottom, sides, and tube of a 9-inch tube cake pan.

Cream the butter and sugar until smooth. Add the eggs, one at a time, mixing well after each addition, but do not overbeat. Set the mixer on slow speed and stir in the flour and cream alternately, beginning and ending with the flour. Add the vanilla and stir well. Pour the batter into the prepared pan and put the cake in a cold oven. Set the oven temperature to 325°F. Begin timing now and bake the cake for 1 hour and 15 minutes. Test for doneness by inserting a toothpick in the center of the cake. The toothpick should be clean when it is removed. Cool in the pan for 30 minutes, then turn out onto a rack to continue cooling.

Great-Aunt Marie Yearwood Bruce, my grandaddy Bo's sister, in her cucumber patch.

# old-fashioned strawberry shortcake

I'm a fan of salt and sweet mixed together. My grandmother Lizzie Paulk often used biscuits in place of pastry in her recipes. Nowadays, most people use angel food cake or pound cake for this dessert, but I like the old-fashioned mix of the not-so-sweet biscuit with the sweetness of the strawberries and the whipped cream. I serve this dessert in the summer with fresh-picked berries from our local strawberry farm. SERVES 8 TO 10

4 cups sifted all-purpose flour

2 tablespoons baking powder

1 teaspoon salt

1¼ cups plus 2 tablespoons sugar

⅔ cup butter (11 tablespoons), cold and cut into small pieces

2 large eggs, beaten

1 cup milk

2 tablespoons butter, melted

3 pints fresh strawberries

1 cup heavy cream, whipped

Preheat the oven to 450°F. Grease the bottoms of two 9-inch round cake pans.

In a large mixing bowl, sift together the flour, baking powder, salt, and ½ cup of the sugar. Add the butter and cut in with 2 knives or a pastry blender to coarse-crumb consistency. In a large bowl, beat the eggs. Add the milk until fully combined. Gradually stir the egg and milk mixture into the flour mixture. Knead the dough for about 20 seconds on a lightly floured board. Pat half the dough into each cake pan. Brush the surfaces with melted butter. Bake for 12 to 15 minutes, until lightly browned. Turn the shortcake layers out onto cooling racks.

While the layers are cooling, wash the strawberries and remove the hulls. Reserve a few berries for garnish. Cut the large berries in half and sprinkle with ¾ cup of the sugar. Let stand for about 30 minutes.

Spoon half of the berries with their juice over one shortcake layer. Place the second layer on top and spoon the remaining berries and juice over it. Sprinkle with the remaining 2 tablespoons sugar and top with the whipped cream.

# carrot cake

My friend Tana first made this cake and left it in our refrigerator for us to enjoy when we returned home from a trip. What a sweet surprise, literally! This cake has become a regular dessert at our house and a popular request for birthdays. I think what makes it unique is that it is cut into six layers. The pureed carrots make for a smoother cake. Of course, at my house, nobody cares about that, they just think it's good! SERVES 12

**CAKE**

3 cups granulated sugar

1½ cups corn oil

4 large eggs

1 tablespoon vanilla extract

3 cups all-purpose flour

1 tablespoon baking soda

1 tablespoon ground cinnamon

1 teaspoon salt

1½ cups walnuts, finely chopped

1½ cups frozen grated coconut, thawed

1½ cups pureed carrots (about 6 medium, boiled)

¾ cup crushed pineapple, drained

Preheat the oven to 350°F. Grease the bottom of three 9-inch round cake pans with cooking spray, line with circles of parchment paper, and grease the paper with cooking spray.

With an electric mixer, cream the sugar, oil, eggs, and vanilla. Sift together the flour, baking soda, cinnamon, and salt. Add the dry ingredients to the sugar mixture. Add the walnuts, coconut, carrot puree, and pineapple, and beat until smooth. Divide the batter evenly among the prepared pans and bake for 40 to 45 minutes, or until a toothpick inserted into the center comes out clean.

Cool the layers in the pans for about 5 minutes. Run a knife around the edges of each pan and turn the layers out onto wire racks that have been sprayed with cooking spray. Cool the layers completely before frosting (see Note).

NOTE: After the layers have cooled, wrap each in plastic wrap and refrigerate overnight. They are easier to handle and cut in half the next day. Also, to handle as little as possible, put the first layer of cake on the plate you intend to store it on, slice it in half, ease a piece of parchment between the layers, and lift the top portion off. Frost the bottom slice, and then add the next layer. Continue until the entire cake is frosted.

*recipe continues*

## CREAM CHEESE FROSTING

2 8-ounce packages cream cheese, room temperature

¾ cup (1½ sticks) butter, room temperature

6 cups confectioners' sugar

2 teaspoons vanilla extract

2 cups walnuts, finely chopped

To make the frosting, combine the cream cheese and butter in an electric mixer and beat until smooth. Slowly add the confectioners' sugar and continue beating until fully combined. Add the vanilla.

Slice each layer horizontally in half using an electric knife. Frost each layer, the sides, and the top of the cake. Press the chopped walnuts into the sides of the cake. Refrigerate until ready to serve.

# grandma yearwood's coconut cake
## with coconut lemon glaze

We found this recipe in my grandma's recipe file. I thought it was interesting because I'd never made a cake with vanilla wafer crumbs. For years my mom made a more difficult divinity icing for her coconut cakes, only to learn much later that my dad actually preferred the juicier, easier glaze that his mother made. I was really happy to find this recipe because I thought it had been lost forever and I had heard about this legendary cake all my life! SERVES 12

### CAKE

1 cup (2 sticks) butter, room temperature

2 cups sugar

6 large eggs, room temperature

1 teaspoon vanilla extract

1 12-ounce box vanilla wafers, finely crushed

1 6-ounce package frozen grated coconut, thawed

½ cup chopped pecans

### COCONUT LEMON GLAZE

2 cups sugar

2 tablespoons cornstarch

Pinch of salt

Grated zest of 2 large lemons

¼ cup fresh lemon juice (juice of about 2 large lemons)

1½ cups water

1 6-ounce package frozen grated coconut, thawed

Preheat the oven to 325°F. Grease and flour a 9-inch tube cake pan.

Cream the butter and sugar until light and smooth. Add the eggs and vanilla, beating well. Mix in the vanilla wafer crumbs, coconut, and pecans. Pour into the pan and bake for 1 hour and 15 minutes. Allow the cake to cool in the pan for 10 minutes before turning out onto a rack.

For the glaze, mix the sugar, cornstarch, salt, lemon zest and juice, water, and coconut in a medium saucepan. Cook over medium heat, stirring until thickened, about 15 minutes. Let cool slightly, then, using a toothpick, poke several holes in the top of the cake and drizzle the glaze over the cake.

Grandma Yearwood, Beth, and me, 1967.

# spice cake with lemon sauce

My memory of this spice cake is of coming home from school and slicing a piece right out of the pan, putting a little lemon sauce on it, warming it up in the microwave for a few seconds, then sitting down to watch a *M\*A\*S\*H* rerun on television before I had to start my homework. Heaven! We used a really tangy lemon sauce for years, but our longtime family friend Miss Betty Maxwell turned us on to this sweeter version of the sauce and it's so good. I make this cake at the first sign of fall. The smell of it baking in the house gets me excited because I know Thanksgiving and Christmas are right around the corner!

**MAKES ABOUT 22 (2-INCH) SQUARES**

### CAKE

2½ cups sifted self-rising flour

1 teaspoon baking soda

¾ teaspoon ground cinnamon

½ teaspoon ground cloves

1 cup granulated sugar

⅔ cup light brown sugar

⅔ cup vegetable shortening, such as Crisco

2 large eggs, room temperature

1 cup buttermilk

### LEMON SAUCE

3 large eggs

2 cups granulated sugar

Juice of 3 lemons

Grated zest of 1 lemon

1 cup (2 sticks) butter, cut into ½-inch cubes

Preheat the oven to 350°F. Grease and flour the bottom of a 9 × 13 × 2-inch baking pan.

Sift together the flour, baking soda, cinnamon, and cloves. With an electric mixer, cream the sugars with the shortening. Add the eggs, one at a time, beating after each addition. Add the buttermilk alternately with the flour mixture, beginning and ending with flour, stirring until no flour is visible. Don't overbeat. Spread the batter into the pan and bake for 35 to 40 minutes. Test for doneness by inserting a toothpick into the center of the cake. If the toothpick comes out clean, the cake is done. Cool the cake slightly in the pan and turn out onto a long rack while still warm.

To make the sauce, whisk the eggs and sugar over medium heat in the top of a double boiler. Stir in the lemon juice, zest, and butter. Cook the mixture until it thickens, about 30 minutes.

Cut the spice cake into squares and serve warm with lemon sauce.

FROM BETH: The lemon sauce may be stored in the refrigerator for up to 1 week.

# red velvet cake

This recipe came from Mrs. Gail Sealy. She taught first grade at my school, alongside my mom, who taught third grade for twenty-three years. Before we knew her, my sister and I called "Miss" Sealy the movie star lady because she was, and still is, stunningly beautiful and had this exotic look about her. She also drank Tab all the time. I thought she was the coolest! I don't think she drinks Tab anymore, but I still think she's cool. SERVES 12

### CAKE

2½ cups all-purpose flour

1 teaspoon baking soda

1 teaspoon salt

2 teaspoons unsweetened cocoa powder

2 cups granulated sugar

2 large eggs

1¾ cups vegetable oil

1 cup buttermilk

1 teaspoon vanilla extract

1 2-ounce bottle red food coloring

### CREAM CHEESE FROSTING

1 8-ounce package cream cheese, room temperature

½ cup (1 stick) butter, room temperature

1 1-pound box confectioners' sugar

1 teaspoon vanilla extract

1 cup pecans, finely chopped

Preheat the oven to 350°F. Grease and flour three 9-inch round cake pans.

Sift together the flour, baking soda, salt, and cocoa. Mix the sugar and eggs. Add the oil, slowly beating well as the oil is added. Add the flour mixture alternately with the buttermilk, beginning and ending with the flour and mixing well after each addition. Stir in the vanilla and food coloring. Divide the batter evenly among the pans and bake for 40 minutes, testing for doneness with a toothpick. Cool the layers in the pans for 10 minutes, then turn out onto racks to finish cooling while you prepare the frosting.

Cream the cream cheese and butter. Beat in the confectioners' sugar until the mixture is smooth. Add the vanilla and nuts, reserving 2 tablespoons of nuts for garnish. Spread the frosting between the layers, on the sides, and on the top of the cake.

FROM BETH: Leave the sides unfrosted if you like, to let the vibrant red show.

# chocolate cake with divinity icing

I loved my grandaddy Paulk, my mom's dad. He always made us feel like we were the most special children in the world. When he and Grandma would come to visit, he had a smile for everybody and a laugh that was contagious. He loved a good meal. Grandma was such a wonderful cook, and she always had an amazing meal waiting for him when he would come in from working in the field or at the dairy barn. When he came to our house for his birthday, my mom would make this cake for him. SERVES 12 TO 15

1 cup water

2¼ cups sugar

4 ounces (4 squares) unsweetened chocolate

1½ teaspoons vanilla extract

3 cups cake flour, sifted

4½ teaspoons baking powder

¾ teaspoon salt

1 cup (2 sticks) butter, room temperature

4 large eggs, room temperature

¾ cup milk

Divinity Icing (recipe follows)

NOTE: The chocolate may be melted with ½ cup of sugar in 1 cup of water in the microwave.

FROM GWEN: My mother, Lizzie, used one large marshmallow for each egg white for perfect divinity icing.

In a small saucepan, combine the water, ½ cup of the sugar, and the chocolate. Heat over low heat, stirring constantly, until thick (see Note). Remove the pan from the heat and add the vanilla. Set aside to cool.

Preheat the oven to 350°F. Prepare three 9-inch round cake pans by greasing and lining each with parchment paper.

Sift the flour with the baking powder and salt onto waxed paper. Cream the butter and the remaining 1¾ cups sugar until smooth. Add the eggs, one at a time, beating after each addition. Add the cooled chocolate mixture and beat until smooth. Add the sifted flour mixture alternately with the milk, starting with a third of the flour, then adding half the milk, and ending with the flour. Stir only enough after each addition to blend the ingredients. Pour evenly into the pans and bake for 35 minutes, or until done. Judge doneness by appearance—layers will begin to pull away from the sides—or by inserting a toothpick in the center of a layer. The toothpick should come out clean. Cool in the pans for 10 minutes, then turn out onto racks. Remove the paper and cool completely before frosting. Spread the icing between the layers and on the top and sides of the cake.

*recipe continues*

*Don't try this with a single-bladed mixer like KitchenAid; and don't make it on a rainy day because humidity can make it impossible to achieve perfect divinity.*

# divinity icing

3 large egg whites, room temperature

⅛ teaspoon salt

3 cups sugar

¾ cup water

3 tablespoons white corn syrup

¾ teaspoon white vinegar

30 miniature marshmallows or 3 large marshmallows, cut up

1½ teaspoons vanilla extract

Put the egg whites and salt in the bowl of a mixer that uses 2 beaters. Beat the whites until smooth but not stiff. They should not form stiff peaks when the beaters are lifted up.

In a large saucepan with a cover, mix the sugar, water, corn syrup, and vinegar. Stir until the sugar dissolves, then cover and cook for 3 minutes to melt any sugar crystals that may be on the sides of the saucepan. Remove the lid and continue cooking for about 12 minutes, until the mixture reaches the hard ball stage, about 265°F on a candy thermometer. The syrup will spin a long thread when poured from the edge of a spoon. Remove the syrup from the heat and stir in the marshmallows. The mixture will be foamy. With the mixer running at high speed, stream the syrup into the egg whites, following the groove the beaters make as the bowl turns. Beat well and add the vanilla.

Grandaddy Paulk helping me and Beth ice his birthday cake.

# chocolate torte

Beth had never had a cake with this many layers before moving to South Georgia. Around there, it's known as twelve-layer chocolate cake, or seventeen-layer—almost a point of pride to see how many thin little layers you can get out of the recipe! At first glance, this cake screams, "Don't try this at home" because three layers is pretty much my limit. But Beth's friend Gail, who is known in those parts for her delicious food, shared her mother's recipe with us. Gail says that the older ladies in her community used to cook these layers one at a time on a cast-iron griddle. She's made it "easy" for us with 9-inch cake pans, so with her directions even I can bake a multilayer (twelve? thirteen? fifteen?) chocolate torte! SERVES 15

1¾ cups (3½ sticks) butter, 1 cup at room temperature

5 ounces (5 squares) unsweetened chocolate, melted

7 cups sugar

2¼ cups (18 ounces) evaporated milk

3 teaspoons vanilla extract

1 tablespoon instant French roast coffee granules

6 large eggs, room temperature

2 cups plus 1 tablespoon milk

4 cups self-rising flour

Make the cake glaze before baking the cake layers. In a large saucepan, melt ¾ cup of the butter and mix it with the melted chocolate and 4½ cups of the sugar. Stir in the evaporated milk, 2 teaspoons of the vanilla, and the instant coffee. Cook the glaze over medium-high heat until it boils. Reduce the heat to low and continue cooking, stirring constantly, until the mixture thickens, about 20 minutes. Remove the glaze from the heat. When cooled a bit, return to low heat as needed, as the glaze must be warm to spread on the cake layers.

Preheat the oven to 350°F. Grease and flour at least four 9-inch cake pans (see Note).

NOTE: Borrow pans from friends if you can in order to bake this special cake. You will be able to work quickly by having layers ready to bake while you frost the baked ones.

*recipe continues*

FROM BETH: Gail uses Wilton Cake Release to grease the surfaces of nonstick pans. The thin layers pop right out!

Cream the remaining 1 cup butter and remaining 2½ cups sugar until smooth. Add the eggs, one at a time, beating after each addition just until blended. Mix the remaining 1 teaspoon vanilla with the milk and add alternately with the flour, beginning and ending with flour. Put a very thin layer of batter —about 7 tablespoons—in each pan, shaking the pans to distribute the batter to the edges. Bake the layers for 11 to 13 minutes. Remove the layers from the pans and frost immediately with the warm icing. Bake all of the remaining batter in this manner, building layers. You should be able to get 12 layers from this recipe.

If the idea of all these layers is too much for you, divide the batter evenly into three cake pans. It tastes great, no matter how many layers you make.

# pumpkin roll

From Thanksgiving through Christmas, I'm in heaven because I get to make all of my signature dishes for my family and friends. It's always special when a friend drops by to bring something he or she has made for you. It's really one of the sweetest gifts someone can give you, because the person has put his or her love and time into it. Every year, my friend Kim makes the Pumpkin Roll for her Thanksgiving table, and she always bakes an extra one for me. It makes our family gathering all the more special. SERVES 16

3 large eggs

1 cup granulated sugar

2/3 cup canned pumpkin

1 teaspoon lemon juice

3/4 cup all-purpose flour

1 teaspoon ground ginger

1/2 teaspoon salt

1 teaspoon baking powder

2 teaspoons ground cinnamon

1 cup pecans, finely chopped

1 cup confectioners' sugar, plus more for sprinkling

2 3-ounce packages cream cheese, room temperature

1/2 cup (1 stick) butter, room temperature

1/2 teaspoon vanilla extract

Preheat the oven to 350°F. Grease and flour a 17½ × 12½-inch jellyroll pan. (Jellyroll pan sizes may vary.)

With an electric mixer, beat the eggs, sugar, pumpkin, and lemon juice until smooth. Sift together the flour, ginger, salt, baking powder, and cinnamon. Add to the mixer and blend until fully combined. Spread the batter in the jellyroll pan. Sprinkle the dough with the chopped pecans. Bake for 14 minutes, or until a cake tester inserted in the center comes out clean. Let the cake cool in the pan for 5 minutes.

Invert the cake onto a wire rack lined with parchment paper and let it cool completely. Sprinkle some of the confectioners' sugar on a large tea towel and transfer the cake to the towel. Roll the cake up in the towel and cool in the refrigerator thoroughly, about 45 minutes.

With an electric mixer, combine the 1 cup confectioners' sugar, the cream cheese, butter, and vanilla and beat until smooth. Unroll the cooled cake and spread the mixture on top of the cake. Gently roll the cake up and refrigerate it until you're ready to slice and serve. Dust with confectioners' sugar just before serving.

# chocolate pie

This recipe comes from family friend Mack Tillman. Mr. Mack was a tall drink of water, like my daddy. He was the Jasper County sheriff, and later he opened what I think is the best restaurant in Georgia, the Tillman House. After Mr. Mack passed away, the restaurant was kept in the family and run by his son and daughter, Ben and Sissy. We all lived on Eatonton Street in Monticello when I was a little girl, and Sissy and I were best buddies. Mr. Mack made the best fried chicken I have ever tasted (sorry, Mama!) and this amazing chocolate pie. Most people use a 9-inch prebaked pastry shell, but I make it with a graham cracker crust. SERVES 8

CRUST

1½ cups fine graham cracker crumbs

¼ cup sugar

¼ cup (½ stick) butter, melted

FILLING

1 cup sugar

1 tablespoon unsweetened cocoa powder

3 tablespoons self-rising flour

3 large eggs, separated

1 cup milk

2 tablespoons butter, melted

½ teaspoon vanilla extract

Pinch of salt

In a mixing bowl, stir together the graham cracker crumbs, sugar, and butter until the crumbs are coated. Press the mixture firmly into the bottom of a 9-inch pie plate. Set aside.

In the top of a double boiler, mix the sugar, cocoa, and flour. Lightly beat the egg yolks (save the whites for the meringue) and stir in the milk. Slowly add the egg-milk mixture to the sugar mixture in the double boiler, creating a paste in the beginning; this will ensure that the chocolate and flour blend smoothly. Cook in the double boiler until very thick, 45 to 50 minutes. When the spoon is moved in the filling, it will leave a brief indention or trough. Remove the boiler from the heat and stir in the melted butter, the vanilla, and the salt. Stir well to mix in the butter.

Pour the filling into the crust. Allow the pie to cool in the refrigerator for 45 minutes before putting a meringue on top.

*recipe continues*

SEP · 67

My best pals! *From left to right:* Beth, me, Sissy, Paula Lane, Ben, and Sydney Lane. Sydney's dog, Toby, is in the back row.

**MERINGUE**

3 large egg whites

Pinch of salt

5 tablespoons sugar

To prepare the meringue, preheat the oven to 325°F. With an electric mixer, beat the egg whites with the salt until stiff. Add the sugar gradually as you continue beating until the whites are smooth and glossy. Spread the meringue over the pie, all the way to touch and seal the edges of the crust. Bake for 15 to 20 minutes, until brown. Cool completely before serving.

Instead of using a meringue, you could sprinkle the top of the pie liberally with graham cracker crumbs.

# magic lemon meringue pie

I ate this pie a lot while I was growing up in Georgia, and I never knew who had the recipe. Turns out my mama had it all along! Edward's Pies makes a really good frozen lemon meringue pie, but I can't find it out here in Oklahoma. Edward's products date back to the 1950s, and if you ever have one, be sure to check the box for a Bible verse. They're known for that, and I guess that makes me like them even more, because I always include a Bible verse on my CDs. I made this homemade version of the pie for the first time recently. When I realized that I could actually make this myself and enjoy it whenever I wanted, I was thrilled. Garth isn't a big fan of meringue, so sometimes I double the filling for this pie and leave off the meringue. That's double the magic! Thanks for the inspiration, Edward's. SERVES 10

### CRUST
1½ cups fine graham cracker crumbs
¼ cup sugar
¼ cup (½ stick) butter, melted

### FILLING
1 14-ounce can sweetened condensed milk
½ cup fresh lemon juice (about 2 large lemons)
1 teaspoon grated lemon zest
3 large egg yolks, whites reserved for meringue

### MERINGUE
3 large egg whites
¼ teaspoon cream of tartar
¼ cup sugar

Preheat the oven to 325°F.

In a mixing bowl, stir together the graham cracker crumbs, sugar, and butter until fully combined. Press the mixture firmly into a 9-inch pie plate. Set aside.

In a medium bowl, mix the condensed milk, lemon juice, zest, and egg yolks. Pour the mixture into the crust.

Beat the egg whites and cream of tartar in a medium bowl with an electric hand mixer until soft peaks form. Gradually beat in the sugar until stiff peaks form.

Spread the meringue over the pie and seal to the edge of the crust. Bake for 15 to 20 minutes, or until the meringue browns slightly. Chill for at least 2 hours before serving.

> FROM GWEN: Be sure to watch the pie while it's baking. Meringue can burn quickly.

# cookies, candy, etc.

I tell people who are afraid to cook because they think it's too hard to start with something simple, like baking cookies. It's a good way to get your culinary feet wet, and it's fun. My experience has taught me that even a cookie that turns out badly is usually good! Once you get the hang of it, you might move to the hard stuff, like Mama's Never-Fail Divinity (page 212).

We're all called upon from time to time to take something to a bake sale or fund-raiser. The next time you're asked, before you are tempted to buy a box of cookies from the grocery store, try one of these recipes. Surprise yourself and your friends!

# jennifer's iced sugar cookies

When Beth lived in west Tennessee, she began a tradition of baking cookies with friends during the Christmas holidays. At their first cookie baking, Jennifer Vincent shared this recipe for rolled sugar cookies, letting the children roll, cut, and decorate them. Even though Beth and her family have moved back to Georgia, they have continued the tradition with their new friends, and even though many of the children are all grown up, they still make these cookies at their annual Christmas cookie party. Everybody doubles the dough so they'll have plenty to decorate and share. Her tradition has spilled over to Oklahoma. MAKES 15 TO 17 MEDIUM COOKIES

COOKIES

2 cups all-purpose flour

2 teaspoons baking powder

½ teaspoon salt

½ cup (1 stick) butter

1 cup granulated sugar

1 large egg

½ teaspoon vanilla extract

ICING

1 1-pound box confectioners' sugar

3 tablespoons meringue powder (see Note)

⅓ cup warm (80–90° F) water

Food coloring (optional)

Assorted sprinkles, colored sugar, and small candy pieces

Sift together the flour, baking powder, and salt. In a large mixing bowl, cream the butter and sugar until light and fluffy. Add the egg and mix until combined. Gradually add the sifted dry ingredients, one spoonful at a time, until thoroughly combined. Add the vanilla. Chill the cookie dough in the refrigerator for at least 1 hour.

Preheat the oven to 400°F. Roll out half of the dough at a time, keeping the remainder of the dough in the refrigerator. On a lightly floured surface, roll out the dough to a ¼-inch thickness and cut it into desired shapes with a cookie cutter. Place the cutout cookies 2 inches apart on an ungreased cookie sheet and put the cookie sheet in the refrigerator for a few minutes before baking. This will help the cookies retain their shape. (You can roll out the scraps to make a few more cookies.) Bake for 8 to 10 minutes, or until just before the edges of the cookies start to brown. Cool the cookies for 1 to 2 minutes on the cookie sheet before removing to wire racks to cool completely.

In a medium bowl, combine the confectioners' sugar, meringue powder, and warm water with a wire whisk. Stir until the icing is smooth. Adjust the consistency of the icing by adding more confectioners' sugar or more water, as needed. Add food coloring, if desired, to the icing. Spread the icing on the cooled cookies and then top with assorted sprinkles and candies.

*Counterclockwise from bottom left:* Jennifer's Iced Sugar Cookies, Lizzie's Chocolate Pinwheel Cookies, Venita's Chocolate Chip Cookies, Mamie's Teacakes, Lemon Squares, and Thumbprint Cookies.

# thumbprint cookies

These cookies are always on the baking list at Beth's annual Christmas cookie party. Cream cheese and almond flavoring in the dough make these nut-covered cookies extra special. And for the "icing on the cake," you fill the "thumbprints" with the icing from Jennifer's Iced Sugar Cookies (page 190)! MAKES 2 DOZEN COOKIES

1 cup vegetable shortening, such as Crisco

1 3-ounce package cream cheese, room temperature

1 cup sugar

1 large egg

1 teaspoon almond extract

2½ cups all-purpose flour

¼ teaspoon baking soda

½ teaspoon salt

1¼ cups finely chopped pecans

Icing from Jennifer's Iced Sugar Cookies (page 190)

In the bowl of an electric mixer, cream the shortening, cream cheese, and sugar until smooth. Add the egg and almond extract. Sift together the flour, baking soda, and salt, and stir into the shortening mixture. When thoroughly mixed, chill the dough in the refrigerator for 1 hour.

Preheat the oven to 350°F. Shape the dough into 1½-inch balls, roll the balls in the chopped pecans, and place on an ungreased cookie sheet. Bake for 12 to 15 minutes, or until lightly browned. Remove the baked cookies from the oven while still warm, and use your finger or a wooden spoon handle to make a "thumb-print" in the center of each cookie. Fill the indentation with the icing. Transfer the cookies to wire racks for cooling.

Fill these cookies with your favorite jelly or jam for a different flavor.

FROM BETH: Ask your children to make the actual "thumbprints" in the cookies.

# lizzie's chocolate pinwheel cookies

Grandma Lizzie made these little cookies that looked like they could spin. They're not only pretty but also delicious. Grandma would always have some sort of sweet treat baking when we arrived for a visit. These pinwheels were as fun to play with as they were to eat. MAKES 2 DOZEN COOKIES

½ cup vegetable shortening, such as Crisco

½ cup sugar

1 large egg yolk

1½ teaspoons vanilla extract

1½ cups all-purpose flour

½ teaspoon baking powder

¼ teaspoon salt

3 tablespoons milk

1 ounce (1 square) unsweetened baking chocolate, melted

NOTE: When cutting the roll, use a very sharp knife and wipe the blade after each slice to avoid mixing the colors and to keep the cookies round. You could also use an electric knife.

Cream the shortening and sugar. Add the egg yolk and vanilla. Mix well.

Sift the flour with the baking powder and salt. Add the flour mixture and milk alternately to the shortening mixture, beginning and ending with the flour. Divide the dough into two halves. To one half, add the chocolate, mixing thoroughly. Wrap both sections of dough in separate pieces of plastic wrap and chill in the refrigerator for about 1 hour.

Unwrap and roll each half of dough between 2 pieces of waxed paper. Roll to a ⅛-inch thickness. Remove the waxed paper from the top of each layer of dough. Place the white layer on top of the chocolate layer, and roll up carefully as you would a jellyroll, using the waxed paper to roll smoothly. Wrap the roll with the waxed paper and chill overnight in the refrigerator.

The next day, preheat the oven to 375°F. Cut the roll into ¼-inch slices (see Note) and place about ½ inch apart on an ungreased cookie sheet. Bake for about 12 minutes. Do not brown. Remove carefully with a pancake turner and cool on racks.

*To cut the dough with a thread, slide a 12-inch length under the roll, cross it over at the top, and pull right through.*

# fruitcake cookies

I'm not a fan of fruitcake, but these Fruitcake Cookies are delicious and are a special favorite of my sister, Beth. The ladies of Shady Dale, Georgia—among them, Mrs. Fannie Newton (the grandmother of my high school friend Lynn Newton Deraney) and Mrs. Sara Martin—were known as great cooks. They made and sold baked goods to places as far away as King Plow Company in Atlanta, Georgia. For this reason, some of their recipes were closely guarded secrets. However, they were very generous in sharing the baked goods locally. (We're told that Miss Sara didn't cook but was the delivery person!) They would send goodies to the Bank of Monticello, where Daddy worked and, somehow, he managed to get a copy of this recipe. I'm sure it was his southern gentleman's charm.

MAKES 14½ DOZEN COOKIES

3 cups all-purpose flour

1 teaspoon baking soda

1 teaspoon ground cinnamon

1 cup light brown sugar, packed

1 cup (2 sticks) butter, room temperature

3 large eggs, lightly beaten

½ cup whole milk

7 cups coarsely chopped pecans (about 2 pounds whole pecans)

2 cups candied cherries, chopped

6 slices candied pineapple, chopped

1 15-ounce box golden raisins, chopped

Preheat the oven to 300°F. Grease a cookie sheet.

Sift together the flour, baking soda, and cinnamon. Cream the butter and sugar, then gradually add the eggs. Add the dry ingredients alternately with the milk, blending well. Mix the fruits and pecans in a large bowl, then pour the batter over them. Fold the fruit into the batter by hand, mixing well. Drop the batter by teaspoonfuls onto the cookie sheet. Bake for 20 to 25 minutes, or until done.

Daddy always said this recipe made a blue million. That's a lot, for those of you who are wondering!

*From left to right:* "Miss" Fannie Newton, Lynn Newton Deraney, and "Miss" Sara Martin.

# venita's chocolate chip cookies

Everyone has a favorite chocolate chip cookie recipe, but this one just might replace yours! This is *the* signature cookie for Beth's friend Venita. It takes a little extra time to blend oatmeal and grate chocolate bars, but trust me—it's worth it! These cookies are a staple for family gatherings, college care packages, and beach potlucks.

**MAKES 6 DOZEN COOKIES**

¾ cup (1½ sticks) butter, room temperature

¼ cup vegetable shortening, such as Crisco

1 cup granulated sugar

1 cup light brown sugar

2 large eggs

1 teaspoon vanilla extract

2½ cups old-fashioned rolled oats

2 cups all-purpose flour

½ teaspoon salt

1 teaspoon baking powder

1 teaspoon baking soda

6 ounces semisweet chocolate chips (about 1 cup)

1 5-ounce Hershey's chocolate bar, grated or chopped

1½ cups chopped pecans (optional)

Preheat the oven to 400°F.

With an electric mixer, cream the butter, shortening, and sugars until smooth. Add the eggs and vanilla, mixing well. In a blender or food processor, process the oats to a fine powder. Sift together the flour, salt, baking powder, baking soda, and oatmeal and, with the mixer running, gradually add to the creamed mixture. Stir in the chocolate chips, grated chocolate bar, and pecans, if using.

Roll the dough into golf-size balls and place 2 inches apart on an ungreased cookie sheet. Bake for 7 to 8 minutes. With a spatula, loosen the baked cookies from the pan and allow them to cool on the cookie sheet. Serve warm.

# mamie's teacakes

My parents' first apartment was in a lovely old home in Monticello, Georgia, owned by the town librarian, Miss Mary Murrelle. When my folks built their first house, it was just down the street and "Mamie," as we called Miss Mary, had become a lifelong friend. She made the best teacakes, which were soft and had a cakelike texture. My mom, sister, and I have collected recipes for years trying to replicate that teacake. These come close! Just make sure you don't overwork the dough. The less you work the dough, the lighter and fluffier the cookie. MAKES 3 DOZEN TEACAKES

3½ cups all-purpose flour
1 teaspoon baking soda
¼ teaspoon salt
½ cup (1 stick) butter, room temperature
1½ cups sugar
2 large eggs
1½ teaspoons vanilla extract
¼ cup sour cream

Preheat the oven to 400°F. Grease 2 large (14 × 16-inch) cookie sheets with solid shortening.

Sift together the flour, baking soda, and salt. Using an electric mixer on medium speed, combine the butter, sugar, eggs, and vanilla. Add the sour cream and mix well. On low speed, gradually add the flour mixture until well blended. Turn the dough out onto a lightly floured board, and pat with floured hands to a ¼-inch thickness. Cut with a 2-inch round, floured cookie cutter and place on cookie sheets about 1 inch apart. Bake for 10 to 12 minutes, until the teacakes are lightly browned. Do not overbake. Using an egg turner, remove the cookies to a rack to cool.

*The dough is sticky, but be careful about adding too much extra flour when shaping the teacakes. By using care, patience, and a floured egg turner when patting and cutting, you will be rewarded with tasty, tender teacakes.*

# vicki's shortbread

This past Christmas, we came home from Christmas Eve church service to find a pan of this shortbread sitting on the steps. Thank goodness Beth's cat Ferrari (don't ask) is 100 years old and has long ago lost her sense of smell. We devoured the shortbread in short order (I know, pun intended). "I'll bet Vicki Walker brought this by," Beth said. By the way, Vicki, I'll be at my sister's house again this Christmas . . . I'm just sayin'. SERVES 16

1 cup self-rising flour

½ cup (1 stick) butter, room temperature

¼ cup granulated sugar

¼ cup brown sugar

Preheat the oven to 350°F. Spray a 9-inch pie pan with cooking spray.

With an electric mixer, mix the flour, butter, and sugars together until fully combined. Spread the mixture in the bottom of the pie pan. Bake for 25 minutes. Cool and slice.

*A slice of shortbread with a hot cup of coffee is one of my favorite afternoon snacks during the holidays.*

# grape salad

This is a popular salad in Georgia. A family friend, Bobbie Jean Ozburn, first took it to a Monticello Woman's Club luncheon and it became known as "That Woman's Club Grape Salad." There are a lot of versions of this salad out there. It's called a salad, but it's really more of a dessert. SERVES 12

2 pounds seedless green grapes

2 pounds seedless purple grapes

1 8-ounce package cream cheese, room temperature

1 8-ounce container sour cream

½ cup granulated sugar

1 teaspoon vanilla extract

1 cup brown sugar, firmly packed

1 cup pecans, finely chopped

Wash the grapes and dry thoroughly with paper towels. Put the dry grapes in a large bowl. In a separate bowl, stir the cream cheese until it is smooth. Add the sour cream, granulated sugar, and vanilla. Mix well. Pour this mixture over the grapes and toss together until all grapes are coated. Pour the grapes into a 9 × 12-inch pan. Refrigerate overnight.

Just before serving, sprinkle with the brown sugar and pecans.

# lemon squares

This is the first thing I ever made that had confectioners' sugar in the crust. I could eat this crust all by itself! Our youngest daughter, Allie Colleen, is the aspiring cook in our family, and this is one of her specialties. **MAKES 15 SQUARES**

### CRUST
1 cup (2 sticks) butter, room temperature

2 cups all-purpose flour

½ cup confectioners' sugar

### FILLING
4 large eggs

5 tablespoons fresh lemon juice (from about 2 large lemons)

2 tablespoons grated lemon zest

2 cups granulated sugar

1 tablespoon all-purpose flour

1 teaspoon baking powder

½ teaspoon salt

Confectioners' sugar, for sprinkling

Preheat the oven to 350°F. Spray a 9 × 13 × 2-inch pan with cooking spray.

In a medium saucepan, melt the butter. Remove from the heat and add the flour and confectioners' sugar, mixing until a dough forms. Press the mixture firmly into the pan. Bake the crust for 25 minutes.

While the crust is baking, with an electric mixer, combine the eggs, lemon juice, and zest until smooth. Add the granulated sugar, flour, baking powder, and salt, and beat until smooth. Pour the mixture over the baked crust. Bake for 25 minutes more. Remove the pan from the oven and let it cool completely. Sprinkle the top with confectioners' sugar. Cut into squares and serve.

# bess london's pecan tassies

Bess London is a friend of mine. Garth and I have known her son Emmett for years, and when I moved to Oklahoma, she was one of the first people I met. She's in her nineties and still as active and lively as ever. She is a true inspiration and the kind of woman I want to be. She raised three boys in rural Mississippi and has so many great stories about them. Even though they are grown men now, Bess can still embarrass them with a good story from childhood. She is also an amazing cook, and believes, like me, that one way you can show people you love them is to cook for them. The first treats Miss Bess ever made for me were these Pecan Tassies. I have to say that, even following her recipe to the letter, I find that hers are lighter and tastier than mine. It must be all of that love!  MAKES 24 TASSIES

½ cup (1 stick) butter, room temperature, plus 1 tablespoon butter, melted

1 3-ounce package cream cheese, room temperature

1 cup all-purpose flour

1 large egg

¾ cup packed light brown sugar

1 teaspoon vanilla extract

Pinch of salt

½ cup pecans, finely chopped

With an electric mixer, beat the ½ cup butter and the cream cheese until smooth. Add the flour and beat until fully combined. Cover the bowl with plastic wrap and chill in the refrigerator for 1 hour.

Preheat the oven to 325°F. Spray a mini-muffin pan with cooking spray.

In a large mixing bowl, whisk together the melted butter, egg, brown sugar, vanilla, and salt until smooth. Set aside.

Shape the chilled dough into 24 balls, about 1 inch in diameter. Press each ball into a cup of the muffin pan, then spoon 1 teaspoon of the pecans into each muffin cup. Fill each cup with the egg mixture until evenly distributed. Bake for 25 minutes, or until the filling is set. Cool on a wire rack for 10 minutes, then remove from the muffin pan.

Garth and Miss Bess at our wedding, December 10, 2005.

# betty's apple ambrosia

In my family, ambrosia is usually made with oranges, coconut, and sugar. My friend Betty Maxwell used to make this for my daddy all the time. He loved ambrosia. You don't have to wait until oranges are in the peak season to enjoy this—just use a lot more sugar for sweetness. MAKES 6 CUPS

1 cup orange juice with lots of pulp, or more as needed

3 ripe Delicious apples

1 8-ounce can crushed pineapple

¼ cup sugar

½ cup frozen grated coconut, thawed

Pour the orange juice into a medium bowl. Peel and core the apples, then grate them into the orange juice using the large-hole side of the grater. Add the pineapple, sugar, and coconut. Mix well, adding more orange juice if the mixture is not juicy enough. The apples will continue to absorb juice, and orange juice can be added as needed to keep it as juicy as you like. Store in the refrigerator until ready to serve.

Choose a sweet apple that you like.
My favorite is Golden Delicious.

# crockpot chocolate candy

My cousin Donna Paulk is a great cook. She's kindly given us several great recipes for this collection, including chicken soup, macaroni and cheese, beignets, and this candy. I love this kind of recipe: the candies look so pretty and appear really hard to make. People will think you're a genius cook, which is almost embarrassing considering how easy they are to make. Just layer everything in the cooker and wait! MAKES 30 TO 40 PIECES

2 pounds (36 ounces) salted dry-roasted peanuts

4 ounces (4 squares) German's sweet chocolate

1 12-ounce package semisweet chocolate chips (about 2 cups)

2½ pounds white almond bark

FROM BETH: This is a fun recipe to make with your children. They can put everything in the slow cooker, and drop the candy into the cupcake liners, too.

Put the peanuts in the bottom of a 4-quart slow cooker. Layer the chocolate over the peanuts, beginning with the sweet chocolate, followed by the chocolate chips, and then the almond bark. Set the temperature on low and cook for 3 hours. Do not stir the mixture.

After 3 hours, stir the mixture with a wooden spoon until smooth. Drop the candy into cupcake pan liners using about 2 tablespoons per liner. Allow the candy to cool completely before removing the cupcake liners.

If you can't find almond bark, substitute white chocolate chips.

# "miss" mickey's peanut butter balls

One summer our friends Patty and Pam were having a garage sale. Our girls Taylor and August wanted to have a lemonade stand, so they made a sign to hang on the front of their card table, and they set up shop during the garage sale. Patty and Pam's sweet neighbor Howard saw the girls and came over to buy some lemonade. Shortly after that, Howard's wife, Mickey, came over with some cookies and some peanut butter balls to give the girls. After that day, any time the girls were visiting Patty and Pam, they'd go see Howard and "Miss" Mickey. Mickey passed away several years ago, but Howard is eighty-one and still going strong. Garth and the girls make these peanut butter balls to give as gifts, and they always remember "Miss" Mickey when they make them. MAKES ABOUT 40 BALLS

1 cup sugar
½ cup dark corn syrup
½ cup white corn syrup
2 cups crunchy peanut butter
4 cups Rice Krispies

In a large saucepan, stir the sugar and the syrups together over medium heat. Add the peanut butter and continue to stir until the mixture is fully combined. Remove the pan from the heat, and add the Rice Krispies. Mix well. Spray your hands lightly with cooking spray and shape the mixture into balls. Transfer to waxed paper. Store in an airtight container for up to 2 weeks.

August and Taylor and their lemonade stand.

# peanut butter bars

These peanut butter bars came from Beth's sister-in-law, Margaret Ann Akins. She says her daughter Amanda requests them for her birthday instead of cake. Mama and Beth spent a weekend testing all kinds of brownies and bars, and they sent some to school with Beth's children on Monday morning. When my mom drove the carpool that afternoon, she overheard my nine-year-old nephew, Bret, and his friends in the backseat discussing the cookbook. Bret spoke up and said to her, "Grammy, we have another two thumbs up for the Peanut Butter Bars!" If a nine-year-old says they're good, what more do you need to know? They're perfect for a picnic or a day at the lake.  MAKES 3 DOZEN 1 X 3-INCH BARS

½ cup (1 stick) butter, room temperature

½ cup granulated sugar

½ cup packed brown sugar

½ cup plus 4 tablespoons creamy peanut butter

1 large egg, beaten

1 teaspoon vanilla extract

1 cup all-purpose flour

1 teaspoon baking soda

¼ teaspoon salt

½ cup quick-cooking oatmeal

6 ounces semisweet chocolate chips (about 1 cup)

1 cup confectioners' sugar

4 tablespoons milk

Preheat the oven to 350°F. Grease a 9 × 13 × 2-inch baking dish.

Using an electric mixer, cream the butter, sugars, and ½ cup peanut butter. Add the egg and vanilla. Sift the flour with the baking soda and the salt. Mix the oatmeal into the flour and stir the flour into the creamed mixture. Spread the batter in the baking pan. Sprinkle the chocolate chips over the batter and bake for 20 to 25 minutes, until browned around the edges.

Mix the confectioners' sugar, remaining 4 tablespoons peanut butter, and milk. Blend until smooth, then spread over the warm Peanut Butter Bars.

# sweet and saltines

After a meal, my mama will always say, "I need a little something sweet." If she has dessert, she will inevitably follow it up with, "Now I need a little something salty." It's become a joke at our house. These crackers are so good, you will just keep eating them, and Mama has her sweet and salty thing covered. Beware, they're really addictive.

SERVES 20

40 saltine crackers

1 cup (2 sticks) butter

1 cup light brown sugar

8 ounces semisweet chocolate chips (about 1⅓ cups)

Preheat the oven to 425°F. Line a large jellyroll pan with aluminum foil and the saltine crackers.

In a medium saucepan, melt the butter and brown sugar together and bring to a boil. Boil for 5 minutes. Remove from the heat and pour over the crackers, covering them evenly. Put the jellyroll pan into the oven and watch closely. Bake for 4 to 5 minutes, or until just bubbly. Remove from the oven and pour the chocolate chips over the crackers. When the chips melt a bit, spread them over the crackers with a knife. Transfer the pan to the freezer for 15 to 20 minutes, or until completely cold. They will form one big sheet. Break up into pieces. Store in an airtight container.

FROM GWEN: Use anywhere from 35 to 45 saltine crackers, depending on the size of your pan.

FROM BETH: I used milk chocolate chips instead of semisweet once because that's what I had on hand. They tasted great, too.

Substitute graham crackers for the saltines for a sweeter snack. Use 1 stick of butter instead of 2 for a crunchier, saltier cracker.

# never-fail divinity

This is another family favorite of mine from childhood. I always thought these perfect white candy pieces looked so elegant. They are really rich, so you shouldn't eat too many at a time! My mom makes this recipe, and my only rule is "Always eat divinity when it's in the house, rain or shine!" MAKES ABOUT 2 DOZEN CANDIES

2 cups sugar

½ cup cold water

½ cup light corn syrup

Pinch of salt

2 large egg whites, stiffly beaten

1 teaspoon vanilla extract

1 cup chopped pecans or walnuts

In a large saucepan, stir the sugar, water, syrup, and salt together until the sugar dissolves. Cook on medium heat to 260°F, or until the mixture spins a long thread. Pour one third of the boiling syrup over the beaten egg whites, beating continuously. Add the vanilla. Cook the remaining syrup over medium heat until it reaches the hard boil stage, 300°F. Pour this syrup over the egg-white mixture and continue beating until the candy holds a soft shape. Stir in the nuts and drop by teaspoonfuls on waxed paper or pour into an 8 × 8 × 2-inch pan. Allow the candy to harden.

FROM BETH: Double beaters are a must when making this candy.

FROM MAMA: Dorothy Cliett, from Grandma Lizzie's side of the family, cooks the syrup twice to ensure that the candy will be firm.

# thanks

I'll never be able to thank everyone who helped make this second collaboration possible! So many people rose to the occasion to make this cookbook come alive. Thanks to everyone at Clarkson Potter, especially Emily Takoudes for tackling the editing job on the heels of having a new baby! Thank you to Jenny Beal Davis for designing a beautiful book . . . again! Thanks to Lauren Shakely, Doris Cooper, Kate Tyler, and Peggy Paul. Special thanks to Ken Levitan, Michelle Owens, and Vector Management for continuing to bring me fun opportunities like this one.

When something works the first time, you stick with it. Ben Fink, your talents continue to amaze me. Thank you for photographing our food and for taking such care to make sure it was absolutely perfect. Special thanks to Jeff Kavanaugh, Jamie Kimm, Barb Fritz, Ruby Guidara, and Cynthia Winn for photographing, styling, and preparing everything necessary for the photo shoots in New York and Nashville. Thank you to Russ Harrington for shooting the cover and to Eli McFadden,

Joel Hood, and Brent Harrington for assisting. Thanks to Matt Harrington and Luellyn Latocki for PhotoShop Botox! Sorry about the mosquitos! Thank you Bev Parker for capturing the love I feel for my cowboy.

Thanks to the crew in Nashville: Gary Birdwell, Lark Foster, Steve Gibson, Tracy Greenwood, Jarrah Herter, Terri McGee, and Steve McLellan. You made it all work! Thank you, Hope Baldwin, for driving down to Willacoochee, Georgia, to take pictures at the Paulk family reunion. The crockpot mac and cheese is in the mail! Melissa Perry, thanks for coming to the party a second time and preparing all of these recipes. I think your being seven months pregnant during this process made you enjoy the food even more! Thanks to Earl Cox, Mary Beth Felts, Claudia Fowler, and Amanda Kaye West, for hair, makeup, and wardrobe for all of the Yearwood women!

Thank you to the family and friends who contributed recipes and photos for this cookbook. You all really came through for us! Thank you for your love and generosity:

Faye Abercrombie, Louise Aiken, Margaret Akins, Betty Alexander, Frank and Loretta Bruce, Linda Buchanan, Charlene Burton, Larue Camp, Colleen Cates, Nellie Chaires, Lydia Clements, Melba Clements, Dorothy Cliett, Mandy Smith Corley, Elizabeth Davis, Shirley Davis, Lynn Deraney, Shirley Durden, Pat Foster, Paula Funderburke, Shirley Anne Gilliam, Cordelia Goodman, Rita Goodman, Clarice Hamby, Lynn Hamby, Mary Cam Harding, Sissy Hayes, Pam Helm, Patti Helm, Nancy Hinds, Sissy Tillman Hulsey, Geraldine Johnson, Mary Lou Jordan, Iris Kicklighter, Diane Knight, Hope Kozma, Sydney Lane, Peggy Leach, Cynthia Lee, Kim

LeFlore, Bess London, Leona Lucine, Vicki Martin, Pat McCormack, Ruth McCormick, Joann Mosley, Karen Oakes, Bobbie Jean Ozburn, Donna Paulk, Emily Paulk, Fred and Dorothy Sue Paulk, Michele Paulk, Warren and Linda Paulk, Wilson and Beth Paulk, Julianne Perry, Phyllis Pritchett, Amanda Richey, Jodi Roberts, Lindsey Rundorff, Terry Rundorff, Kate Sandifer, Mark and Venita Sandifer, Kathryn Sauls, Gail Sealy, Mae Sears, Gail Shoup, Medea Shuman, Donna Smith, Eryn Smith, Stan and Mari Smith, Vicki Smith, Angela Spivey, Tricia Stafford, Howard Stamper, Angela Stewart, Mandy Stewart, Brian and Becky Tankersley, Lynne Tanner, Ben Tillman, Aletha Tyler, Sandy Vandegrift, Jennifer Vincent, Chrystal Vining, Vicki Walker, Margaret Watson, Tana Weber, Amanda Paulk Wildes, Nona Wilson, Susan Winslett, Stone Workman, Dianne Yearwood, Pete Yearwood, and SuSan Yearwood.

A huge thank-you to our immediate families, John, Ashley, Kyle, and Bret Bernard and Garth, Taylor, August, and Allie Brooks: Thank you for trying anything we put on the table and for being patient while we spent hours in front of the computer. We love you all.

Finally, thank you to Mama (Gwen) and Beth, for taking this journey with me again. You cooked, tested, counseled, laughed, and cried with me! I am so lucky you're my family. I love you.

*Trisha*

# index